THE CHANGING TRAVEL MARKET

by

John B. Lansing

Dwight M. Blood

Sponsored by

The Boeing Company
The Federal Aviation Agency
The Port of New York Authority, Aviation Department
The Port of New York Authority, Port Development Department
Time, The Weekly Newsmagazine
United Air Lines

March 1964

Survey Research Center
Institute for Social Research
The University of Michigan
Ann Arbor, Michigan

Composition and Lithoprinted by
BRAUN-BRUMFIELD, Inc.
Ann Arbor, Michigan

PREFACE

Since 1955, a series of National Travel Market Surveys has been conducted by the Survey Research Center. The surveys are based on interviews with people about trips they and their families have taken 100 miles or more away from home. Questioning was conducted in six years, 1955, 1956, 1957, 1958, 1960, and 1962, interviewing successive cross-sections of the population of the United States. Each survey was similar in some respects to the others, but each also sought unique information. The purpose of this volume is to summarize the findings of the whole body of research and make the information easily accessible.

The report is organized around these broad questions: What determines who travels and how much? What determines the choices travelers make among the different methods of transportation? What determines the volume of travel by auto, air, rail, and bus? An attempt is made to ascertain how the answers to these questions have been changing over time.

It is impossible to reproduce in a single volume all of the work that has been done since 1955 in analyzing the travel market surveys. To make the earlier data more usable, the reports to the sponsors of the six surveys have been reprinted in two volumes similar in format to this one. These volumes are *The Travel Market 1955, 1956, 1957* by John B. Lansing and Ernest Lilienstein and *The Travel Market 1958, 1959-1960, 1961-1962* by John B. Lansing, Eva Mueller, and others. A combined index to the series of reports has been prepared and is incorporated in this volume.

In preparing a report like this there is always a dilemma about using formal, multivariate methods of statistical analysis. Powerful statistical techniques make a major contribution to the interpretation of the data, and they compress a mass of statistical results into compact form. In particular, they are indispensable for handling the problem which statisticians refer to as multicollinearity; that is, the tendency of explanatory variables to be correlated with one another to the point where the effect of one variable easily can be confused with the effect of another variable. Yet most people interested in the travel market are not trained as statisticians. A report built around a set of equations would be about as readily understood as a report written in Sanskrit.

The resolution of this dilemma adopted here has been to carry out the complex analysis but exclude it from the main body of the report and to present it as clearly as possible in an appendix. Major findings from the appendix are stated verbally in the main body. Various cross-tabulations shown in the narrative text are approximations to the findings obtained from the statistical analysis. The report also includes, in Appendix IV C, a set of tables showing in more detail the findings summarized in the text tables. In some instances, apparent discrepancies between the text tables and the tables in Appendix IV C arise because cases for which information was not ascertained are shown in the Appendix, while in the preparation of the text tables these cases have been assumed to be distributed similarly to those for which information is known.

Sponsors

This report could not have been prepared without the support given to the whole program of study by all those organizations which have sponsored one or more of the surveys. The names of these organizations and the years in which they were sponsors are as follows:

> The Boeing Company, 1957, 1958, 1960
> The Federal Aviation Agency, 1962
> The General Motors Company, 1960, 1962
> The General Electric Company, 1960
> The Greyhound Corporation, 1962
> The Hertz Corporation, 1962
> New York Central System, 1955, 1956, 1957
> Pennsylvania Railroad Company, 1957
> The Port of New York Authority, 1955, 1956, 1960, 1962
> Time, The Weekly Newsmagazine, 1958, 1962
> United Air Lines, 1960

The preparation of this summary report has been sponsored by:

> The Boeing Company
> The Federal Aviation Agency
> The Port of New York Authority, Aviation Department
> The Port of New York Authority, Port Development Department
> Time, The Weekly Newsmagazine
> United Air Lines

Mention should be made also of the important intellectual and financial contributions to the statistical work reported in Appendix I made by the Research Seminar in Quantitative Economics of the Department of Economics of The University of Michigan. The seminar is under the direction of Daniel B. Suits and W. H. Locke Anderson.

The Staff

This volume has been prepared as a project of the Economic Behavior Program of the Survey Research Center. The center is a division of the Institute for Social Research of the University of Michigan. Directors of the various units are: Program, George Katona; Center, Angus Campbell; and Institute, Rensis Likert. The authors are especially indebted to William Ladd and Nancy Barth for extensive assistance in the preparation of the tabulations and graphs and in the assembly of the report itself. The index was prepared by Nancy Barth. They are also much indebted to Grace Beardsley who edited the manuscript. The tables were typed for photographic reproduction by Mary Sano and Sandra Berman.

CONTENTS

Preface   iii

I. *Who Travels?*   1
    A. Introduction   1
    B. Purposes of Travel and Attitudes Toward Travel   4
    C. Frequency of Travel, All Modes Combined, 1955 and
        1962   14
    D. People Who Never Travel   22
    E. Frequent Travelers and Their Role in the Travel
        Market   23
    F. Vacation Travel   28
    G. Overseas Travel   31

II. *Choice of Mode of Travel*   35
    A. Division of the Market Among the Four Modes of Travel,
        1955 to 1962   36
    B. Determinants of Choice of Mode   41

III. *Auto*   59
    A. Experience with Auto Travel   60
    B. Frequency of Travel by Auto, 1955 and 1962   64
    C. Regional Differences in Auto Travel   73
    D. Speed and Superhighways   79

IV. *Air*   81
    A. Attitudes Toward Air Travel   83
    B. Experience with Air Travel   88
    C. Frequency of Travel by Air, 1955 and 1962   95
    D. Regional Differences in Air Travel   104
    E. Response to the Introduction of Jet Powered Air Craft .   107
    F. Time to Reach the Airport   111
    G. Air Trips Versus Communication Without Travel   112
    H. Use of Rented Cars on Air Trips   114
    I. Responses to Hypthotical Changes in the Price of Air
        Travel   115

V. *Rail*   117
    A. Attitudes Toward Rail Travel   118
    B. Experience with Rail Travel   124
    C. Frequency of Travel by Rail, 1955 and 1962   128
    D. Regional Differences in the Use of Rail   136

VI. *Bus* 139
    A.   Attitudes Toward Bus Travel 140
    B.   Experience with Bus Travel 143
    C.   Frequency of Travel by Bus, 1955 and 1962 146
    D.   Regional Differences in the Use of Bus 154

VII. *Conclusion* 157

Appendix I. - Multivariate Analysis 161
    A.   Frequency of Travel 162
    B.   Choice of Mode 176

Appendix II. - Survey Methodology 181
    A.   Description of Methods 181
    B.   Expansion of Number of Air Trips 183
    C.   Sampling Errors 189

Appendix III. - List of Publications 191

Appendix IV. - Tables 193
    A.   List of Tables 193
    B.   List of Graphs 201
    C.   Tables 205

Appendix V. - Index 367

WHO TRAVELS?   I

A. Introduction

Modern American society is increasingly a mobile, travel-oriented society. Much of the nation's resources are devoted to getting people from one place to another. More and more physical space is taken up by stretches of asphalt, concrete, and steel rails. Even air space is filled in some urban areas. Changing patterns and modes of travel have altered the economic and social structure of the nation. People have become accustomed to mobile ways of living, and businesses have become accustomed to depending on modern means of travel for carrying on their activities.

A moment's reflection helps to realize the extent of the changes. A blue-collar worker on a six or seven day work week early in this century had neither time nor resources to travel, except perhaps to a new job. People living in rural areas never dreamed of leaving the farm for extensive traveling. Very few people were able to travel for other than utilitarian reasons.

A series of developments extending over decades has changed the picture. Today people have more leisure time, more money, better educations, and better jobs than their forebears. Paid vacations are common. Speed of modern travel makes it possible to reach almost any major point in the world within a day or two, and cost is so reduced that travel is no longer a luxury enjoyed by the few. There is little doubt that Americans in the 1960's are more mobile than ever before.

Viewed in this perspective the series of travel market surveys reported here came late upon the scene. The changes between 1955 and 1962 cover only a part of the long history of the increasing mobility of the population. That there were substantial changes in this short span of years is in itself revealing as to the extent of the larger process of change.

While the impact of the vast increase in American mobility upon the structure of our society is an important and at the same time too much neglected subject of inquiry, it is not the focus of this report. This investigation has been conceived and carried out for the purpose of contributing to the solution of problems of public and private economic policy arising from the changing travel market. These problems are numerous and varied. They include such questions as investment - new investment in airports, aircraft, and highway transportation; price policy - pricing of trips by common carriers; product policy - exact time, place, and other detailed characteristics of the transportation service to be offered; and problems of information - telling the public about the services offered.

Since this research is concerned only with the demand side of the travel market, for the most part it does not lead directly to problem solutions. Policy must be based on information about costs as well as about demand. It is the main purpose of this report to provide part of the information needed to appraise the outcomes of alternative courses of economic policy. Considering how long trains, planes, buses, and automobiles have been in existence; and considering the extent to which society has been altered by these mechanical contrivances; surprisingly little is known about how much they are used, by whom, where, and why, and what the trends over time in all of these matters are like.

In many ways, the period from 1955 to 1962 is an excellent period for studying changes in the travel market because many important shifts took place in the market structure during this time. The Interstate and Defense Highway Program was begun. Commercial jet aircraft came into use. In 1955 the common carrier market was divided fairly evenly among the airlines, buses, and railroads; however rail travel held a slight edge over the buses in revenue passenger miles and a margin of about three billion passenger miles over the airlines; and bus travel also exceeded air travel. By 1962, however, the airlines accounted for almost half of common-carrier passenger miles by all three modes, and even bus travel exceeded rail travel by three or four billion passenger miles. As for the automobile, estimates of volume of travel are imprecise, but the number of automobiles registered in the United States rose sharply from 48 million at the beginning of 1955 to 63 million at the beginning of 1962.

Among the questions which may be posed relative to changes in the travel market over the period studied are the following:

1. Are there any differences in the characteristics associated with travel by each of the modes in 1955 as compared with 1962?
2. What is the future of the currently dwindling rail-passenger market?
3. What possibilities exist for diversion of automobile travel to common-carrier travel, and particularly to air travel?
4. What are the possibilities for the continued expansion of air travel?
5. Does the continued concentration of population into urban areas bear implications for the future of the automobile travel market in relation to that of the common-carrier?

The relative positions of each of the common-carrier markets and of the automobile market 10 or 20 years from now will be decided largely by policy decisions already made or now in the process of being made. To some extent, consumer tastes and preferences will help dictate future trends. But consumer tastes and preferences often are predicated upon imposed innovations, which in turn are based on supposition about what consumers might want. A decision to proceed with a supersonic airliner may materially alter future travel patterns. Policy decisions relative to the speed with which the Interstate Highway Program is completed may influence the scheduling of surface travel and the desire by consumers to expand their travel by bus and automobile. Policy decisions or lack of policy decisions relative to the introduction of efficient mass-transit facilities will continue to have an important effect on whether people feel that they can afford to maintain an automobile in congested urban areas. Decisions concerning development of intermediate and short-range aircraft may lead to alteration of the structure of the market for trips of less than 500 to 1000 miles. It is hoped that the information presented in this report will make some useful contribution in reaching such policy decisions.

Of course, not all decisions affecting travel are made by government. Once common carriers have received authorization from the government to operate, they are free to make a wide range of decisions about the level of services they provide and the courtesy and convenience with which they provide these services. Many carriers have tried to anticipate the needs and desires of their passengers and to adjust their operations accordingly. Some of the factors that contribute to consumer attitudes toward travel and are, perhaps, relatively independent of the schedule or cost, may be assumed to be important without research. To illustrate, few travelers welcome unsanitary restrooms and eating places, discourteous service, or out-of-date facilities. No one likes to have to organize a search party to find out the cost of a ticket and the schedule of arrivals and departures. Such considerations were taken for granted in planning the research into consumer attitudes toward travel which will be discussed extensively in this report.

In the remainder of this chapter, information will be presented concerning travel without distinguishing among the different modes used. The question, "Who travels?" will be approached by discussing the reasons some people have for taking trips and the reasons others offer for not taking trips. This presentation will be followed by a discussion of the frequency of travel in the years 1955 and 1962. The total travel market is so broad and so diverse that it is essential to consider portions of it separately. With regard to frequency of travel, there are two extreme groups - those who never travel at all and those who travel very frequently. Each of these groups is discussed. The final sections of the chapter concern two other special sections of the travel market, vacation and overseas travel. Subsequent chapters will consider the division of the market among the several modes of transportation.

B. Purposes of Travel and Attitudes Toward Travel

Purposes of travel: The starting point in analysis of the travel market must be the distinction between business and non-business travel. Most people readily distinguish trips made in connection with their work from those made primarily for other reasons. Whether business or personal funds are tapped is a matter of obvious importance. When business foots the bill, speed has direct financial consequences. An employer sending an employee from New York to San Francisco, for example, certainly will be aware of the fact that he must pay the man's salary all the while he crosses the continent whether by air, rail, or highway.

The following tabulation shows how total travel was divided between business and non-business in 1955 and 1962, as well as modes of travel for each:

| | Per Cent of All Trips | |
Purpose and Mode	1955	1962
Business	24	27
Auto	17	21
Air	4	4
Rail	2	1
Bus	1	1
Non-business	76	73
Auto	65	65
Air	2	3
Rail	5	2
Bus	4	3
Total	100	100

For example, of all trips in 1955 about 24 per cent were business and 76 per cent non-business. The auto carries practically all non-business travelers and even the majority of those on business. In 1962 about 27 per cent of travel was on business. The share of all trips which were by auto increased 4 per cent in the period, and the increased use of this mode of travel was entirely for business. These estimates, however, are subject to substantial margins of uncertainty because of memory error in reports of trips by frequent travelers. This point is discussed in detail in Section E of this chapter.

A more detailed description of the purposes of travel, based on people's statements regarding their most recent trip, appears in the following tabulation:

Purpose of Trip	Per Cent of Trips, 1955
Business travel	19
For employer (business, government)	8
By self-employed (business or professional man)	8
Convention or meeting	3
Personal affairs	17
Emergency, illness, death, to visit doctor or hospital	7
Escort or drive someone	3
Moving to new home	2
Other personal affairs	5
Vacation and pleasure travel	64
Visit friends, relatives	25
Other vacation and pleasure trips	39
Total	100

Business travelers are, in general, frequent travelers. Hence, in this table business travel registers only 19 per cent, as compared to 24 in the earlier table, because only each person's most recent trip is included. In business travel self-employed or professional men are important as well as employees of business enterprises or the government. Actually, not a great deal is known about the reasons for business travel nor its possible response in volume to changes in price, speed, or other aspects of the service. Information available concerning the possibility of substituting improved long distance communication, by television, telephone, or other means, for business trips by air and rail points to the conclusion that the possibilities of such substitution are limited. This evidence is discussed in a later chapter.

Much more can be said about the market for non-business travel. In the first place, to assume all non-business travel is pleasure travel is to oversimplify. Many trips taken in connection with personal affairs hardly can be described as pleasure trips. Often they involve an emergency, illness, death of someone in the family, a visit to a doctor, or obtaining some other medical services. For example, one elderly man reported the purpose of his most recent trip as follows: "I went to Sharon Springs, New York, for the baths. I go every year to try to help my arthritis." Another kind of non-business trip may be pleasureable but is not primarily for pleasure; for example, trips to a new home, to school, or escorting someone somewhere. Nonetheless, and in spite of all these exceptions, the majority of non-business trips are for vacation and pleasure.

Motives for travel: To classify trips into broad groups by purpose is useful, but it fails to do justice to the variety and complexity of
the motives for travel, especially the motives for non-business travel.
The motives for vacation and pleasure travel fall into three groups.
First is the desire for social prestige. People in the upper income
brackets and with high levels of education are known to be frequent travelers. Travel is associated with status and is, therefore, desirable.
A second type of motivation is social: Many trips are undertaken to re-
new personal ties with friends and relatives living at a distance. The
third group of motives consists of desires for individualistic gratifications found in travel such as curiosity, desire for varied experiences,
or temporary escape from their accustomed environment.

One measure of the importance of these different motivations is
obtained by noting the frequency with which they are mentioned in different contexts. The first group of motivations, those concerning social
prestige, must be approached with discretion. Using one approach,
people were asked to complete sentences with the first words that
popped into their heads. Spontaneous comments such as the following
can be revealing:

People Who Travel a Lot are:	Per Cent, 1962
Lucky, happy	28
Wealthy, can afford to travel	14
Well-informed	11
Interesting	3
Restless, nervous	4
Crazy, stupid	3
Unfortunate, unhappy	2
Other (tourists)	23
Don't know, no answer	12
Total	100

The comments on these anonymous people, about whom nothing is suggested except that they travel, are overwhelmingly favorable. The response that they are lucky or happy is the most frequent single answer.
Attribution of high status appears in the comments of the 14 per cent
who ascribe wealth to the frequent travelers, and equally in the 11 per
cent who assume them well informed and the 3 per cent who consider
them interesting.

A middle-aged technical librarian in a small city put it this way,
"People who travel a lot are interesting to talk to." The wife of a steel
mill worker in Baltimore said, "People who travel a lot probably got
more money than I'll ever have." Such comments are based on social

reality. The relation between income and travel has already been mentioned, and a similar relation exists between education and frequency of travel. Some replies, however, do suggest that for some people frequent travel has dubious connotations. An engineer on a construction company dredge remarked, "People who travel a lot - I don't know - I suppose they're gypsies."

In the context of a different sentence completion item as shown below, attribution of very similar attitudes and motivations on the part of travelers is suggested:

Mr. and Mrs. Smith Want to Go to Europe Because They Want to:	Per Cent, 1958
Go sight-seeing; to travel around	23
See the World's Fair in Brussels	2
See historic places	1
See how other people live	2
See Europe, or a particular country in Europe	2
Go there, they have never been	9
Visit friends, relatives	8
Visit someone in the service; see where their boy fought	1
See where their own ancestors lived	1
Do what other people do - the Joneses went	3
Show they can, they have the money	6
Have a good time, have a vacation	13
Enjoy traveling, take long trips	8
Benefit because travel is broadening, educational, interesting	2
Other comments	14
Not ascertained	5
Total	100

The nature of this sentence completion item gives people a chance to respond to Europe as a specific destination or to speak about travel in terms other than the characteristics of the people who take the trip. Nevertheless, 9 per cent still refer to the motivation of conspicuous consumption, show they can do what the "Joneses do."

The importance of the second group of motives, those arising out of the desire to maintain personal ties with people that are distant, is easier to show because the subject is easier to discuss with people. As already mentioned, when asked 25 per cent of the respondents stated

that the purpose of their most recent trip was to visit friends or relatives. Even in the context of the Mr.-and-Mrs.-Smith-went-to-Europe
item one respondent out of ten mentions personal ties (8 per cent,
friends or relatives; 2 per cent, service men or ancestors).

The strength of this motivation appears also in a quite different
context. In the 1956 survey people were asked, "Are there any trips
that you have thought you would like to take but you haven't been able
to? Two-thirds of the adult population answered "yes" to this question.
These people were then asked what sort of trip they were thinking
about, with results as follows:

Purposes of Trips People Would Like to Take	Per Cent of Adults Who Report Trips They Would Like to Take, 1956
Vacation and pleasure	62
To visit friends or relatives	22
Other vacation and pleasure trips	40
Personal affairs or business	1
No purpose mentioned; not ascertained	37
Total	100

Here 22 per cent specifically would like to visit friends or relatives.

The existence of this motivation presumes separation of people
from their close friends and relatives. Although only a small proportion of the population moves to a different geographic area in any one
year, when mobility over many years accumulates the mobile part of
the population turns out to be a majority. A study by the Survey Research Center has shown that of all heads of families only 35 per cent
are living in the area in which they were born, and even of these 8 per
cent at one time have lived elsewhere. Thus, only 27 per cent of all
heads of families always have lived in the area where they now reside.*
In short, a great majority of people have personal ties with friends and
relatives at a distance and a considerable minority would like to make
more frequent trips to visit them. A retired man living on social secu-
rity in Tallahassee, Florida, made a typical reply: "If I could pick the
way to spend my vacation this year, I'd spend it in St. Petersburg with
my brother."

The third group of motives, individualistic gratifications, includes
the general desire to go sightseeing, the most frequent answer to why

* See The Geographic Mobility of Labor: A First Report, Chapter 2,
"Patterns of Mobility."

Mr. and Mrs. Smith went to Europe. To the 23 per cent general sightseeing answers perhaps should be added the 9 per cent who ascribe to
the Smiths a desire to go to Europe because they never have been
there, a negative way of saying they want to see what's there. Addition-
ally, another 5 per cent mention wanting to see more specific places but
without personal associations. Thus, some sort of sightseeing desire is
contained in 37 per cent of the responses.

Other responses about what people would like to do in Europe
were obtained by a different sentence completion item:

If I Were in Europe the Thing I'd Most Like to Do Is:	Per Cent, 1958
See particular countries or parts of countries	29
Go sightseeing, travel around	25
See something in particular	16
Other answers; not ascertained	30
Total	100

Here 45 per cent answered with some particular sight, city, or region
that they would like to see. Vague curiosity is characteristic of only 25
per cent.

Travel for fun is different from satisfying one's curiosity and is
less emphasized in people's comments. Nevertheless, 13 per cent say
in essence that the Smith's went to Europe "to have a good time" or "to
have a vacation," and another 8 per cent touch this motive in saying the
Smiths enjoy traveling. A "good time" has different meanings to different people. Some types of travel are considered exciting, adventur-
ous, or even dangerous, and may be sought or avoided by people accordingly. If the place to be visited is regarded as exotic or remote, it is
much more likely to be thought exciting to travel there than to visit
places already familiar or nearby. Difference in motivation for the two
types of trip appears in the following tabulation from the 1958 survey:

Response	Traveling in the United States Is:	Traveling in Foreign Countries Is:
Wonderful, nice, pleasant	29	13
Entertaining, fun	9	5
Stimulating, exciting, adventurous	2	7
Dangerous	1	6
Other comments	59	69
Total	100	100

Danger, excitement, and adventure are not very often mentioned in connection with travel in the United States (3 per cent), but are spoken of more often with reference to foreign travel (13 per cent). But in neither case are these stirring qualities brought up often enough to indicate them as important motives for travel. Other individualistic motives were evident in the data gathered, but too few or too elusive to warrant summary.

It would be possible to study each of the three groups of motives discussed here much more intensively. The available evidence does at least indicate the importance of the three broad areas of desire: social recognition and prestige, maintenance of personal ties, and satisfaction of individualistic inner desires.

<u>Barriers to travel</u>: The barriers to travel fall into five broad categories. There is, first, the matter of expense. Consumers operate within monetary constraints, and travel must compete with other allocations of funds. Second, travel is hindered by lack of time. People may be tied to their jobs or fettered with other commitments. Poor health and the physical limitations associated with old age keep many persons at home. Fourthly, people with young children cannot travel as freely as adults who have none. And finally, people may not travel because either they or members of their immediate families, especially their husbands or their wives, are not interested in taking trips.

These barriers are important as determinants of the total volume of travel. They are important also as influences on where people will go and how they will get there. Where the motivation for travel is sufficiently powerful, people may overcome obstacles such as expense, health, dependents, or lack of time; but these forces still may influence their choice of travel mode or destination. Hence, these barriers will be discussed in the subsequent sections, which deal with the choice of method of transportation, as well as in the analysis of the total volume of travel.

The importance of expense as an obstacle to travel hardly needs elaborate documentation. The relation between income and the number of trips people take will be a recurring theme in this report. The following tabulation is based on two questions, asked in 1956; one on what trips people would like to take, but have not been able to; and a follow-up question about the reasons they haven't taken these trips:

Reasons Why People Don't Go On the Trips They Would Like to Take	Per Cent of Adults Who Report Trips They Would Like to Take, 1956
Too expensive	62
Can't leave business or job	18
Lacks time, too busy; refers to activity other than the job	7
Too busy, not clear whether refers to job or other activities	6
Respondent or other member of the family doesn't like to travel	17
Children or other dependents	12
Health	7
We are too old	2
Other	9
Total	140[1]

Fully 62 per cent of the people asked mention expense as a reason for not taking a desired trip. Even allowing for the interpretation that saying travel is too expensive is an indirect way of saying travel is not important, costs are a principal reason for staying home. The second reason, lack of time, is mentioned by 18 per cent who say they cannot leave their business or their job. A smaller group, 13 per cent, say that they can't get away because they are committed either to some activity other than their job or unspecified. Other reasons given are dislike of travel (17), encumbrance of children or other dependents (12), and physical infirmity (9), the last including ill health and old age.

Another approach to the barriers of travel, but in a context eliminating costs, was taken in this incomplete sentence: "Mr. and Mrs. Brown were offered an expense free tour of the United States, but they don't want to go because . . ."

Reasons Why Browns Do Not Accept an Expense-Free Tour of the U.S.	Per Cent, 1962
Want to but can't	42
Cannot get away from job	5
Cannot get away for non-job reasons; they have other plans	10
Poor health	8
They are too old	8
They have children whom they don't want either to leave or to take	11

1. Some people mentioned more than one reason.

(Cont'd)

Don't want to	26
Rather stay home	6
Do not like travel	9
Afraid to go far, not adventurous	3
Crazy, nuts, silly, stupid	8
Other	16
Don't know, no answer, not ascertained	16
Total	100

In these results since the question is phrased in terms of Mr. and Mrs. Brown's not *wanting* to go, it is not surprising that lack of time has dwindled in importance, but 15 per cent of the respondents still refer to the difficulty of getting away from a job or other commitments. A recent immigrant from Europe, employed as a ceramic mixer in a jet plane factory, said simply, "They lose their job."

There is no doubt that people aged over 65 travel less than others. The relationship of age to extent of travel will be shown in the next section of this chapter. The decline in frequency of automobile travel with increased age is particularly pronounced, as will be discussed in the chapter on automobile travel. There are subtle questions, however, as to whether the decline has to do with reduced physical powers, decrease in income associated with retirement, or psychological withdrawal. (Incidentally, it may be recalled that only 2 per cent of all adults say that they themselves are too old to take trips they would like to take, while 7 per cent mention their poor health.) In any case, in this tabulation, old age and poor health combined make infirmity a reason advanced by 16 per cent.

That presence of young children hampers a family's freedom of movement is reflected in 11 per cent of the answers. Typically, a young housewife in the $10,000 - $14,999 income group says of Mr. and Mrs. Brown, "They had small children to take care of." As will be discussed below, the presence of children also may be one consideration in the choice of means of transportation by people who do take trips.

Finally, in spite of widespread desires for travel, not everyone wishes to travel. Some people would just rather stay home, and for others a weak desire to travel is overbalanced by nervousness or fear of what the experience may bring. Attributions of these attitudes to the Browns account for 18 per cent of the answers. Such a reluctance to travel runs counter to the tide, but is large enough to be important. It will be recalled that in the immediately preceding table 17 per cent of the answers indicated someone in the family as disliking travel. A widow, aged 50, who works as a bookkeeper in a light fixture business, said succinctly of the Browns, "They hate to travel."

These motives for travel and barriers to travel are of basic importance in the travel market. In one sense the bulk of this report is devoted to showing how these forces work themselves out in determining demand for different modes of travel.

C. Frequency of Travel, All Modes Combined, 1955 and 1962

The most fundamental single measure of behavior in this research is the distribution of the adult population by number of trips taken per year. The distribution has shifted since 1955 as follows:

Number of Trips	Per Cent of Adults	
	1955	1962
No trips	39	34
1 trip	21	18
2-4 trips	22	23
5-15 trips	14	19
16 or more trips	4	6
Total	100	100

Corresponding to the dwindling of the non-travelers from 39 to 34 per cent, one notes a 5 per cent growth among travelers, from 61 per cent in 1955 to 66 per cent in 1962. But 5 percentage points amount to a relatively small increase, even taking into account the fact that the proportions apply to a larger population of adults due to the growth in the population of the country from 1955 to 1962. Of greater interest is the 7 per cent increase in the proportion who took 5 or more trips, from 18 per cent to 25 per cent of all adults.

To an economist, the first explanation that comes to mind for the increase in travel from 1955 to 1962 is the general increase in income over the period. As people's incomes rise, one would expect them to travel more, and it is well known this period witnessed a distinct upward shift in income for the population. The proportion of adults in each income class in 1955 and 1962 is shown in the appendix, Table 11. Does the rise in incomes account for the increase in travel? To answer this question, the basic data needed are the proportions in each income class in each year who took 5 or more trips. These proportions are shown in Graph 1 and in the following tabulation:

Family Income	Per Cent of Adults Who Took Five or More Trips	
	1955	1962
Under $2000	6	10
$2000-2999	10	13
$3000-3999	13	15
$4000-4999	16	17
$5000-5999	24	21
$6000-7499	22	28
$7500-9999	31	33

(Cont'd)	1955	1962
$10,000-14,999	39	43
$15,000 or more	44	48
All adults	18	25

GRAPH I

PER CENT OF ADULTS AT DIFFERENT INCOME
LEVELS WHO TOOK 5 OR MORE TRIPS BY
ANY MODE DURING THE SURVEY YEAR

Per Cent

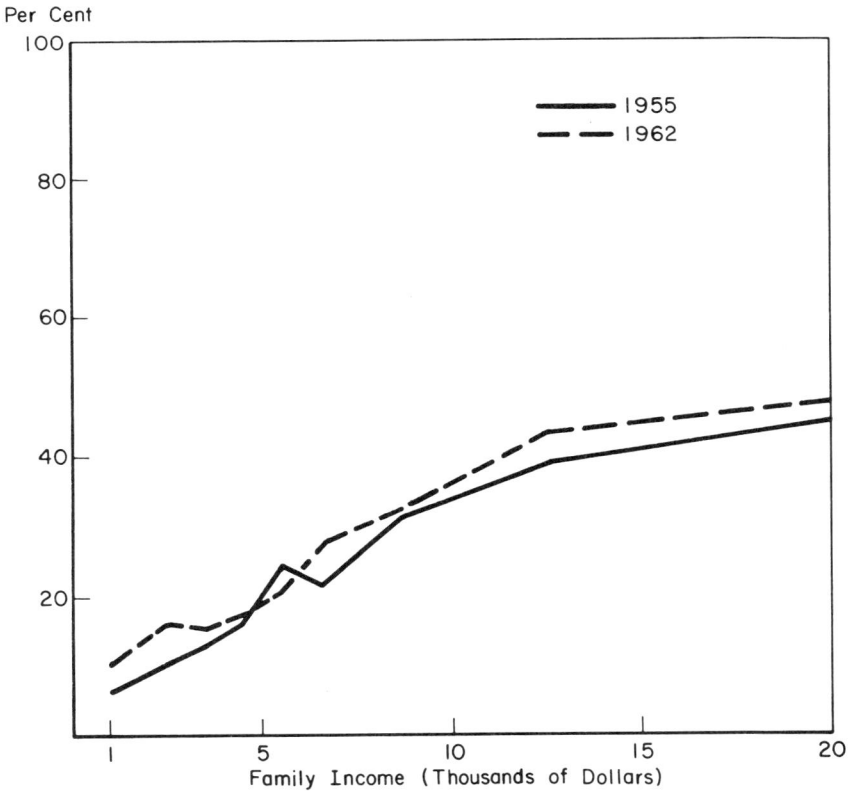

Family Income (Thousands of Dollars)

The powerful effect of income on frequency of travel is evident in both years. Ten per cent or less of the poorest people took 5 or more trips in either year, and the proportion rises to almost half of those persons with the most money.

GRAPH 2

PER CENT OF ADULTS AT DIFFERENT INCOME LEVELS WHO TOOK NO TRIPS BY ANY MODE DURING THE SURVEY YEAR

Per Cent

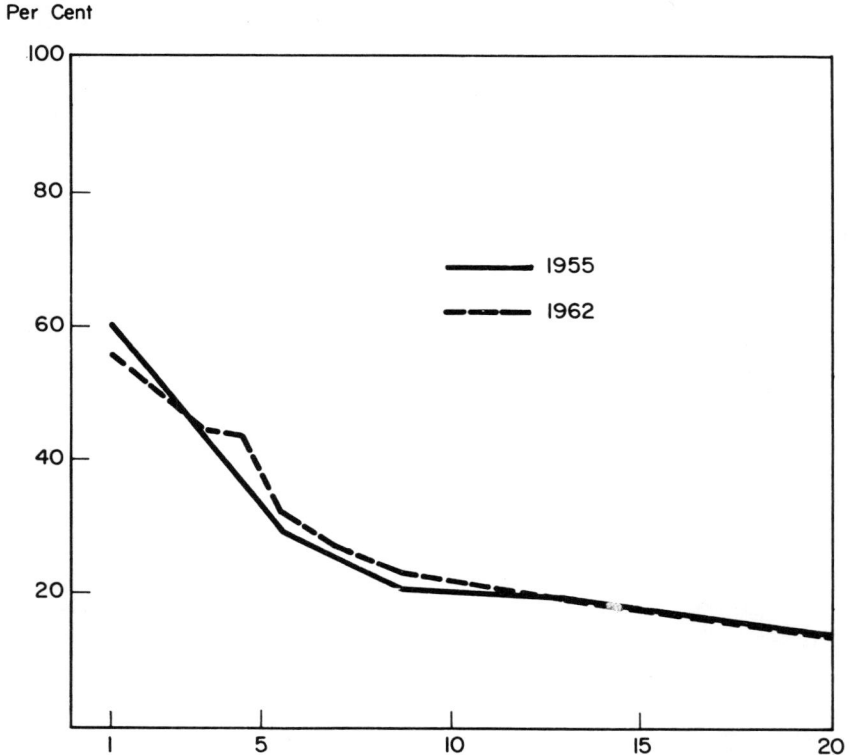

At each income level, however, with but one exception, the proportion of frequent travelers rose from 1955 to 1962. The increase in income cannot account for the rise in frequency of travel within income groups. Even adults at the bottom level took more trips. Increased income contributes only part of the explanation for increased travel.

The fact that almost half the adults in the top income group took five or more trips in 1962 suggests that the demand for travel is not easily saturated.

Strangely enough, the proportion of adults who took no trips at all did not decrease within income groups between 1955 and 1962. In fact, as is shown in Graph 2, in many income groups, the proportion who took no trip increased slightly. For the explanation of this development, it is necessary to go beyond the income distribution.

To a student of population change, the logical place to start in the analysis of travel might be with the effect of the changing age distribution of the population rather than with the effect of the changing distribution of income. Old age is a powerful deterrent to travel. That the proportion of adults who take no trip in a year increases with age is clearly shown in Graph 3 and in the following tabulation:

	Per Cent of Adults Who Took No Trip	
Age	1955	1962
18-24	34	34
25-34	34	31
35-44	34	26
45-54	40	32
55-64	44	36
65 and over	59	51
All adults	39	34

In spite of their age, however, there was a 8 per cent increase in travelers among persons 65 and over. But the picture continues to be one of old people staying at home.

The slow increase in the proportion of people 65 and over (shown in Table 11 in the appendix) tends to reduce the percentage of the population who travel in any one year. The slight shift in the age distribution from 1955 to 1962 worked in the opposite direction from the shift in the income distribution. The effect of the changes in income and other forces tending to increase travel was greater than the effect of the forces tending to reduce the amount of travel.

The distribution of the population between the two sexes remained constant over the period, and it continued to be true that men are somewhat more frequent travelers than women. That men form the larger group taking five or more trips a year is no doubt attributable to the greater proportion of men who travel on business. Details appear in the appendix, Table 14.

There have been dramatic changes over the period 1955 to 1962 in the types of transportation available to passengers. The technological changes in some forms of transportation and the increased investment for the attraction of travelers affect primarily the changing use of the different modes of travel. This change will be discussed in

GRAPH 3

PER CENT OF ADULTS IN DIFFERENT AGE GROUPS WHO TOOK NO TRIPS BY ANY MODE DURING THE SURVEY YEAR

Per Cent

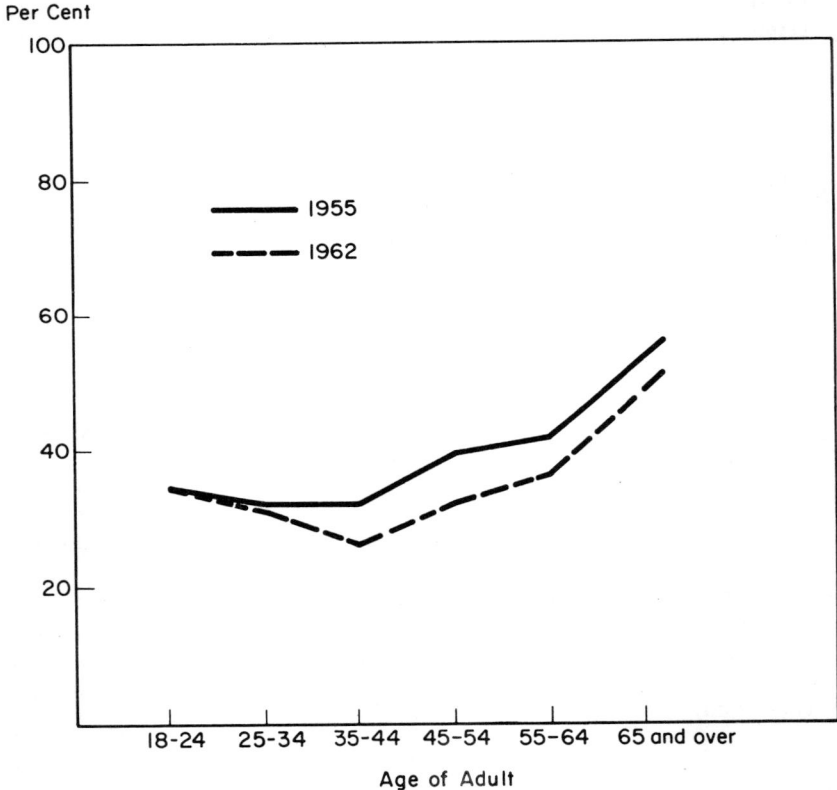

Age of Adult

Chapter II. No doubt technical improvements contributed to the increased total volume of travel over the years discussed in this report, but in a cross-section study their effect cannot be satisfactorily isolated.

Strictly speaking, the national travel market is an abstraction. People actually travel and carriers compete for markets between specific origins and destinations. While a national sample does not permit study of individual lines of travel, it does permit study of regions. Data have been prepared on four regions: Northeast, North Central,

GRAPH 4

PER CENT OF ADULTS LIVING IN DIFFERENT REGIONS WHO TOOK 5 OR MORE TRIPS BY ANY MODE DURING THE SURVEY YEAR

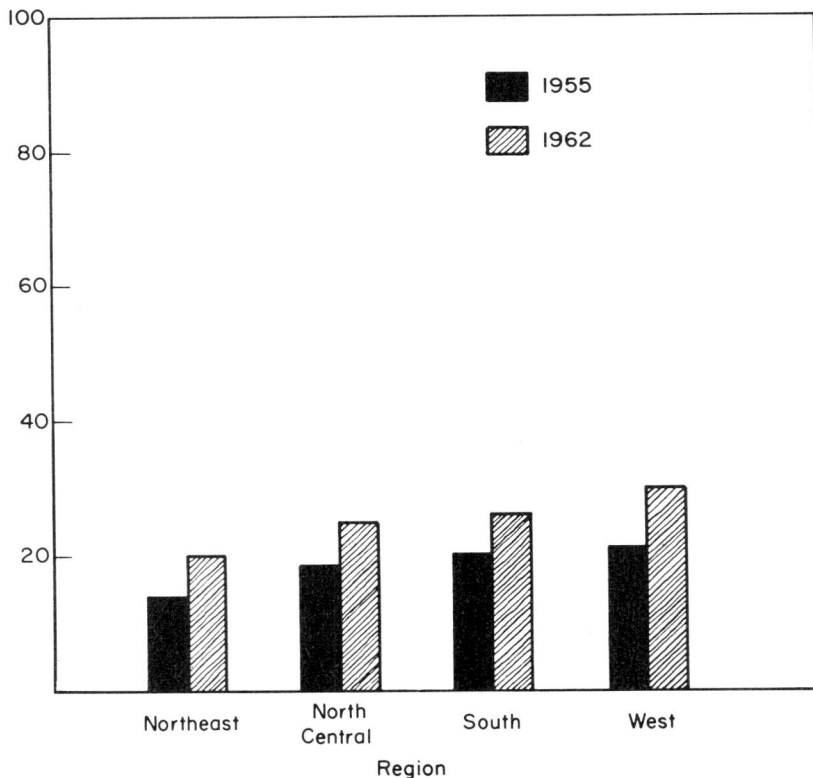

South and West. (For definition of these regions see the appendix, Table 15.) A comparison of frequency of travel in these regions is shown in Graph 4 and the following tabulation.

Region	Per Cent of Adults Who Took Five or More Trips	
	1955	1962
Northeast	14	20
North Central	19	25
South	20	26
West	21	30
All adults	18	25

These results show that the proportion of frequent travelers is larger in the West than the other regions, and has been increasing most rapidly in the West. In this region, where distances are great and the population is thinly distributed, the effect of the increased ease of transportation in recent years may be most sensitively reflected.

There has been considerable interest recently in an urbanized area in the northeastern United States, a megalopolitan corridor which extends roughly from Boston to Washington, D. C., east of the Appalachians. Special tabulations have been prepared comparing the travel patterns of people who live in: The New York metropolitan area, the remainder of the megalopolitan corridor, and the rest of the United States. The tabulation below shows the per cent of the frequent travelers among those living in these areas:

	Per Cent of Adults Who Took Five or More Trips	
	1955	1962
New York area	15	17
Megalopolis excluding New York area	12	25
Remainder of country	19	26

These results suggest that the proportion of the population who are frequent travelers in the megalopolitan area outside of New York was about the same by 1962 as in the country as a whole. In the New York area the per cent of frequent travelers increased only slowly from 1955 to 1962, falling behind the percentage of frequent travelers elsewhere. The reasons for this slow rate of growth in the New York area will be considered in later portions of this report. As will be there shown, the difference in rate of growth of travel is primarily a difference in automobile travel, which grows more slowly in New York than in other parts of the country. Thus, travel in the West increased the most in the period 1955 to 1962, while in the New York area travel increased least, owing to the relatively slow growth of long distance automobile travel in the latter area.

But the sub-divisions of New York are by no means homogeneous with respect to frequency of travel, as the following tabulation shows:

Sub-Division of the New York Area	Per Cent of Adults Taking Five or More Trips in Different Parts of New York, 1962
Manhattan	24
Bronx	21
Queens	*
Brooklyn	2
Newark, Jersey City	*
Suburbs in New York	18
Suburbs in New Jersey	26

* Less than one half of one per cent.

These estimates are approximate because of the small number of interviews in any subdivision (See Appendix, Table 17). It appears, however, even from these limited data, that people living in Queens and Brooklyn are less likely to be frequent travelers than either those living in Manhattan or those in the suburban areas in New York or New Jersey.

D. People Who Never Travel

The distribution of the population by frequency of travel runs a wide gamut of behavior. At one extreme are the very frequent travelers, subject of the next section; and at the other extreme are the very infrequent travelers, treated here.

Although two-thirds of the adult population take at least one trip to a point 100 miles or more away in any twelve month period (as has been indicated already, most of them traveling by auto), of the remaining third some people never in their lives have been 100 miles from home. In the 1955 survey 7 per cent of all adults were found *never* to have taken a trip 100 miles away by air, rail, bus, or auto.

As one might expect, these non-travelers are poor. In 1955 two-thirds of them had incomes below $4000. They tend also to be in the older age groups, but here the concentration is less pronounced. In 1955, 19 per cent of them were aged 65 and over, while 12 per cent of the survey population as a whole were of comparable age. They tend to live either in the central cities of the largest metropolitan areas or in the rural parts of the nation. In 1955, 27 per cent of them lived in the central cities of the 12 largest metropolitan areas, but of the general population only 16 per cent lived there. Forty-one per cent of them lived in rural areas, but of all adults only 33 per cent were country dwellers. Thus for the most part they live either in the poorer districts of the urban centers or in the less prosperous farming country. Viewed in a larger perspective, the most remarkable fact is not so much that there are such people but that they form such a small percentage of the total.

E. Frequent Travelers and Their Role in the Travel Market

To a remarkable extent the travel market is dominated by a relatively small group of people. Estimates of the exact share of the total travel market accounted for by the very frequent travelers depend on what definitions are used and on the accuracy of the measurements. As will be discussed below, the problems of measurement are redoubtable. Nevertheless, whatever measure of travel is used, a small group of frequent travelers accounts for a large proportion of the total travel market.

The following estimate of the extent of concentration of trips of all types among relatively few people is based on data for 1962. It excludes entirely the 34 per cent of all adults who took no trips:

Number of Trips Taken	Distribution of Travelers (per cent)	Distribution of Trips (per cent)
1-2	42	9
3-4	20	10
5-9	18	17
10-19	12	22
20-39	6	20
40 and more	2	22
Total	100	100

At the bottom of the tabulation, it may be observed that the 2 per cent of all travelers who take 40 trips a year or more account for 22 per cent of all travel. These few people take more trips than the travelers who take 1-2 trips plus those who take 3-4 trips, who combined are 62 per cent of all travelers but account for only 19 per cent of all travel. These estimates are illustrated in Graph 5, and the same distribution is shown in somewhat more detail in Table 18 in the Appendix. Although in all likelihood these results overstate the true concentration of travel, they are so extreme that they could be substantially in error and the point of high travel concentration among a few persons still be valid.

Evidence of concentration also appears if the total market is broken down by mode of travel, as is done in detail in later chapters. Very frequent travelers are primarily people who travel on business. In the air travel market about 60-66 per cent of all trips are business trips. Persons taking such trips represent only about 4 per cent of all adults. Within the group of business air travelers there is further concentration. It was estimated in the 1962 survey that three-quarters of all business travelers take from one to four trips and thereby account for only about one quarter of the business air trips. This leaves roughly one quarter of the business air travelers - one per cent of all adults - accounting for three business air trips out of four, or nearly half of all air travel.

The concentration of travel has major consequences in two directions. In the first place, the characteristics of the frequent travelers are of special importance to the travel industry. Carriers compete for the patronage of the frequent traveler. Who these people are and how they can be reached are matters of concern from a marketing point of view. Their socio-economic characteristics are analyzed below.

In the second place, from the point of view of research methodology, it is essential to take into account the role of the very frequent traveler in the planning of research and the interpretation of research findings. People who are not directly concerned with the conduct of research have a natural inclination to leave research methods to the researchers and the dull appendices at the back of the report. Nonetheless, some of the implications for travel research of the concentration of travel deserve wider understanding. They are discussed subsequently.

Characteristics of frequent travelers: If frequent travelers are taken to be those who report 16 or more trips in the survey year, they comprise 6 per cent of all adults, and their characteristics may be summarized as follows:

> 36 per cent have incomes over $10,000
> 47 per cent have attended college
> 67 per cent live in metropolitan areas
> 73 per cent are in the age range 25-54

Thus, frequent travelers tend to be well off, college educated city people of middle age. This characterization, it should be kept in mind, refers to frequent travelers by any mode for any purpose. People who travel frequently by air on business, for example, are a smaller and more selected group of people. (See Chapter IV.)

Methodological implications of the concentration of travel: There are three types of errors encountered in sample surveys of the population; sampling error, error of non-response, and response error. All three types tend to shoot up when the behavior to be studied has a distribution like that illustrated in Graph 5.

Sampling error is the error which arises because only a sample of the population is interviewed instead of the entire population. The sampling error becomes high when, for example, estimates of the mean

GRAPH 5

PER CENT OF TRAVELERS BY NUMBER OF TRIPS TAKEN, 1962

Per Cent

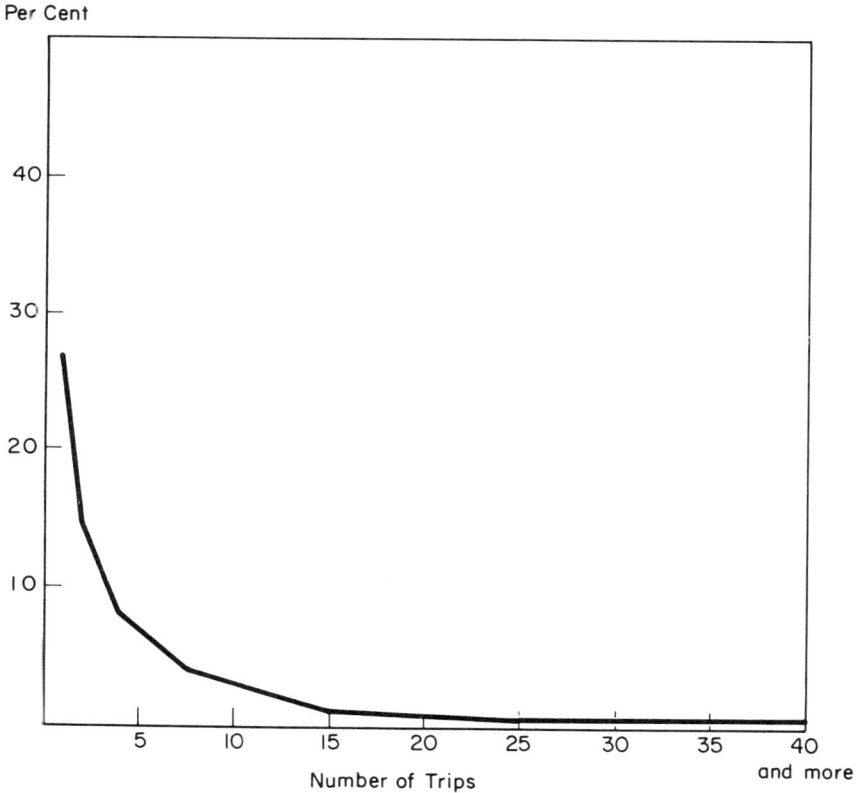

Number of Trips

number of air trips per person are heavily influenced by the chance exclusion of a few very frequent travelers. Estimates of total air travel from the survey are subject to the same kind of uncertainty because total air travel is estimated by multiplying mean air trips per adult by the number of adults.

Inherent in the nature of the distribution of trips is a further difficulty, which is referred to as non-response bias. Frequent travelers are less likely to be at home than those who do not travel. Hence, frequent travelers are not likely to be found by interviewers on first call. Persistent call backs are necessary to catch them all at home.

The importance of this bias may be illustrated with reference to air travel experience. People who are experienced as air travelers are known to be likely to travel repeatedly by air and to travel frequently by other modes as well. Necessarily these people must leave home frequently. It seemed reasonable to suggest, therefore, that there might be a consistent difference in air travel experience between people who are easy to find at home and people who are hard to find at home. This hypothesis was tested using data on air travel experience collected in connection with the *1960 Survey of Consumer Finances*. The results follow:

Air Travel Experience	Number of Calls Made by Interviewer Before Interview Was Taken								
	All	One	Two	Three	Four	Five	Six	Seven or More	Not Recorded
Have taken an air trip	29	25	27	35	36	39	35	32	24
Never took an air trip	71	75	73	65	64	61	65	68	76
Total	100	100	100	100	100	100	100	100	100

People interviewed on the first or second call differ consistently from those interviewed on all later calls. Of those interviewed on the first call, 25 per cent had taken an air trip, compared to 27 per cent on the second call, and over 30 per cent for the third call and higher calls. If a survey were limited to two calls, for example, the estimated proportion of experienced air travelers would be 26 per cent, compared to an estimate for all adults of 29 per cent from the data collected from the 1960 survey.

The difference in the proportion of air travelers from call to call would persist regardless of the size of sample. A complete census of the population in which only one call was made per family and no attempt was made to return to those not at home would yield an estimate of about 25 per cent experienced travelers. A better estimate of the true figure could be made from a sample of only a few hundred interviews in which repeated calls were made on those not at home. Thorough investigation of the sample is of paramount importance to reduce errors of non-response.

The third kind of error arises when the answers people give to questions are not accurate. The concentration of travel creates problems of such response error. It is difficult to obtain precise information from frequent travelers in a single interview covering all of their trips over a period as long as a year. People who take 10, 20, 30, 40, or 50 trips in a year cannot recall them all individually. If these trips are repetitive, the traveler knows the pattern. For example, if he goes from Chicago to New York *every* Wednesday all year round, he knows he takes 52 trips a year. Such repetition seems to be unusual. A man who takes frequent trips at irregular intervals to many destinations will find it impossible to remember them all. When he is asked how many trips he took in a long period, such as a year, he can give only an estimate.

Will the estimate be systematically too high or too low? People value travel positively. As shown above, the comments about "people who travel a lot" are overwhelmingly favorable. The natural tendency of a respondent talking about himself (or someone in his family) is to exaggerate the extent to which he participates in activities which carry social prestige. This exaggeration, of course, may be unconscious. The person does not really know the exact answer as to how many trips he took; he is asked to make an educated guess; he makes a guess which reflects credit upon himself.

This difficulty seems to apply much more to estimates of the total number of trips in a given period than to estimates of modes of travel used. Experiments with variations in the way questions are asked failed to produce any variation in estimates of the proportion of the population who took at least one trip, say, by air, in a period of a year. These experiments are discussed in Appendix IIA in more detail.

There is a tendency on the part of people not familiar with the strengths and weaknesses of sample surveys to take an all or nothing position. Either surveys are perfect sources of data, free from all inaccuracy, or they are a tissue of errors. The facts are more complex.

It is the view of the authors of this report that statistics based on estimates of *numbers* of trips are subject to a substantial margin of error and should be treated with extreme caution. For example, the tabulation shown at the beginning of this section of the per cent of all trips accounted for by frequent travelers is subject to error. It is not accidental that such statistics play a smaller role in this report than in the first report in the series. The tables that group adults into broad categories according to the number of trips of a certain type which they took in the last year should not be interpreted too literally. If four groups are shown, for example, it is reasonable to take the view that these four groups are properly ranked according to frequency of travel without insisting that the true points of division between the groups are exactly the points reported. People who say they took 40 or more air trips are frequent air travelers even though some of them may have taken only 30 trips. Since the most accurate distinction appears to be that between those who took no trip and those who took one or more trips, the distinction between travelers and non-travelers is emphasized in this report.

F. Vacation Travel

As the preceding discussion has shown, from the point of view of the people who travel the reason most frequently given for taking a trip is for a vacation. The market for vacation travel, therefore, deserves analysis in its own right.

Asked if they have ever taken a vacation trip to a point 100 miles or more away, about three adults in four will reply that they have. The proportion of adults who at some time have taken a vacation trip grows with income, as one might expect and as the following tabulation shows:

Experience with Vacation Travel to a Place 100 Miles Away (1958 Survey)	Family Income				
	All Adults	Under $3000	$3000 -4999	$5000 -7499	$7500 +
Have taken a vacation trip	77	60	74	88	93
Never have taken a vacation trip	23	40	26	12	7
Total	100	100	100	100	100

The 93 per cent vacationers in the $7500 income and over class contrasts with 60 per cent vacationers among those whose family income is below $3000. Later studies reinforce the impression that it is people in the upper income groups who are important in the market for vacation travel.

The most detailed information on spending on vacation trips collected by the Survey Research Center was in connection, not with the National Travel Market Surveys, but with the 1962-1963 Surveys of Consumer Finances. The following discussion is based on the data from the 1962 Survey of Consumer Finances in which vacation trips were considered if they involved a total outlay of $100 or more without regard to trip distance. People were asked, first, whether they took any vacation trips during the year under study, and second, whether they spent $100 or more on vacation trips during that year. That the proportion of all spending units who meet this double criterion rises with income is shown in the following tabulation:

Income in 1961	All	Amount Spent on Vacation Travel	
		Zero or Under $100	$100 or Over
Under $1000	100	95	5
$1000-1999	100	93	7
$2000-2999	100	86	14
$3000-3999	100	86	14
$4000-4999	100	75	25
$5000-5999	100	81	19
$6000-7499	100	70	30
$7500-9999	100	52	48
$10,000-14,999	100	41	49
$15,000 or more	100	23	77
All incomes	100	73	27

It is most unusual for people at the bottom of the income distribution to spend as much as $100 in a year on vacation travel. Only about 1 in 20 of those with an income below $2000 reports such an outlay. At the other end of the income distribution, three fourths of those with incomes over $15,000 report a vacation expenditure of $100 or more.

The average (mean) expenditure on vacation travel (including those with no such outlay) also rises with income, as the following tabulation shows:

Income in 1961	Mean Expenditure on Vacation Trips in 1961
Under $3000	$30
$3000-4999	60
$5000-7499	70
S7500-9999	150
$10,000-14,999	260
$15,000 and over	610

People in the higher income groups, tnus, not only have larger incomes but spend larger percentages of their incomes on vacation travel. As a result average expenditures on such travel rise very sharply with income. From the income group below $3000 to that over $15,000 the increase from $30 to $610 is an increase by a factor of 20!

It is not to be assumed that all of people's expenditures on vacation trips are made on a single trip. The distribution of the number of vacation trips taken in 1961 for all spending units is as follows:

Number of Vacation Trips	Per Cent of All Spending Units
None	73
One	20
Two	5
Three	1
Four or more	1
Total	100

Thus, 7 per cent of the population took two or more vacation trips during the year. The proportion of people at different income levels who took any vacation trip and the proportion who took two or more trips are shown in Graph 6.

GRAPH 6

PER CENT OF ADULTS AT DIFFERENT INCOME
LEVELS WHO TOOK A VACATION TRIP, 1961

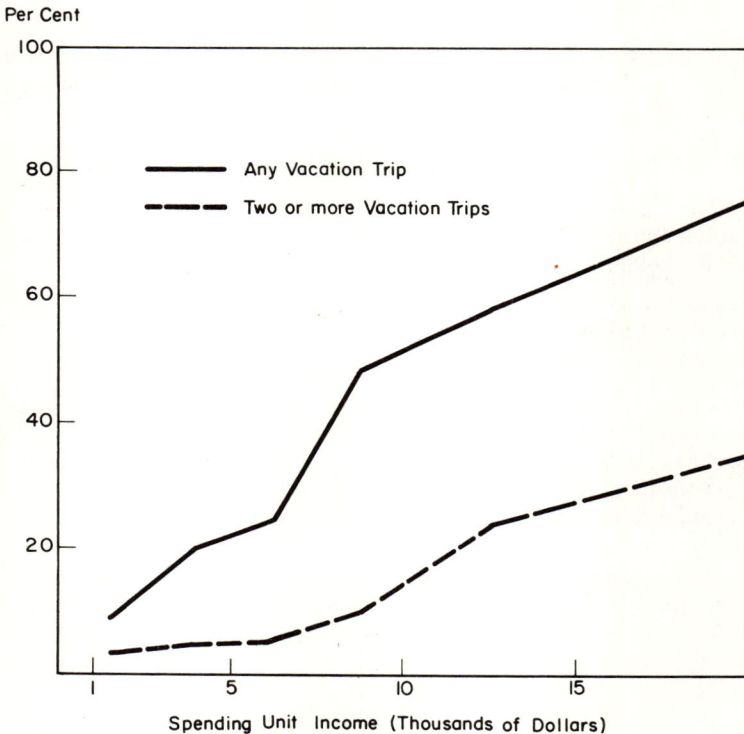

G. Overseas Travel

Another special segment of the travel market which is of interest in its own right is the market for overseas travel. The term overseas here includes all foreign countries except Canada and Mexico and also includes island portions of the United States.

Since the overseas travel market is a part of the total travel market, as a first approximation one would expect the same broad economic, social, and psychological variables to be important as for domestic travel. As a matter of fact, the barriers which prevent trips overseas are like the barriers to domestic trips, but they are higher. It takes more time and more money to go overseas. Children are even more of a concern. Old people are even more hesitant. Nervousness about venturing into the unknown is heightened.

The effect of the cost of overseas travel is reflected in the survey results in several ways. It appears in the small percentage of people who go overseas in any one year, in the strong effect of his income on the probability that a person will go overseas, and in the low propensity of families with children to go overseas.

Of all adults in any one year only about one per cent go overseas. The proportion of adults in different income groups who went overseas in 1959-60 varied as follows:

Family Income	Per Cent of Adults Who Took an Overseas Trip, 1959-1960
Under $3000	*
$3000-4999	*
$5000-7499	1
$7500-9999	1
$10,000-14,999	2
$15,000 +	8

* Less than one half of one per cent.

Thus, of those in the income groups below $10,000 only 1 per cent or less went overseas, but of those with incomes over $15,000, 8 per cent took an overseas trip.

Another measure provides a little more personal information on the traveler than that of income. The proportion of those at different stages of the family life cycle who went overseas in the same year was as follows:

Stage in Family Life Cycle	Per Cent of Adults Who Took an Overseas Trip, 1959-1960
Young, single	1
Young, married, no children	2
Young, married, children	*
Older, married, children	1
Older, married, no children	2
Older, single	1

* Less than one half of one per cent.

Children certainly show up as a hindrance to overseas travel. Youth or age doesn't seem to make much difference, if only there are no children. Thus, two important segments of the overseas travel market are childless young couples and older couples whose children have grown up and left home.

The best single predictor of whether an individual will go overseas in any one year, however, is prior overseas experience.

Prior Experience with Overseas Travel	Per Cent of Adults Who Took an Overseas Trip, 1959-1960
Had taken an overseas trip	12
Had not been overseas	*

* Less than one half of one per cent.

Less than 1 per cent of those who never had been overseas took their first trip in 1959-1960, but 12 per cent of those who had been overseas took another trip. (In the definition of experience overseas travel in the armed forces was not counted, but experience prior to immigration to the United States was counted.)

While the importance of travel experience as a predictor is clear, the interpretation of this variable is complex. In part, no doubt, "experience" merely reflects the probability that the same forces which led the person to go overseas in the first place may continue to influence his behavior. For example, if he is in the highest income bracket one year, he is likely to be there in other years. Yet it also seems probable that experience with overseas travel does itself change people's attitudes. Expectations of pleasure may be reinforced by pleasurable experiences. Nervousness and apprehension about strange places may be reduced by successful visits to such places.

This second interpretation implies that as the number of people who have been overseas grows, the number of potential future travelers also increases. From this point of view overseas travel by young people is of special interest to travel promoters since the young have more years ahead of them in which to travel overseas again. The proportion of adults of different ages in 1959-1960 who had ever been overseas was as follows:

Age of Adult	Per Cent Who Ever Had Been Overseas as Civilians
18-24	2
25-34	6
35-44	5
45-54	7
55-64	9
65 and over	7

Since older adults have had more years in which to go overseas, one would expect the proportion who have done so to rise with age. It is remarkable that of those aged 25-34, 6 per cent already had been overseas in 1959-60. Since others in this group of people surely will go overseas in the coming decades, by the time they are aged 65 and over many more than 6 per cent will have had this experience.

There are, then, three variables which influence the probability that an individual will take an overseas trip: his income, his stage in the family life cycle, and his prior experience. Those most likely to go overseas have incomes over $15,000; are married but have no children under 18; and have been overseas as civilians already.

Given the problem of explaining the total volume of travel by auto, air, rail and bus, there are two procedures which may be used. One is to advance in two stages, explaining in the first stage the total volume of travel, and in the second stage how the trips are distributed among the different modes. Thus, in the first chapter of this report there is an analysis of the total number of trips which people make. In this chapter there is an analysis of how people select their mode of travel. The two stages of analysis when combined constitute a complete explanation of the number of trips by each method of transportation.

The second procedure is to start directly with the explanation of the number of people who travel by each mode. Ignoring the total volume of travel by all modes combined, one may seek to explain the total volume of travel by each separate mode. This approach is taken in subsequent chapters, which consider separately travel by each of the four modes of transportation. In principle the two procedures should lead to the same conclusions. It is useful to approach the problem by both methods, however, since some aspects of the travel market are more easily appreciated by one route than by the other.

This discussion of people's selections of modes of travel is divided into two parts. The first part presents a summary of data about what the choice of travel mode has been. A discussion of the changing use of the four modes from 1955 to 1962 in the market as a whole is followed by an estimate for one given time of the division of the market among the modes for different lengths of trip. The second part of the chapter is concerned with the determinants of choice of mode.

A. Division of the Market among the Four Modes of Travel, 1955 to 1962

Changes in the use of the four modes of travel, 1955 to 1962: As discussed in Chapter I, between 1955 and 1962 there was a modest increase in the volume of travel unevenly distributed among the modes. As far as can be detected from the surveys, the changes in the use of the different modes were the result of changes in the percentage of adults using each mode at least once, not changes in the number of repeated trips made by those who traveled. The per cent using each mode in the two years is shown in the following tabulation:

Per Cent of Adults Traveling by Different Modes

Year	Auto	Air	Rail	Bus	Any Mode
1955	57.2	6.7	10.5	6.6	60.9
1962	64.0	10.7	7.4	8.5	66.2

There were substantial increases between 1955 and 1962 in the proportion of adults traveling by air and auto. By air the increase was from about 7 to nearly 11 per cent. By auto the increase was greater, from 57 to 64 per cent. Even a small shift in the proportion of the whole population traveling by a common carrier can make a large change in the number of persons traveling by that carrier. The changes in the per cent of adults traveling by each mode during the survey year are indicated also in Graph 7.

The upward shift between 1955 and 1962 in the proportion of adults traveling by air and by auto corresponds to the increase over the same period in the number of passenger miles traveled by these modes as estimated by other sources. A decline in the proportion of adults who took a rail trip from 1955 to 1962 is consistent, of course, with the decline in the aggregate passenger miles of rail travel. An increase in the proportion of bus travelers, however, is inconsistent with an estimated decline in aggregate passenger miles of bus travel. A possible explanation for the inconsistency is that recently more people are taking bus trips of moderate length. Many bus trips are shorter than the one way minimum of 100 miles requisite for trips to be considered in this study. It is possible that from 1955 to 1962 the new highways improved the position of the bus for trips of over 100 miles at the expense of rail travel, while for distances under 100 miles increased competition from private automobiles cut a swath in the bus travel market. Unfortunately, there is no body of information known to the authors against which this interpretation can be checked.

GRAPH 7

PER CENT OF ADULTS TRAVELING BY EACH MODE
DURING THE SURVEY YEAR

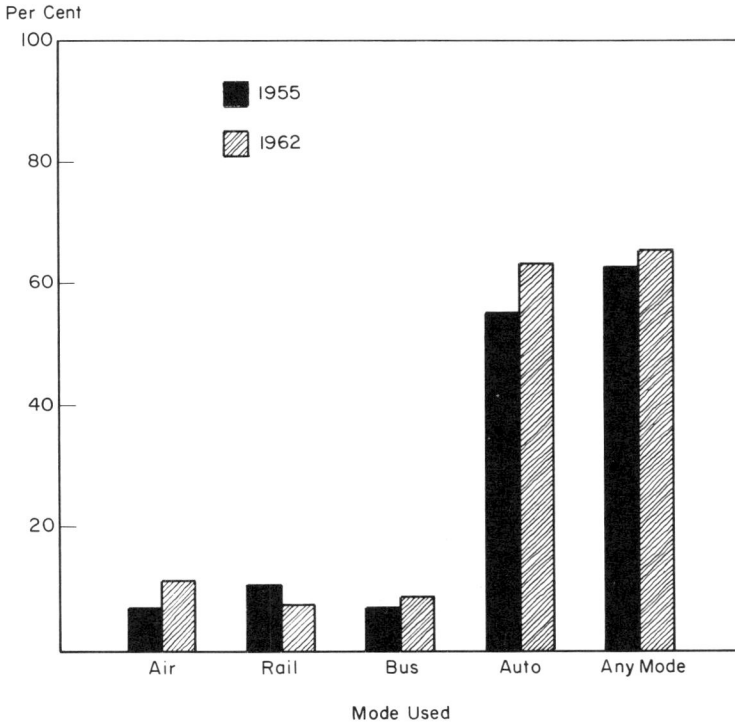

Do the indicated increases in auto and air travel and the decrease in rail travel hold for business travel as well as for non-business. Apparently, yes. The proportion of all adults who used each travel mode for each purpose was as follows:

Per Cent of Adults Traveling by Different Modes
for Business and Non-Business Purposes

	Auto		Air		Rail		Bus	
	1955	1962	1955	1962	1955	1962	1955	1962
For business reasons	7	10	2	4	2	1	1	1
For non-business reasons	53	61	5	8	8	6	6	8

Of all adults 7 per cent took a business trip by auto in 1955, 10 per cent
in 1962.   Business trips by air doubled, from 2 to 4 per cent. But rail
trips for business dropped from 2 to 1 per cent. Bus travel for business purposes remained rare.

Complete statistical analysis requires information about the number of trips taken by each individual who took one or more trips. Such
estimates are difficult to prepare in detail, as already discussed, owing
to the importance of frequent travelers in the travel market and the
small number of business travelers. The following tabulation indicates
the approximate number of trips by each mode taken in 1955 and 1962.
Business and non-business trips are shown separately:

Non-Business Trips

Number of Trips	Auto		Air		Rail		Bus	
	1955	1962	1955	1962	1955	1962	1955	1962
One	36	32	68	69	71	72	70	68
Two-four	38	37	27	26	27	23	23	25
Five and over	26	31	5	5	2	5	7	7
Total	100	100	100	100	100	100	100	100

Business Trips

Number of Trips	Auto		Air		Rail		Bus	
	1955	1962	1955	1962	1955	1962	1955	1962
One	28	32	38	40	53	63	59	68
Two-four	34	29	36	34	31	25	22	25
Five and over	38	39	26	26	16	12	19	7
Total	100	100	100	100	100	100	100	100

Broadly speaking, it is apparent that people who take non-business auto
trips often take several trips a year, but most people who take the same
kind of trip by a common carrier do so only once in a year. Take 1962
for example. Most people who took any non-business trip by auto took
from two to five or more trips; but by air, rail, and bus only one trip is
common.

Business travel resembles the pattern of non-business travel except in use of planes. For business air travel the frequency of trips
approaches that for trips by car.

The observed differences in frequency of travel between 1955 and
1962 in the above tabulation are mostly within the margin of sampling
error. It is the similarity in these distributions which led to the comment made earlier that the changes in the market over this period were

primarily changes in the percentage of travelers using the various modes. There does seem to have been an increase, however, in the proportion of non-business auto travelers who took five or more trips.

Approximate division of the market in 1955 - 1957 by mileage brackets: If it were possible to prepare the necessary data, it would be useful to divide the total market into sub-markets for trips of different distances and compare the proportion of each sub-market accounted for by the different modes of transportation in 1955 and 1962. Shifting portions of the market for trips of different lengths reflect successes and failures in the competitive struggle among modes within the travel market. While ideally the data should show for each year for each distance the proportion of the market won by each mode, it is not possible to prepare such a tabulation with the data at hand. An estimate can be made for the 1955-1957 period based on combined data from the three surveys in those years. This estimate is presented below, with some trepidation.

To prepare such a breakdown on the basis of a cross-section of the population as a whole is inherently a risky undertaking owing to the small group of high frequency travelers, whose importance has been stressed repeatedly in this report, and whose trips are difficult to cover satisfactorily in a single interview. The attempt, however, has been made, and the results are summarized in Graph 8 and in Table 30 in the Appendix.

The method used was to combine data from the 1955, 1956, and 1957 surveys on most recent trip by common carrier with 1955 data on the most recent trip by automobile. The estimates of distance were made as precisely as possible. For some trips data from the interviews on place of residence and place of destination made it possible to enter published tables of airline distances between cities. Where necessary this approach was supplemented with estimates of distance based on use of a large map of the United States.

The estimates were weighted to give to the trips by frequent travelers weights equal to the total number of trips that they took per year. In effect, the most recent trip of each traveler is taken to represent all trips that he took. The division of the total market between auto and the common carriers was based on the finding in the 1955 survey that 81 per cent of all trips were by auto and 19 per cent by common carrier. Note that the estimates are in passenger-miles.

The main results of these calculations are consistent with expectations. The position of the automobile is one of dominance in the short haul market, but of decreasing importance as distance lengthens. Conversely, air travel is of minor importance for the short trips, but its

GRAPH 8

PER CENT OF PASSENGER MILES ACCOUNTED
FOR BY EACH MODE OF TRAVEL BY DISTANCE
TO DESTINATION

Per Cent

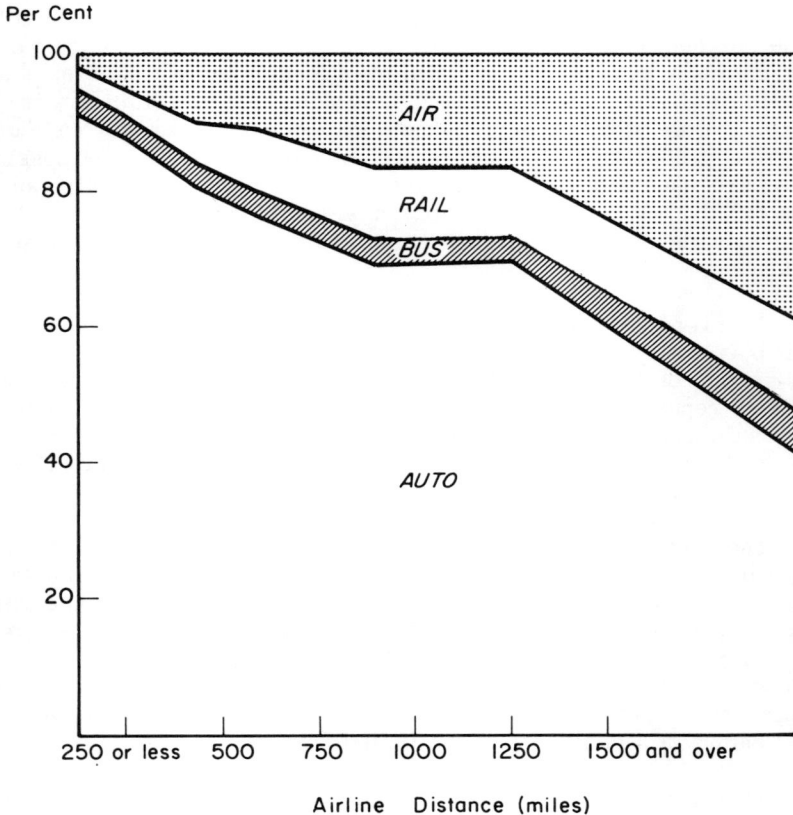

Airline   Distance (miles)

per cent of passenger miles increases steadily with distance. Rail
travel increases in relative importance up to distances of 750 miles,
and then falls off, showing an apparent decline in relative importance
for distances up to 1,250 miles and then an increase for the very long
distances.   The relative importance of bus travel is roughly constant at
all distances. Since 1955-1957 the situation may have changed, but as
previously noted, it is not possible to construct comparable estimates
for recent years with the data at hand.

B. Determinants of Choice of Mode

Variables which influence choice of mode: The many forces which act on people to determine their choice of mode of transportation can be grouped under three headings:

1. Availability. Factors related to availability of service, including accessibility of terminals and convenience of scheduling.

2. Financial Considerations. Factors related to the price of transportation and the financial resources of the traveler.

3. Quality and Preferences. Factors related to differences in quality of transportation and to the preferences of buyers for different qualities of service.

Each of these categories may be viewed from either the demand or supply side of the market; that is, from the point of view of the buyer or the seller of transportation.

Availability is meant to include the whole complex of variables related to the accessibility of different modes of transportation. With respect to common carriers, it includes the accessibility of the terminal at both ends of the trip, the existence of service to or near the desired destination, and the frequency of service and the convenience of the times of the scheduled departures and arrivals. From the point of view of the carriers, the choice of market strategy has to do with the nature of the offerings of service to be made; for example, the location of terminals, the routes on which service will be offered, and the times of departure. From the point of view of the buyer for some trips easy accessibility and particular scheduling are of utmost importance; again, there may be a range of indifference. In this sense buyers have preferences with regard to availability. With respect to travel by automobile, the question of availability is primarily one of whether there is an auto available for the trip. The existence of a highway to the desired destination can be assumed, and so usually can convenient service stations, restaurants, and motels.

As for financial considerations, price from the point of view of the common carriers is represented by their schedules of fares. Their interest is in the price per seat-mile. From the point of view of the buyer, the relevant price is the total amount to be paid to the carrier for the movement of his party, which may consist of one person or of several people. He must also consider items of expense in addition to the fare itself, such as the cost of reaching the terminal, meals en route, and so forth. Similarly, the cost of travel by automobile may include a variety of outlays in addition to the expense of operating the car such as the cost of food and lodging en route.

Income, for non-business travel, is a measure of the amount of money people can spend. For most business trips, however, income is not a measure of available resources since costs are met out of the funds of the business enterprise or organization rather than out of the income of the traveler. For business trips income is a measure of the cost of the time of the traveler to the organization which is paying for his services. For both types of travel income may also be a measure of social-economic status and preferences associated with status.

The quality of a method of transportation should be distinguished from its accessibility. For common carriers the difference is between on one hand, the speed, comfort, and other attractive (or unattractive) features associated with riding in the vehicle and, on the other hand, the ease (or difficulty) a passenger experiences in finding one of these vehicles which goes to his desired destination at an acceptable time and making his way to the terminal. Events in the period prior to boarding and after he leaves the vehicle at his destination may be combined for purposes of analysis. From management's point of view, the choices of market strategy with respect to quality of service have to do with the type of vehicle to be provided, how it is to be furnished and operated, and what services to the passenger are to be provided. From the buyer's point of view the question is one of his preferences for different types of conveyance and service. For travel by automobile, "quality of transportation" includes quality of the highways as well as performance of the vehicle itself. Thus, construction of improved highways improves the quality of transportation, even as do improvements in the car itself. All of these factors bear on quality of transportation as the buyer perceives it. Sellers seek to offer service which will be adjusted to buyer's preferences and, therefore, be rated high in quality by the customers.

Several levels of preferences must be distinguished. First there are general desires influencing choice, especially the desire for speed, safety, comfort, and for new experiences. The relative importance of these desires changes from one trip to another. For example, the man in a hurry wants speed, but on the next trip he may not be in a hurry. At another level are preferences for particular modes of transportation. Although related to the more general desiderata, these preferences are independent attitudes in their own right and may be studied as such. Experience as an air traveler appears to be an indirect but useful measure of attitude toward air travel. Preferences may reflect subtle and complex motivational patterns. The traveler may be concerned with his own attitude toward himself, and with other people's attitudes toward himself. He may, therefore, be concerned with popular impressions as to what sort of people use the different modes of transportation. The traveler frequently is unaware of these psychological forces which influence him. For present purposes all such considerations are grouped under "preferences".

The above determinants of choice of mode of travel are among factors directly related to choice. But other less direct variables enter the analysis. Among these demographic variables may be considered. Age, for example, was shown to be important in the analysis of barriers to travel; and it is also important in choice of mode, but it is not a direct determinant of choice. Thus, people over 65 tend not to like to drive at high speeds, and hence prefer travel by common carrier to travel by auto on freeways. But not all old people share this attitude, and those who do not share it no doubt act accordingly. Attitude, not age, is the direct cause of the behavior, but age predisposes people to their attitudes. The analysis may at times deal with age rather than the attitude because the former can be measured easily. But age is a less satisfactory variable analytically than the proximate determinants of choice because it is more difficult to interpret. It may predispose people to various attitudes that will be variously reflected in their travel choices. In addition, age may change a person's financial situation and his willingness to spend. The operation of demographic variables is, in a word, ambiguous. On the other hand, the age distribution of the population is known exactly and can be predicted with tolerable precision for the future. Age, therefore, has its place in the analysis of choice of mode. Similar comments apply to other demographic variables, especially those having to do with the location of people's places of residence.

A different kind of variable indirectly related to travel choice is the purpose of the trip. The distinction between business travel and non-business travel is fundamental and is maintained throughout this report. In part, as already discussed, business trips are differently financed, place a premium on speed, and demand high accessibility of service. These purposes are related to the importance of different considerations in choice of mode. Contrast the relative importance of price and speed on a family tour of the national parks in the West and a trip to visit someone who is critically ill.

Finally, length of journey is extremely important. The differences in the frequency of use of the four travel modes associated with different distances were shown earlier in this chapter. Distance, however, is not a direct determinant of choice. Rather, differences in distance are associated with differences in the relative quality of service offered. Air travel is much faster than auto for trips of 2000 miles, but not for trips of 10 miles. Relative costs are associated, also, with length of trip. There is, for example, a discontinuity in the total cost per mile of travel by auto at the distance at which people will stop driving for the day and buy food and lodging.

In the 1955-1957 surveys the direct approach to the study of mode choice was taken. In 1955 people were asked about their most recent trip, which, of course, ordinarily was by automobile. In 1955-1957 people were asked about their most recent trip by common carrier. In the context of questions about these trips people were asked, "How did you happen to choose this way of traveling instead of some other?" The findings may be summarized as follows:

Per Cent of Comments Made in Discussion of Trips by Common Carrier, 1957		Per Cent of Comments About Auto Made in Discussion of Most Recent Trip, 1955	
Availability	30	Availability	40
Availability	10	Freedom of schedule	
Convenience	20	or of route	19
		Convenience; car goes	
		door to door	16
		Inconvenience of other	
		modes, car is the only	
		way to get to the	
		destination	5
Price	16	Price	31
		Cheaper by car	24
		More people could go	
		by car	7
Preferences	54	Preferences	17
Speed	27	Speed	5
Safety	5	Car is easier with	
Comfort	17	children, or old	
Varied experience	5	people	4
		Enjoys the scenery	
		by car	7
		Dislikes going by car	1
		Usefulness of a car	
		after arrival	5
		Other	7
Total	100	Total	100

The relative frequency with which these considerations are mentioned in this context is a measure of their relative importance in people's own minds in the making of the actual decision. Unconscious motives and socially unacceptable motives will tend to be understated, as will things people take for granted.

Availability and accessibility of service are discussed frequently in the context of the most recent trip by common carrier. Altogether three out of ten of the comments refer to one aspect or another of availability, such as to convenience of times of arrival or departure, to accessibility of terminals, and the like, but availability is even more frequently discussed in connection with automobile travel. Here four comments out of ten refer to availability; that is, to the convenience of travel by car, to the fact that the car goes door to door, to the freedom of timing or of route. A woman in her thirties explained the family's choice of auto for their last trip by saying, "It was more convenient with all of us and the fishing stuff. You can't get to the lake except by car." The wife of a dentist in the Navy said, "We had a side trip that would be difficult by train, and airports are hard to get to with three small children."

The availability of automobile travel was approached another way. In 1962, respondents were asked, with regard to their most recent trip, if they could have reached their destination conveniently any other way. The results for those who actually went on a non-business auto trip follow:

Convenience of Other Modes	Per Cent
Air	
Convenient	41
Not Convenient	59
Total	100
Rail	
Convenient	45
Not convenient	55
Total	100
Bus	
Convenient	67
Not convenient	33
Total	100

In over half the trips the destination was not conveniently reached by air or rail, thus narrowing the choice of mode. However, two-thirds of the destinations could have been reached conveniently by bus, but auto was used anyway, perhaps because it was the more convenient of the two and doubtless because of other factors also.

Price is referred to frequently in people's discussion of choice of mode. One comment in six about common carriers has to do with price. Even more striking is that 31 per cent of the comments about auto have to do with its cost. People state quite explicitly that they travel by car because it is cheaper, or because more people could go on the trip. People are well aware that the expense of operating a car does not increase appreciably as it is filled to capacity.

On the other hand, factors like speed, safety, comfort, and varied experience are referred to most frequently in discussions of the common carriers. They are less frequent in references to automobile travel. Some people do say that automobile travel is faster, and some, that they enjoy the scenery. Another small group refers to the special convenience of the automobile for movement of children or old people. These comments are overshadowed, however, among those on price or availability of automobile transportation.

The immediately preceding discussion suggests that people choose to travel by auto rather than by common carrier primarily for reasons of easy availability and lower cost, rather than because it is their favorite mode of transportation. The evidence here presented is insufficient to state this suggestion as a conclusion, but it does show that availability and price are what people talk about when they state their reasons for traveling by car.

Preferences for automobile travel also can be investigated directly. A measure of people's preferences was obtained in the 1962 survey by the use of a sentence completion item, "The best way to travel is . . . ". The results are summarized below:

Best Way to Travel	All	People Who Took No Trips Last Year	People Who Took 16 or More Trips Last Year
Auto	40	35	35
Air	28	20	43
Rail	14	20	8
Bus	5	9	1
Ship, other	3	7	5
Don't know, not ascertained	10	9	8
Total	100	100	100

Considering the population as a whole, winners of the preference competition are auto, air, rail, and bus showing a poor fourth. The auto leads, but the margin of preference does not match its margin of use. It is instructive, also, to note the differences in preference between frequent travelers and non-travelers in 1962. The auto leads among those who took no trip the preceding year, and even for them the combined score of air, rail, and bus outweighs the auto by a wide margin.

Among heavy travelers, air travel leads with only auto running any competition worthy of mention.

In view of the importance of the division of the market by mileage brackets, a special question was asked in the 1960 survey. People who had ever taken a trip 500 miles away by car were asked, "In general, how do you like automobile trips? Why?" The replies may be summarized as follows:

Attitude Toward Long Auto Trips	Per Cent of All Long Distance Auto Travelers, 1960
Likes long auto trips	47
Qualified liking	15
Uncertain; depends	5
Qualified dislike	4
Dislikes long auto trips	23
Not ascertained	6
Total	100

Half of the population of qualified travelers gave a clearly favorable response. Only a quarter clearly disliked long auto trips. Here, again is evidence that a majority of the traveling public likes auto travel, but there is a large unenthusiastic minority. A 21 year old man with an income of $6000-7499, who works for an insurance company in New Jersey, pungently expressed the minority view, "Auto trips are a pain in the neck."

Yet another approach to the problem of measuring preferences was taken in the 1962 survey in the context of the most recent trip by auto. People were asked, "If the cost had been the same no matter how you went, what kind of transportation would you have taken on this trip?" Eighty per cent replied that they still would have traveled by auto. Fourteen per cent, however, would have preferred to go by air if the cost had not been a factor. Here, again, is evidence that a considerable group of automobile trips are taken because of low cost. One automobile trip out of 7 amounts to a substantial part of the total market. The strongest general impression which emerges from study of these answers is that while the strong position of the automobile rests on easy availability, low costs, and personal preferences, the last is its weakest support relative to the common carriers.

In view of the dominant position of the automobile in the travel market as a whole, it may be useful to consider further the nature of these advantages of travel by auto and what is implied about the competitive position of the auto against common carriers. Freedom of schedule, that is, freedom to time one's departure as one pleases, is an inherent advantage of a system of private transportation such as the auto. Common carriers can approach it, but never equal it. Even service every hour is not equal to service at the exact time one pleases. In the same way, common carriers must operate from a terminal or pick-up point. The traveler by auto can start from his doorstep and arrive at any address in the country.

These advantages of the auto refer to what happens at the beginning and end of a trip. One way of looking at the matter is to say that there is a "fixed cost" in getting started on a trip by common carrier. This "fixed cost" is in part paid in cash to reach the terminal and in part paid in time and inconvenience. It is "fixed" in the sense that it does not increase with the length of the trip. For example, it is just as far to the railroad terminal for a trip of 50 miles as for a trip of 1000 miles. People who have a choice can be induced to incur this "cost" only if it is offset by other advantages of the common carrier, which must be advantages related to the price or to the quality of transportation by common carrier once the terminal has been reached. It should be easier for the common carrier to overcome its initial disadvantage the longer the distance to the destination. For example, a plane in flight moves faster than a car on the highway; the saving in elapsed time by plane obviously will depend on the length of the trip.

There are other advantages of travel by auto which do not have this "fixed cost" character. Freedom of choice of route is such an advantage. To the extent that people want to select their own route, the auto gives them maximum flexibility, and this flexibility applies equally to long and short trips. The usefulness of a car at the destination is also independent of the length of the trip and represents an inherent advantage of travel by car. For example, one married woman in her fifties said, "We drive a car and like this way of traveling. We can stop and go when convenient and see the sights." And a retired farmer said, "We could stop off and see places when we wanted to and didn't bother anybody else." The wife of a lieutenant in the U. S. Air Force remarked: "We had to bring a car down here. We prefer this way of traveling because you can stop and rest. You can stop and see friends." Such advantages apply to trips of different lengths. These advantages must be offset or outweighed by other attractions of the common carriers before people will prefer to travel by common carriers.

It was shown earlier in this chapter that the relative attraction of the automobile is greatest for the short hauls and least for the very long hauls. Even for the longest trips the auto retains a substantial part of the market. The considerations of availability just discussed are certainly consistent with such a pattern.

Considerations of the relation of relative price to distance, which already have been suggested, are consistent also with this division of the market. The cost of travel by common carrier is approximately a fixed charge per mile. For air travel when meals are included with the ticket and no lodging is ordinarily needed the cost works out almost exactly to a fixed rate per mile. (There is not much "taper" in the fares per mile themselves as the rate structure has developed.) The cost of travel by auto, however, includes meals and lodging. There is much variation in what people spend for these services. Some reduce costs by staying with friends and relatives, and some sleep in cars and drive in shifts for indefinite distances. The market offers a variety of accommodations. But, for most people, the relative cost of travel by air and by car for a distance greater than one day's drive is less favorable to the auto than shorter distances.

The same analytic framework may be used to consider the choices people make among the common carriers. The following tabulation summarizes the comments made in 1957 in connection with the most recent trip by common carrier:

Advantages and Disadvantages	Air	Rail	Bus
Availability			
Favorable	6	24	33
Unfavorable	8	12	4
Price			
Favorable	8	8	28
Unfavorable	5	2	*
Preferences and quality			
Favorable	66	45	18
Unfavorable	7	9	17
Total	100	100	100

The strength of air travel clearly is in the area of quality of service. Of all comments made about air three out of four refer to this topic, and overwhelmingly they are favorable. The availability and accessibility of air travel is mentioned much less often, and the comments are more unfavorable than favorable. For bus travel the situation is almost the exact reverse. Preferences and quality of service are discussed no more often than the other two areas, and the comments are as likely to be favorable as unfavorable. The strength of bus travel is in its availability, which is frequently discussed and almost always favorably. The low cost of bus travel also is frequently discussed. The findings for rail indicate an intermediate position: relatively stronger than bus but weaker than air in service; relatively weaker than bus but stronger than air in availability. (The content of people's comments is shown in more detail in Table 33 in the Appendix.)

The differences among the common carriers are so important to people that the market tends to be broken up into segments. People do not seriously consider every mode of transportation for every trip. Answers about choice of mode may indicate which modes compete most directly with each other. People frequently volunteered comparisons between the mode they took and other modes of transportation. The question is, what modes did they spontaneously compare? People who thus mention a mode not used may be regarded as potential travelers by that mode. The following tabulation is based on data from the 1956 survey and refers to comments made about other modes in discussing choice of mode for the most recent trip by common carrier:

Mode Used	Modes Spontaneously Mentioned, But Not Used			
	Auto	Air	Rail	Bus
Air	19		37	15
Rail	53	82		85
Bus	28	18	63	
Total	100	100	100	100

Of those who mentioned air but did not use it, better than 80 per cent actually went by rail. Thus, many rail travelers in 1956 were thinking of air as an alternative and there was a potential gain by air from rail. Of those who spontaneously mentioned rail but did not use it, a great majority went by bus. Of those who mentioned bus but did not use it, 85 per cent went by rail. Thus, for them, the choice was bus versus rail. Of those who mentioned auto travel but did not use it, 53 per cent actually went by rail.

These results show the extent to which rail travel was "in the middle" in the market in the years 1955 to 1957. People often chose between air and rail, between bus and rail, or between auto and rail. They rarely chose between, say, air and bus, or auto and air. These results, no doubt, would be different if the same questions were repeated in the 1960's. As it is, they provide an insight into the difficulties of rail passenger service in the late 1950's. The picture is one of a mode beset by competition from all sides.

Statistical analysis of choice of mode: As mentioned earlier, the second approach to choice of mode consists in comparing the choices made by people with different characteristics. This approach is particularly helpful for analysis of the effect of income and, to a lesser

ᅟ

ᅟ

ᅟ

GRAPH 9

PER CENT OF MOST RECENT BUSINESS AND NON-BUSINESS TRIPS AT DIFFERENT DISTANCES ACCOUNTED FOR BY AIR, RAIL, BUS, AND AUTO, 1962

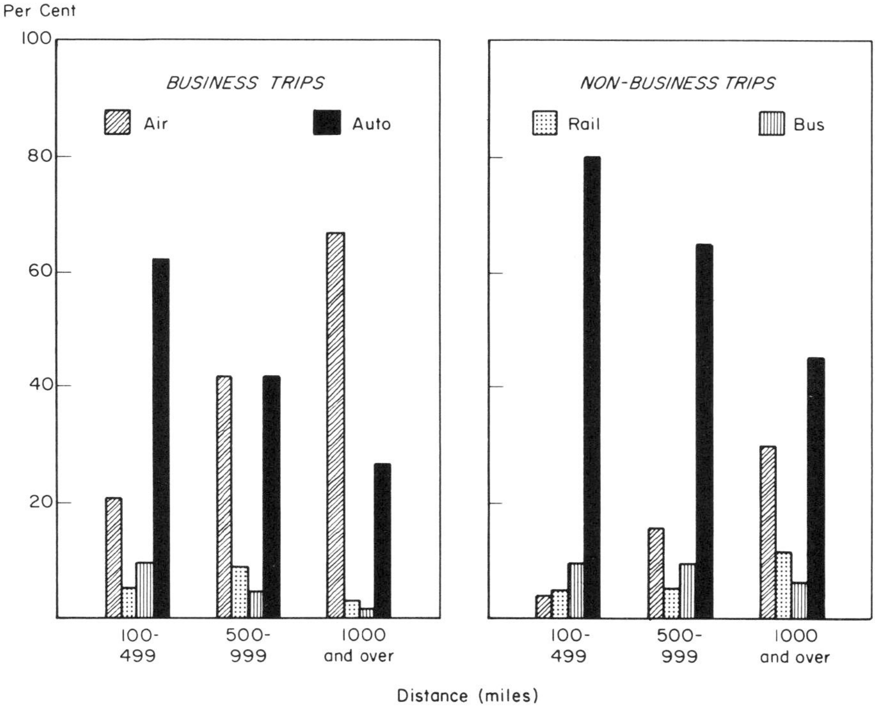

Distance (miles)

degree, of price. It also shows the importance of the distinction between business and non-business travel and the importance of distance. Further, it can be used to show the importance of preferences and quality of service. The distance of the trip and the purpose of the trip, as indicated above, should not be thought of as themselves determinants of choice of mode. They are sorting variables, or classifying variables, which do not themselves determine the choice but mediate the influence of the other variables which affect choice of mode. The effect of distance and purpose is shown in Graph 9 and Table 38 in the Appendix.

The effect of income may be illustrated by the following tabulation based on data from the 1955 survey. In this tabulation attention is

GRAPH 10

PER CENT OF MOST RECENT TRIPS BY EACH
MODE TAKEN BY PEOPLE AT DIFFERENT IN-
COME LEVELS, 1955[a]

Per Cent

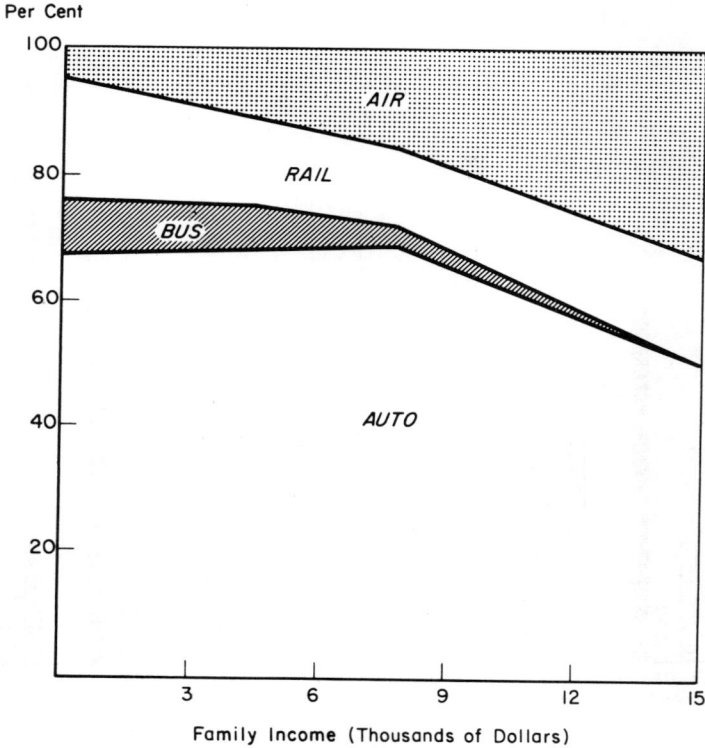

Family Income (Thousands of Dollars)

[a] Includes only trips 500 miles or more away by two or more people.

restricted to trips to places 500 miles or more away involving parties
of two or more people, but both business and non-business trips are included:

| Mode | | Family Income | | | $10,000 and |
Used	All	Under $3000	$3000-5999	$6000-9999	Over
Air	13	5	8	14	31
Rail	15	18	15	13	17
Bus	5	8	7	2	*
Auto	67	69	70	71	52
Total	100	100	100	100	100

Air travel moves up with income, while bus travel falls. The per cent of rail and auto travel remains roughly constant, except that auto declines in the top income group. (See also Graph 10.)

The effect of income was again shown in the 1956 survey, when the data were tabulated for vacation and pleasure trips only, excluding both business trips and trips on personal affairs. Only trips primarily by common carrier were included. For distance of 100 to 499 miles the income effect was as follows:

Modes Used	All	Under $3000	Family Income $3000-5999	$6000-9999	$10,000 and Over
Air	31	1	14	25	61
Rail	46	41	50	46	39
Bus	32	63	43	31	4
Auto	9	7	11	12	13
Total	118	112	118	114	117

In this tabulation the per cent of trips using each mode is shown, second modes appear if they were used. For these trips the effect of income is, again, marked. Use of air travel rises from 1 per cent among those under $3000 income to 61 per cent among those of over $10,000 income. This result is illustrated in Graph 11.

Number of companions may be taken, essentially, as a proxy for price. It is widely understood that the cost of automobile travel is invariant with respect to the number of people; hence, the effect of increasing the number of people who go along is to reduce the price per person by the inverse of the size of the party. The cost *per person* of an auto trip for two is half the cost per person of an auto trip for one. As a first approximation, the cost of travel by common carrier is a constant cost per person. (This generalization is only approximate since some common carriers offer family plan reductions. For air these reductions in the period studied ordinarily applied to first class fares but not to coach fares.)

People interviewed do not use such formal language in discussing choice of mode as this report, but their sentiments are parallel. A widowed school teacher in her sixties expressed the situation in these words, "More of us could go for less money." A retired farmer described how he came to take an auto trip: "My sister and her husband asked me to go along and hold the map. Didn't cost me a thing."

Expressed in more abstract language, the effect of increasing the number of people in the party who go by auto is to divide the price per person by a factor of n, where n is the number in the party. If the cost

GRAPH II

PER CENT OF PLEASURE AND VACATION TRIPS ACCOUNTED
FOR BY AIR, RAIL, AND BUS AT DIFFERENT LEVELS OF IN-
COME AND DISTANCE, 1956

Per Cent

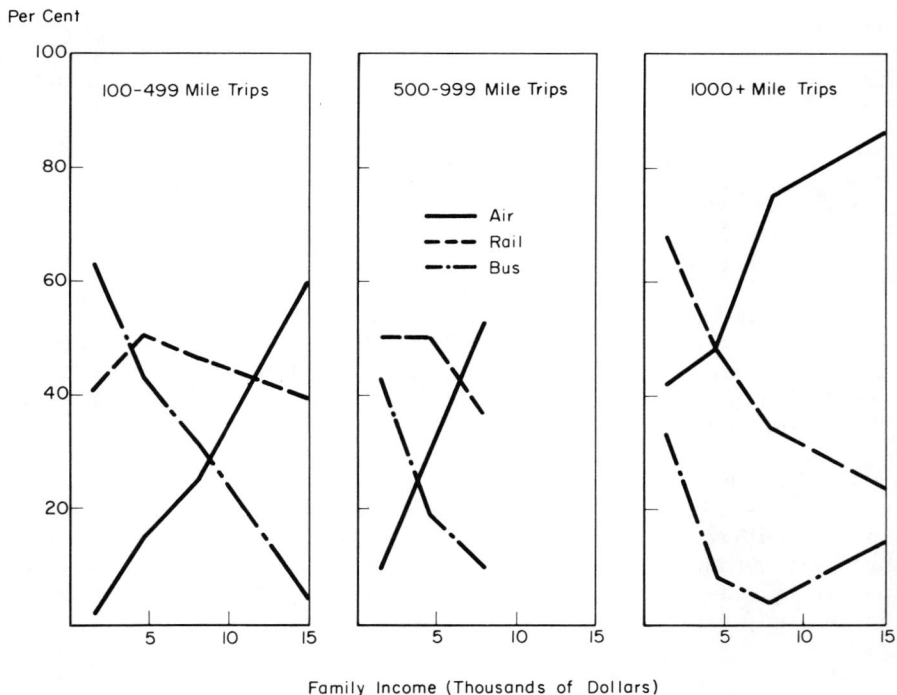

Family Income (Thousands of Dollars)

per person of common carrier travel is invariant with respect to the
size of the party, the ratio of the cost per person by auto to the cost per
person by common carrier will fall by 1/n as the number of people in
the party increases. This decline is limited by the capacity of the automobile. There is a discontinuity in the cost of auto travel at the point
where it becomes necessary to take two cars. In the following tabulation it is assumed for illustration that the cost of a certain trip by car
is $25, air fare is $25 per person, and that six or more people would
take two cars:

Number of People	Cost Per Person by Auto	Cost Per Person by Air	Ratio of Cost Per Person, Auto/Air
One	$25.00	$25.00	1
Two	12.50	25.00	1/2
Three	8.33	25.00	1/3
Four	6.25	25.00	1/4
Five	5.00	25.00	1/5
Six	8.33	25.00	1/3

If the cost per person is the same by auto as by air for parties of one, for parties of two the cost per person by auto will be half that by air. We could have kept the prices of travel by air and by car in the same relation to each other only by a reduction in the cost per person of air travel. This reduction must be 50 per cent below the cost per person for a single air traveler to match the 50 per cent reduction in cost per person when two people go by auto. The same percentage reduction would be needed in the price of air to keep the ratio constant even if the cost for one person had been unequal.

A recent statistical inquiry into choice of mode was conducted in 1962. Attention was restricted to trips of 500 miles or more by air or by auto for non-business reasons. Thus, the length of trip and the purpose were held approximately constant. The relation between the total number of people who went and the choice between air and auto is shown in Graph 12 and the accompanying tabulation:

Total Number of People

Mode Used	All	One	Two	Three	Four	Five +
Air	28	71	22	8	*	11
Auto	72	29	78	92	100	89
Total	100	100	100	100	100	100

Of the trips made by only one person, 71 per cent were by air. Of the trips made by two persons, 22 per cent were by air. If the sole reason for this difference is the difference in the price, by setting the price for two equal to the price for a single person the air carriers could increase the proportion of such trips which are by air from 22 per cent to 71 per cent. By setting a price per person for parties of two at half the price per person for parties of one, they would triple the proportion of parties of two who fly. Similarly, by making the price for parties of three the same as that for parties of two, the proportion of such parties who fly could be raised roughly from 8 to 22 per cent. These effects have nothing to do with possible consequences of changes in the price for parties of one, that is, changes in the basic fare. Air here already enjoys 71 per cent of the combined market. Further gains

GRAPH 12

PER CENT OF MOST RECENT LONG DISTANCE TRIPS TAKEN BY AIR OR AUTO BY THE NUMBER OF PEOPLE WHO WENT, 1962

Per Cent

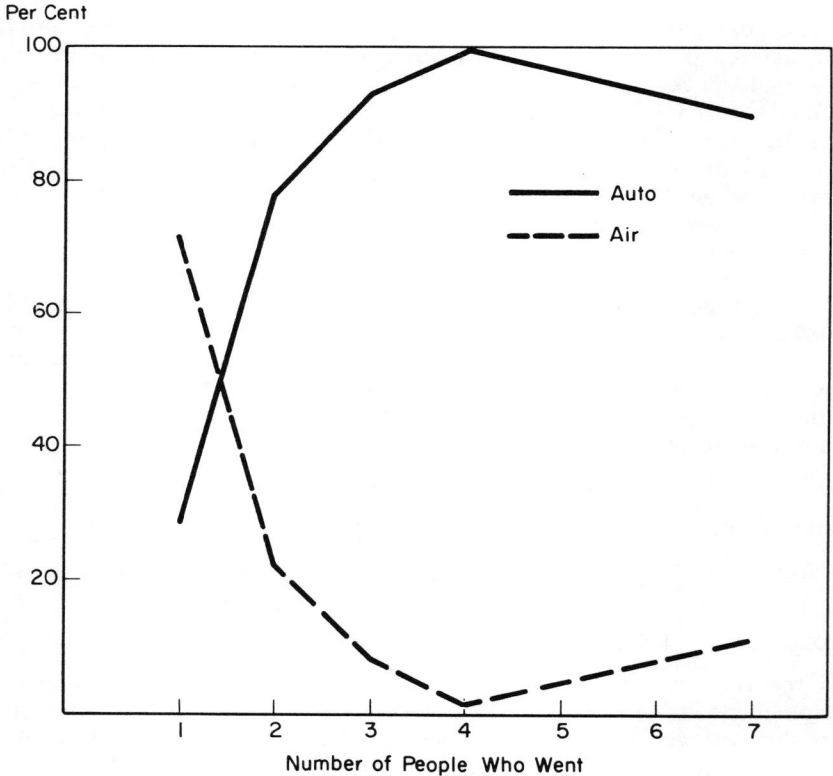

are likely to come from stimulation of increases in total travel as much as gains from the auto.

Essentially similar results were obtained in 1955. The following tabulation shows the effect on mode choice of the number of companions for recent trips made by people in the income class $3000-5999 in 1955. Two distances are considered, under 500 miles and over 500 miles:

Mode Used	Under 500 Miles		500 Miles or Over	
	Alone	Not Alone	Alone	Not Alone
Air	5	1	30	8
Rail	20	4	22	15
Bus	11	4	15	7
Auto	64	91	33	70
Total	100	100	100	100

Considering people who traveled less than 500 miles, of those who went alone, 5 per cent went by air compared to only 1 per cent of those who had a companion. This finding, taken by itself, would suggest that the effect of reducing the price for groups to the level of that for single people would be to multiply by five the proportion of such groups who go by air, in this income class. A factor of five would be higher than is suggested by the 1962 data above and, probably, too high. Some of the single travelers were business travelers whose preferences for the speed of air are particularly strong. The exact magnitude of the effect may be open to some question, but the analysis definitely indicates price is a major determinant of choice of mode for parties of two or more people. For greater detail see Table 39 in the Appendix.

The data also confirm the importance of personal preferences as determinants of choice as between auto and air. Experience as an air traveler, it is argued here, may be taken as an indirect measure of attitudes toward air. There is definite evidence of a relation between experience as an air traveler and choice of mode for the most recent non-business trip by air or by auto to a place 500 miles or more away. The relation is shown below:

Mode Used	All Trips	Prior Experience as an Air Traveler	
		Had Taken an Air Trip	Had Not Taken an Air Trip
Air	28	39	19
Auto	72	61	81
Total	100	100	100

Of those who had taken an air trip prior to the year of the study, 39 per cent went by air compared to 19 per cent of those who had not taken such a trip. People who once have taken an air trip tend to be predisposed to fly again! The effect of experience is undoubtedly somewhat exaggerated in a simple tabulation such as that shown here. Experience is known to be associated with income, and income is known to be one of the basic determinants of the propensity to fly. The effect of experience persists, however, in statistical investigations in which other variables such as income are carefully taken into account.

The investigation of personal preferences was carried forward also in 1962 using questions which refer to preferences. People were asked, "If the cost had been the same no matter how you went, what kind of transportation would you have taken on this trip?" Considering, as before, only those who actually went by air or by auto, 56 per cent preferred auto; 40 per cent air, and 4 per cent other modes. To what extent did people travel as they would have preferred? The following tabulation shows the results for those who preferred air or auto:

| | | Preferred Mode | |
Actual Mode	All	Air	Auto
Air	28	59	4
Auto	72	51	96
Total	100	100	100

Of those who preferred air, 59 per cent went by air. Of those who preferred auto, 96 per cent went by auto. Of those who preferred air, why were 41 per cent frustrated? The most probable answer is the relative cost.

In a situation where many variables are known to be at work, the method of showing relationships by the use of cross-tabulations of the type shown in this chapter tends to become cumbersome and finally to break down altogether. Equations must be used to handle large numbers of variables simultaneously. This approach has been adopted, and the results are shown in Appendix I. Broadly speaking, the results reported there confirm the importance of variables proposed in the model indicated here. The main effects which are shown here in tabulations appear again in the more elaborate analysis taking more variables simultaneously into account.

There is, then strong evidence that the choice of mode of transportation depends on the three main types of variables; availability and accessibility of service, price and income, and personal preferences. This evidence comes in part from people's answers to questions related to their actual choices of mode of travel and their general personal preferences for different modes in the abstract, and in part from statistical analysis of choice of mode for specific trips based on cross-tabulations and multivariate equations.

One of the salient facts about the travel market, to which repeated reference has been made in this report, is the dominance of the automobile over the other means of transportation. All other studies show this dominance. While there may be some difference of opinion as to the total volume of automobile travel, there is no doubt that the great bulk of intercity transportation of passengers is by automobile. The best available information also indicates that the overall share of all intercity travel accounted for by the automobile has been about constant for several decades.

This dominance, however, as the previous discussion has shown, is by no means absolute. The importance of the other means of transportation varies from one part of the travel market to another, and the situation changes over time. Thus, it is particularly interesting to ask, in what portions of the travel market is the automobile growing stronger as time progresses, and in what situations is the automobile weaker in comparison to the other modes of transportation?

The subject is approached first, in this chapter, by considering the slow rise in the cumulative proportion of the population who have ever taken auto trips. Attention is then turned to trends in the rate at which people take auto trips. A special section discusses regional differences in automobile travel, with emphasis on the unique characteristics of the New York area. Finally, a section on people's reaction to speed and to the use of superhighways offers some additional clues as to the probable effect of current highway construction on the future role of the automobile.

A. Experience with Auto Travel

Frequency of travel may be measured with reference to a recent period, such as the last week, or year, or to a longer span of time, as in both the 1955 and 1962 surveys when people were asked if ever in their lives they had taken a trip by auto to a place 100 miles or more away. To this question, 11 per cent answered that they had not, in 1955 and in 1962, 9 per cent had not.

It might be expected that people of lower socio-economic status would be most likely to report they had never taken an auto trip. This expectation is mildly confirmed by the data from the 1962 study:

GRAPH 13

PER CENT OF ADULTS AT DIFFERENT INCOME LEVELS WHO HAVE EVER TRAVELED BY AUTO

Per Cent

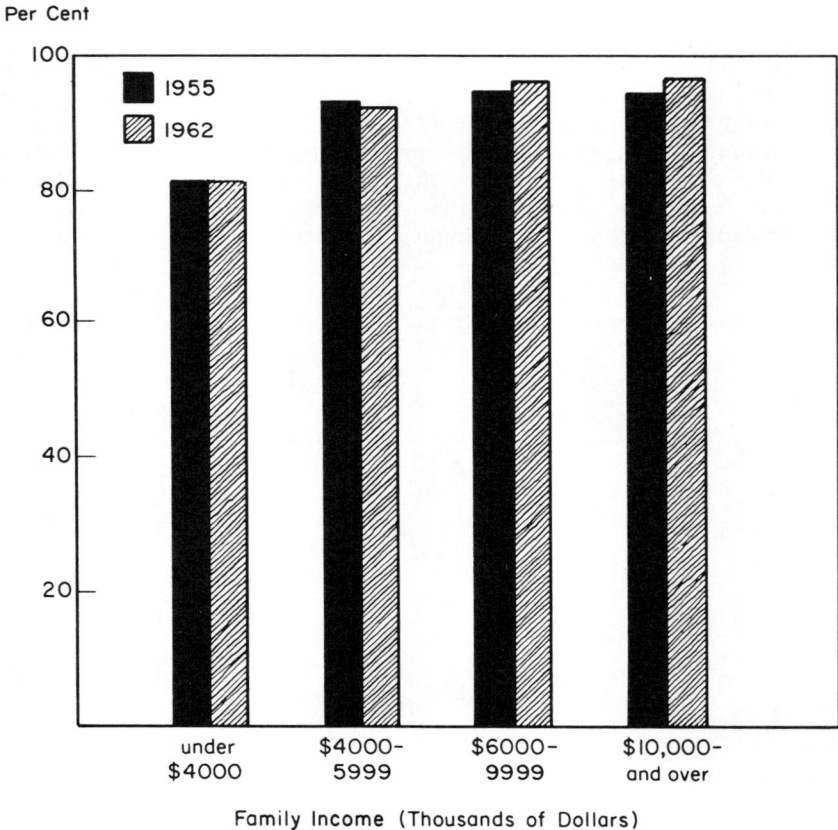

Family Income (Thousands of Dollars)

Income	Per Cent Who Ever Had Taken an Auto Trip
Under $4000	83
$4000-5999	92
$6000-9999	96
$10,000 and over	96
All incomes	91

The same data are the basis for Graph 13. Even of those with family incomes below $4000 in 1962, more than 8 out of 10 were experienced automobile travelers.

The aged form another group in the population who might be expected more often to report they never have taken a long auto trip. The following tabulation shows the per cent experienced in each age group in 1962:

Age	Per Cent Who Ever Had Taken an Auto Trip
18-24	89
25-34	94
35-44	93
45-54	92
55-64	90
65 and over	85
All ages	91

Fifteen per cent of those over 65 never have taken an auto trip, compared to 6 to 8 per cent of those aged 25 to 64. Together, these two tabulations show only a small and slowly diminishing group of people, concentrated in the older aged groups and the lower income groups, who never have taken a long automobile trip. (See Graph 14.)

The proportion of the population who own an automobile has been increasing slowly in recent years, as shown by the following data from the annual Surveys of Consumer Finances:

Year	Per Cent Owning Any Automobile	Two or More Automobiles
1952	60	4
1953	61	5
1954	66	8
1955	67	8
1956	70	9

(Cont'd)

Year	Any Automobile	Two or More Automobiles
1957	72	10
1958	70	10
1959	71	12
1960	74	12
1961	74	14
1962	72	14

These data, it should be noted, are on a spending unit basis. Grown children living at home with their parents are considered separate spending units if they have their own incomes and handle their own finances. The difference between a spending unit basis of tabulation and a family basis in which children and parents are combined into one unit is unimportant for most purposes. On a family unit basis in 1962, the proportion of automobile owners was not 72 but 74 per cent, and the proportion of multiple owners not 14 but 17 per cent. Both the increase in auto ownership and the increase in multiple ownership increase the availability of the auto for trips to places 100 miles or more away, and thereby tend to weaken the relative position of the common carriers in the market.

GRAPH 14

PER CENT OF ADULTS IN DIFFERENT AGE GROUPS
WHO HAVE EVER TRAVELED BY AUTO, 1962

Per Cent

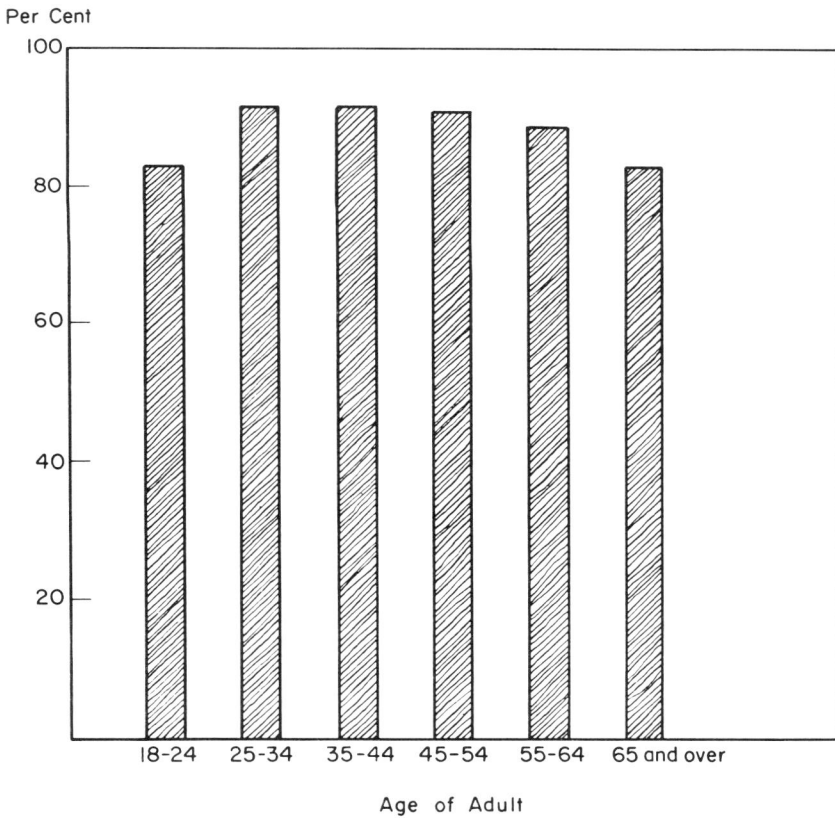

Age of Adult

B. Frequency of Travel by Auto, 1955 and 1962

As previously indicated, in 1955, of all adults 57 per cent reported taking one or more auto trips in the year prior to the survey, while
in 1962 the number had risen to 64 per cent. Of the 64 per cent, 54 per
cent traveled by auto for non-business reasons, 3 per cent for business
reasons, and 7 per cent took auto trips for both reasons in the course of
the year.

As is true for all modes combined, for the automobile singly too,
a large fraction of the trips is reported by a small proportion of the
travelers:

Number of Auto Trips	Business Trips by Auto in 1962		Non-Business Trips by Auto in 1962	
	Per Cent of Travelers	Per Cent of Trips	Per Cent of Travelers	Per Cent of Trips
1	32	4	32	7
2-4	29	8	37	20
5-19	25	25	26	43
20 and over	13	63	5	30
Total	100	100	100	100

Difficulties associated with remembering large numbers of trips, as
discussed in Chapter I, seem to lead to an overstatement of the importance of the very frequent travelers. Even when this difficulty is taken
into account, it is remarkable that 32 per cent of the travelers on business report that they took only one trip, and these trips comprise only 4
per cent of the total number of reported business trips by automobile.
At the other end of the distribution, 13 per cent of the business travelers reporting 20 or more automobile business trips account for a whop-
ping 63 per cent of the total reported number of business trips by auto
in 1962. If accurate data were available, free from errors of memory,
the true proportion might turn out to be less than 63 per cent. In any
case, it is apparent that a small fraction of business travelers taking
repeated trips by auto account for a large fraction of the total volume
of automobile business travel. Conversely, a much larger number of
people taking only one business trip by auto account for relatively few
business trips by auto.

Even non-business travel by automobile is more concentrated
than one might predict. Of all those who took any non-business trip by
auto in 1962, 32 per cent report one trip only, and these adults account
for merely 7 per cent of all the non-business auto trips. At the opposite extreme, the 5 per cent who report 20 or more trips account for 30
per cent of all non-business trips reported. These people who take

non-business auto trips at intervals of one to three weeks are indeed a small fraction of the total population, but they account for almost one third of the total non-business auto travel.

The extraordinary thing about automobile travel is the extent to which it is characteristic of people in the middle income groups, as well as in the upper income groups. Even at the level below $2000 four adults out of ten report that they took one or more auto trips last year. The relation between income and taking at least one auto trip is indicated in Graph 15 and in the following tabulation:

GRAPH 15

PER CENT OF ADULTS AT DIFFERENT INCOME LEVELS WHO TRAVELED BY AUTO DURING THE SURVEY YEAR

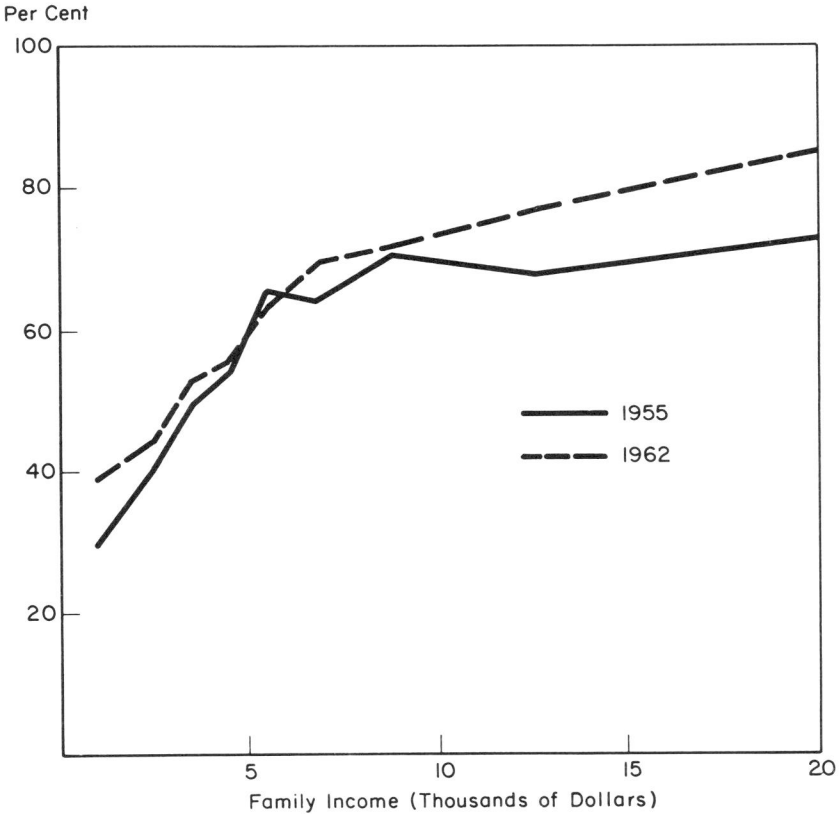

Per Cent

Family Income (Thousands of Dollars)

Family Income	Per Cent Who Traveled by Auto, 1962
Under $2000	40
$2000-2999	46
$3000-3999	55
$4000-4999	57
$5000-5999	66
$6000-7499	72
$7500-9999	74
$10,000-14,999	79
$15,000 or over	87
All incomes	64

The proportion who took one or more automobile trips during the survey year steadily rises with income, as the graph shows, and already includes two-thirds of all adults by the income group $5000-5999.

Between 1955 and 1962, as Graph 15 indicates, an upward shift in the proportion of automobile travelers took place at both ends of the income distribution, but not in the middle. Among the lower income groups, the upward shift was associated with increasing automobile ownership. But the greater proportion of auto travelers at the top of the income distribution is more difficult to explain. It may be the result of improved quality of service. Whatever the explanation, high income people are taking more auto trips.

Another approach to the relation between income and automobile travel is to examine the proportion of adults in each income group and the proportion of trips for which they account. This tabulation should be treated with the usual caution because of memory error, but memory error was a problem in both 1955 and 1962 and should not affect a comparison between the years:

Family Income	1955 Adults	1955 Trips	1962 Adults	1962 Trips
Under $4000	44	24	28	13
$4000-5999	29	34	24	19
$6000-9999	19	28	31	39
$10,000 and over	8	14	17	29
Total	100	100	100	100

Of all adults in 1962, 17 per cent were members of families with incomes of $10,000 and above. They accounted for 29 per cent of the number of auto trips reported in the survey. In the same year, 28 per cent of all adults reported incomes below $4000 and, although some of these took no auto trips, as has already been discussed, this income group accounted for 13 per cent of all automobile travel in that year.

Between 1955 and 1962, two things happened; the size of the lower income groups diminished, to the gain of the upper income group; and the latter traveled more by car. Hence, those with incomes over $6000 accounted for 68 per cent of auto trips in 1962 compared to 42 per cent in 1955.

The degree of concentration shown in this tabulation, however, is much less than that which appears in the tabulation in which people are ranked by the number of automobile trips they took in the course of a year. Thus, even though travel by automobile is concentrated in a relatively small number of people in the population, it is still only moderately concentrated in the upper income groups. People with incomes of $4000 to $9999 account for nearly six auto trips out of ten.

Broadly speaking, the frequency of travel by automobile in different occupation groups is consistent with the results for different income groups which have just been discussed. Adults in the higher status groups, such as professional and managerial workers, are somewhat more likely to take at least one auto trip in a year than are the people in the lower status groups, such as the laborers and service workers, but the differences are only moderate. Graph 16 and the following tabulation present the results:

Occupation	Per Cent Who Took Any Auto Trip, 1962	Per Cent Who Took a Business Trip by Auto, 1962
Professional, technical	79	29
Managerial, self-employed	76	33
Clerical, sales	74	15
Craftsmen, foremen, operatives	69	8
Laborers, service workers	43	5
Farmers	55	15
Not in the labor force at time of interview (housewife, retired)	61	4
All adults	64	10

Of all professional and technical workers, 79 per cent took at least one auto trip (21 per cent took none), and 29 per cent took one or more business trips by auto (71 per cent did not).

The relation between occupation and use of automobile for business purposes is interesting for the light it throws indirectly on the diversity of reasons why people travel "on business". It is, no doubt, consistent with expectations that one third of all managerial and self-employed workers took a business trip by auto in 1962, and that the frequency of travel for professional and technical workers is also high.

GRAPH 16

PER CENT OF ADULTS WITH DIFFERENT OCCUPATIONS WHO TRAVELED BY AUTO DURING THE SURVEY YEAR

Per Cent

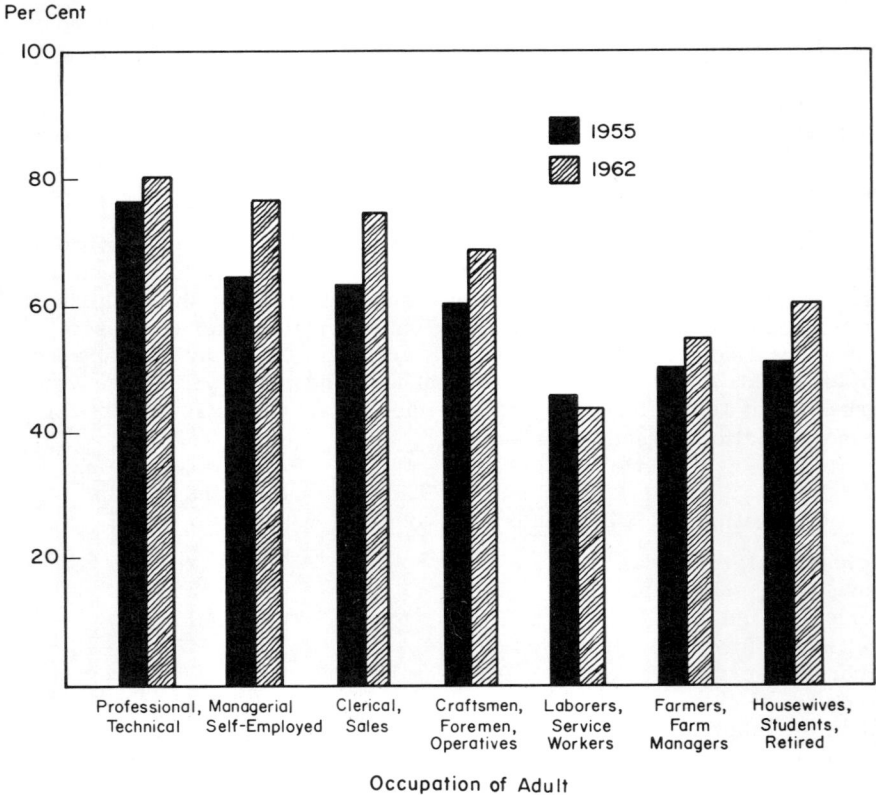

Occupation of Adult

Of all farmers and farm managers, 15 per cent took at least one business auto trip to a place 100 miles or more away in 1962. Their business probably concerned the operation of their farms. Fifteen per cent
of clerical and sales workers also took business trips by auto. It must
have been the sales workers rather than the clerical workers who did
most of the traveling. Even among the craftsmen, foremen, and operatives, 8 per cent report that they took a trip for business reasons to a
place 100 miles or more away during the year. Presumably their em-
ployers needed their services at a distance from their normal place of
work. The only group with a very low proportion who took a business
trip is, reasonably enough, those not in the labor force; the housewives,

GRAPH 17

PER CENT OF ADULTS IN DIFFERENT AGE GROUPS WHO TRAVELED BY AUTO DURING THE SURVEY YEAR

Per Cent

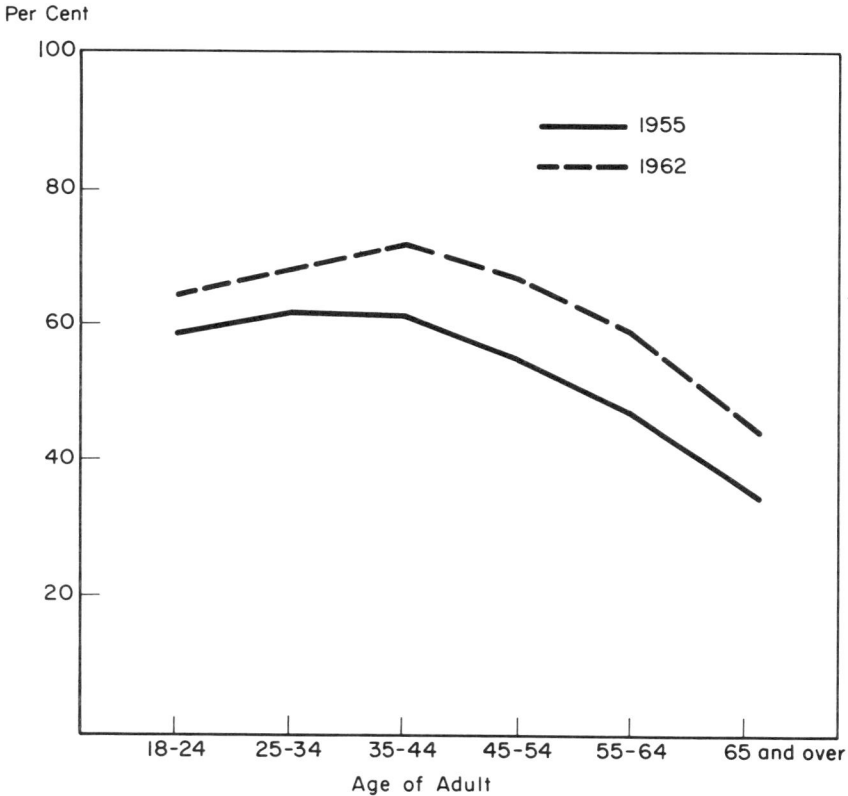

Age of Adult

retired, and students. Some of these people unquestionably left the labor force during the year, so that they may have taken a business trip during a period when their occupation classification was different from that at the time of interview.

There was little or no increase from 1955 to 1962 in the proportion of automobile travelers among professional workers, for whom it remained high, or among laborers and service workers, for whom it remained low. There was an increase among managerial workers, clerical workers, sales workers, and the craftsmen, foremen, and operatives, as well as among those not in the labor force.

The older age groups are a segment of the population for whom automobile travel is less attractive. The difference in frequency of auto travel by age is shown in Graph 17 and below:

Age	Per Cent Who Took an Auto Trip	Per Cent Who Took a Non-Business Auto Trip
18-24	65	63
25-34	69	65
35-44	72	68
45-54	67	63
55-64	60	57
65 and over	44	43
All ages	64	61

Of those aged 65 or over, only 44 per cent took any auto trip in the year prior to the survey compared to 60 per cent of the group aged 55-64. A decline in the frequency of travel by people as they pass age 65 might be expected in part on the ground that business travel is unusual among those in this age range, as most of them have left the labor force. But the decline in auto travel occurs when only non-business trips are considered. Further, the decline in the proportion who take an automobile trip begins much below age 65. The peak years for auto travel are the age range 35-44.

From the point of view of the travel analyst, as noted in Chapter II, age is a complex variable. It reflects, first, the physiological processes of aging; second, changes in personal relations and social status within the family associated with advancing stages in the family life cycle; and third, differences in the kind of travel experience people have been used to depending on when they were born. The combined effect of all three factors causes the differences in use of auto with age.

The change between 1955 and 1962 in frequency of travel arranged by age should be regarded as partly the effect of increases in income. These increases tended to shift the curve upward by providing more income to those of every age in 1962 than had been enjoyed earlier. In part, the data also reflect the increased experience with auto travel of succeeding generations, to which reference was made earlier. The effect of stage in the family life cycle on automobile travel is shown in the following tabulation:

Stage in the Family Life Cycle	Per Cent Who Took an Auto Trip, 1962	Per Cent Who Took a Non-Business Auto Trip, 1962
Young, single	58	56
Under 45, married, no children	74	68
Married with children	72	69
Over 45, married, no children under 18	61	57
Older, single	41	40
All stages	64	61

The people most likely to take at least one auto trip are married couples with or without children, of whom about seven out of ten did take such a trip. Children are an obstacle to travel - the wife of a hair dresser in New York spoke for many when she said, "Auto trips are a pleasure . . . without children." But when people with children do travel, they select the automobile in preference to common carriers. Hence, the proportion of this group who take auto trips is as high or higher than that of any other group in the population. For parents ease is joined with economy in auto travel. As a married gas station attendant commented, "We have a car, and traveling is cheaper with the family." Of persons over 45, the couples are much more likely to travel by auto than single persons, who may be widowed, separated, or divorced. Only 40 per cent of the latter took a non-business auto trip in 1962.

From 1955 to 1962, there was a small increase in the proportion of auto travelers among the young, single people and the young couples without children; and a larger increase in the proportion of auto travelers among those in life's later stages.

In brief, the changes from 1955 to 1962 in auto travel were as follows: an increase at the upper and lower ends of the income distribution occurring at the same time as an upward shift in incomes; a larger increase among managerial and self-employed workers; clerical and sales workers; and craftsmen, foremen, and operatives; than among the professionals or the laborers; and a larger upward shift among the age group 35-and-over, than among those below that age. The increases in auto travel among the low income groups and the older age groups are consistent with the interpretation of the automobile as still in the process of gradual diffusion through the population. The poor and the aged are usually the last to adopt innovations which are expensive or which make physical demands on people. The increase among the upper income group reflects something more, probably the improvement in highway transportation as a system of transportation in the period 1955 to 1962.

As for other differences in travel habits, there are some differences between men and women in the frequency of non-business automobile travel, but these differences are small, and the data have been relegated to the Appendix. On balance, men are slightly more likely to take at least one automobile trip in the course of a year. The explanation is the greater frequency of travel for business reasons among the men.

There are large differences between whites and Negroes in the frequency of travel by auto, as the following tabulation shows:

| Race | Per Cent Who Took an Auto Trip | |
	1955	1962
White	58	68
Negro	30	35

Only 35 per cent of Negroes took one or more auto trips in 1962, compared to 68 per cent of whites.

The difference between the races in this form of travel persists when people are divided into two income groups, those over and under $4000 a year, as shown below from the 1955 survey:

Race	Family Income Under $4000	Family Income $4000 or over
White	45	67
Negro	27	46

Of all whites with incomes of $4000 or over, 67 per cent took one or more auto trips, compared to 46 per cent of all Negroes. Below $4000 the percentages are 45 and 27, respectively. The crude difference between the races in 1962 was 33 percentage points (68 minus 35). Taking the higher proportion of poor Negroes into account by comparing income divisions reduces the difference to about 18 to 21 percentage points, but this is still an important difference. Forces in addition to cost appear to be reducing automobile travel by Negroes.

C. Regional Differences in Auto Travel

In the discussion of differences in frequency of travel by all modes in Chapter I, reference was made to the importance of the geographical analysis of the travel market, and it was shown that people in the West travel more, and people in the New York metropolitan area travel less than the population at large. Since travel by automobile is such a large part of all travel, one would expect to find essentially the same regional differences in frequency of automobile trips. This expectation is borne out by the data.

GRAPH 18

PER CENT OF ADULTS LIVING IN DIFFERENT REGIONS WHO TRAVELED BY AUTO DURING THE SURVEY YEAR

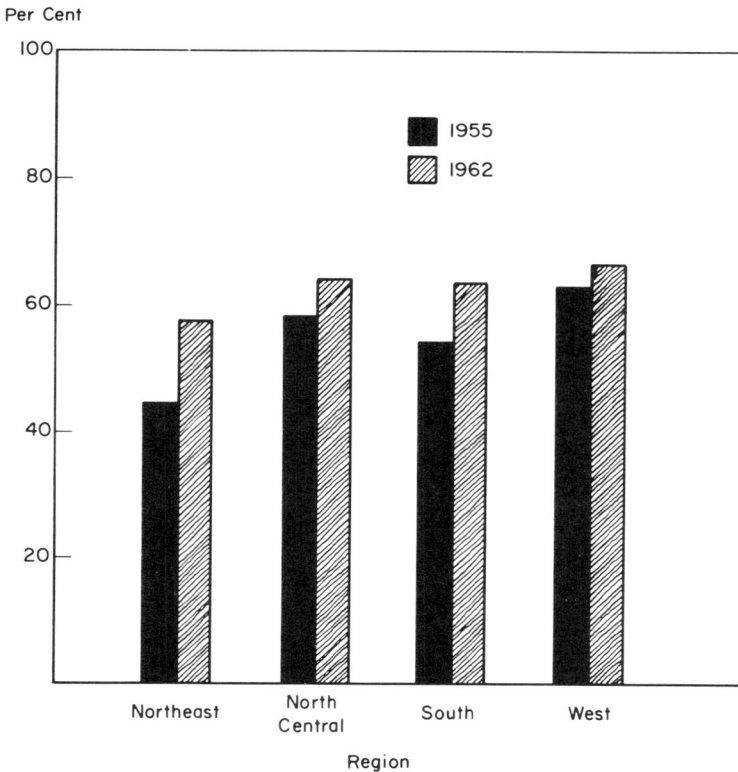

Differences in the proportion of people who take a trip by automobile in the course of a twelve month period in four regions in the United States are shown in Graph 18 and the following tabulation:

Region	Per Cent Who Took an Auto Trip, 1962
Northeast	58
North Central	65
South	65
West	68
All regions	64

(See Appendix, Table 15 for the definition of the regions.) The Northeast shows up as a relatively low automobile traveling region, 58 per cent against 65 to 68 per cent for other areas. The West shows the highest frequency but not markedly so.

The auto travel figures compare interestingly with those of auto ownership. The Survey of Consumer Finances in early 1962 showed the proportion of car owners by region to be as follows:

Region	Per Cent Owning
Northeast	66
North Central	77
South	69
West	76
All regions	72

The Northeast retains its position of lowest in car ownership, as well as in auto travel. And the West, if not at the top in car ownership, is almost there; at 76 per cent car owners, it is only one point behind North Central at 77. The greatest change in relative position is a difference of 8 percentage points between North Central and the South in car ownership, when in travel they were equal. It is tempting to conclude Southerners make more use for travel of the fewer cars they do own, (but there may be some sampling error in the reported findings.) However, the one fact that stands out most unequivocally is the Northeast's low rates of automobile travel and ownership. What accounts for this distinction?

Turning to the data on the alternate regional breakdown, we find New York pulls down the average per cent of automobile travelers for the Northeast. The second half of Graph 19 illustrates the results shown in the following tabulation:

GRAPH 19

PER CENT OF ADULTS TRAVELING BY AIR AND AUTO IN THE SUR-
VEY YEAR BY WHETHER NOW LIVING IN THE NEW YORK AREA,
1955, 1957, AND 1962

Per Cent

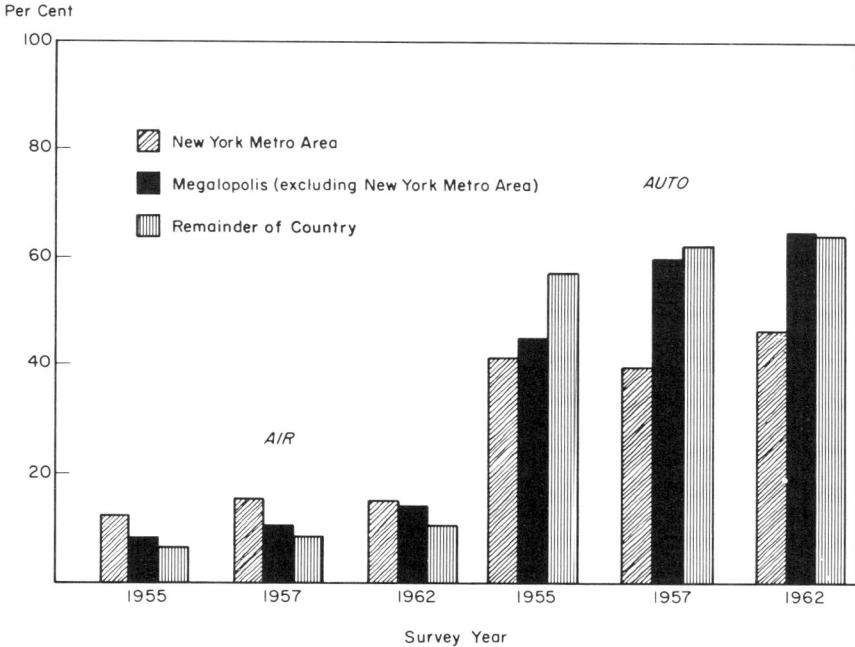

Survey Year

Year	New York	Megalopolis Excluding New York	Remainder of the Country
1955	42	46	58
1957	40	61	63
1962	47	66	65

The proportion of New Yorkers who took at least one auto trip to a
place 100 miles away was low in 1955, and it has remained substantially
below that of other areas. In 1962 the proportion who took such a trip
was 47 per cent for New York, 18 points below the estimated 65 per
cent for the rest of the United States.

A geographical breakdown of the New York area shows large differences within the metropolis as follows:

Sub-Division of the New York Area, 1962	Per Cent Who Took an Auto Trip
Manhattan	41
Bronx	41
Queens	45
Brooklyn	26
Newark, Jersey City	*
Suburbs in New York	50
Suburbs in New Jersey	64
All adults in the area	46

Of those living in the suburban portions of the metropolitan area, a higher proportion took an auto trip than of those in the central city.

The low level of travel by auto in New York is consistent with other data which show a low level of automobile ownership in that city. The 1962 pattern of ownership is as follows:

Number of Cars Owned, 1962	All Families In the U.S.	Central City and Suburbs of 50,000 +	Suburban and Outlying Areas
None	23	54	11
One	56	46	49
Two	19	*	37
Three or more	2	*	3
Total	100	100	100

Of those families in the central city in New York, half own no car. Of all families in the country, only a quarter own no car. Of those in the suburbs in the New York area only one out of ten has no car. Thus it is the central city of New York (including Newark and the very large suburbs) which is low in ownership.

Data from surveys in early 1959 and early 1960 confirm the low level of ownership in New York and show the extent of the difference between New York and the 11 metropolitan areas of the United States next largest in population:

Percentage of Automobile Ownership, 1958-1959

Number of Cars Owned	New York Metropolitan Area	Eleven Next Largest Metropolitan Areas
None	48	26
One	44	59
Two	8	13
Three or more	*	2
Total	100	100

These figures show New Yorkers without cars as numbering about half the city's population (48 per cent), whereas for the 11 next largest metropolitan areas, only a quarter (26 per cent) of the inhabitants do not own cars.

Another kind of comparison seeks to identify the kind of neighborhood in which auto traveling New Yorkers are most likely to live. For the following tabulation, a high density neighborhood contains one or more apartment houses among the seven structures centered on the home of the respondent; that is, the one he lives in and the three to the right plus the three to the left. A low density neighborhood contains only single family homes. All other neighborhoods are considered medium density.

In brief, the low level of travel by auto and of auto ownership in the Northeast as a whole, in the megalopolitan region as a whole, and in the New York metropolitan area as a whole, is the result of the inclusion in all these units of the millions of people living in the densely populated central portions of the New York City area who do not own automobiles. As a first approximation, it is not the Northeast as a whole which is different from the rest of the United States, nor is it the megalopolitan corridor, nor is it even the New York metropolitan area; it is the densely populated central portions of New York City, which are unique from the point of view of the use of the automobiles!

Although changes occur only slowly, the population of the New York metropolitan area is being redistributed. The changes result in a net movement out of those portions of the area in which automobile trips are infrequent into those portions of the area where trips by auto are more common. The shift may be shown by a comparison of Census data on the change in population from 1950 to 1960 with the data on frequency of automobile trips. The Census of Population showed the following percentage changes in population from 1950 to 1960:

New York City	Percentage Change
Manhattan	− 13.4
Brooklyn	− 4.0
Bronx	− 1.8
Richmond	+ 15.9
Queens	+ 16.7
Counties in New York	
Westchester	+ 29.3
Rockland	+ 53.2
Nassau	+ 93.3
Suffolk	+ 141.5

Counties in New Jersey

Hudson	−	5.7
Essex	+	1.9
Passaic	+	20.6
Union	+	26.7
Bergen	+	44.7
Somerset	+	45.3
Morris	+	59.2
Middlesex	+	63.8

Comparison with the Survey Research Center results shows that it is those areas that lost population (Manhattan, Brooklyn, Bronx, Hudson, Essex) that show the lowest percentage taking automobile trips. The suburban areas, which grew in population, are the homes of the auto travelers.

While New York is unique, the same forces are at work in other metropolitan areas. Elsewhere in the country, also, the accessibility of the different modes of transportation is being changed by the redistribution of the population. Both the increasing concentration of the population into urban areas and the spreading out of the urban areas over the countryside change the accessibility of terminals. The data from the Travel Surveys, as discussed in Chapter II, confirm the importance of accessibility in choosing mode of transportation. The data do not permit detailed study of the consequences of these shifts. It seems reasonable to speculate that the common carriers all tended to gain in accessibility, because of the concentration of the population into urban areas from rural areas, but to lose at the same time because of the dispersion of the urban population. The advantage to the railroads of terminals located in the center of the large cities certainly has declined as the population has moved out away from the terminals. It also seems clear that the farther out in the suburbs a family lives, the greater the relative advantage of the automobile, because of its instant accessibility. Whether the trends in the location of the population have as a whole made air terminals more accessible or less accessible is not obvious. Nor is it obvious whether the bus has gained more than it has lost in accessibility. It does seem clear, however, that in relation to the common carriers as a group, the competitive position of the automobile has been strengthened by the redistribution of the population. There is every prospect that the redistribution of the population will continue, and that it will continue to influence the competitive position of the several modes of travel.

D. Speed and Superhighways

If transportation by automobile is viewed as a system of transportation in most of the United States it has been changing rapidly in the last few years with the introduction of new and improved highways. In the 1962 survey people were asked about their experience with the new roads: "In the last few years, new superhighways have been built in many parts of the United States. Have you yourself ever been the driver of a car on one of the new roads?" To this question 57 per cent of all respondents replied in the affirmative. The variation among age groups and between the sexes in this answer is shown in the following tabulation:

| Sex | Per Cent Who Ever Had Driven a Car on a Superhighway | | | | | |
	18-24	25-34	35-44	45-54	55-64	65 and Over
Men	86	86	82	81	67	44
Women	47	61	52	43	31	18

The new highways seem to be most attractive to men below the age of 55. Of men aged 65 or more, only 44 per cent ever had driven a car on a new superhighway, compared to 81 per cent of those 45-54 and 86 per cent of those 18 to 24. Age for age as many women just don't drive on superhighways as men. Of women aged 65 and above, only 18 per cent had driven a car on a superhighway. And only of those 35-44 or below had half ever driven a car on a superhighway.

There is no reason to believe these roads are inaccessible to any group in the population who own cars. It is hardly likely that men live closer to the roads than women, or young people closer than old. The data, therefore, raise a basic question about the appropriateness of this transportation system for older people generally and older women in particular.

In the same survey, those respondents who reported that they themselves had driven a car on one of the new roads were also asked the following question: "Some people enjoy driving fast while others don't like to. How do you feel?" The following tabulation shows the per cent of those in each age and sex group who reported in answer to this question that they like fast driving:

| Sex | Per Cent Who Like Fast Driving of Those Who Ever Had Driven on a Superhighway, 1962 | | | | | |
	18-24	25-34	35-44	45-54	55-64	65 and Over
Men	41	28	32	25	22	9
Women	27	22	22	22	27	12

Here again there is a marked difference in attitude between the sexes, and also a substantial difference associated with age. Of men aged 18-24 who have driven on one of the new highways, 41 per cent report that they like fast driving. Of the smaller group of women aged 18-24 who have had this experience, only 27 per cent enjoy speed. Of those over 65, only 9 per cent of the men who have driven on a new highway like fast driving, while of the women only 12 per cent feel that way about it.

One of the basic barriers to travel, it was shown in Chapter I, is poor health and the physical limitations associated with age. The new roads and improvements in the automobile do not appear to have solved the problems of auto travel for the aged or infirm. The position of the automobile in the travel market is relatively weak in long distance travel over the new roads by men and women of advanced years. Increased adoption of compulsory physical examinations, as in Pennsylvania, may further reduce auto driving among older people. These persons are a potential market for travel by common carrier. It appears unlikely that they will be drawn away from the common carriers by the completion of the new Interstate and Defense System of highways.

While changes take place continually in the technology of all the methods of transportation, air travel is the newest of the four major modes and, beyond any question, the one where technological changes have been occurring the most rapidly. It is a quarter of a century since the introduction of the DC 3, and it is also a quarter of a century since the establishment of the Civil Aeronautics Board gave the industry an organization approximating that of today. Given the record of rapid development in the past, is the period of a high rate of growth now over? How fast and how far will the market for air travel develop in the future?

There are two opposing views as the answer to that question. According to one view, the future of air travel is modest. During the last decade or so the airlines successfully took from the railroads the lion's share of the market for common carrier travel. That process is already far advanced and no longer can be expected to give to the airlines a major source of new traffic in the future. It is reasonable to expect future growth in the demand for air travel as the economy in general expands, but this growth will arise from the increase in the total population, and, more directly, from the increase in the numbers of people in the population in the upper income groups.

According to the second view, there is a large future potential for air travel. True, there may not be much more traffic to be gained from the railroads, but the airlines can hope to take traffic from the automobiles. The volume of travel by automobile is so large that diversion of even a relatively small proportion of traffic would mean a large increase in air travel. Further, according to this view, the airlines will be able to generate new traffic in the future, which will represent a net addition to total travel rather than a diversion from some other mode of transportation.

Which of the views is the more nearly correct? This question cannot be answered from a study of the demand side of the market for air travel only. What happens on the supply side of the market, and what policies are adopted by the responsible private and public officials, obviously will be important. At best, what can be offered here are partial and contingent answers. It is possible to use the underlying data from the travel surveys to make formal forecasts of air travel. Such forecasts have been published by the Aviation Department of the Port of New York Authority, and no forecast will be attempted here.

Data from the travel market studies about travel by air are relevant also to a series of more specific questions concerning who travels and why, and where in the total market air travel is relatively strong, and where weak. It is hoped that the data will be useful to answer a variety of specific questions, as well as to shed light on broad questions of the future of travel.

A. Attitudes Toward Air Travel

It will be recalled that the analysis of choice of mode in Chapter II showed that air is often at a disadvantage with regard to accessibility of service and cost, but that people comment favorably about the quality of transportation by air. More people say they prefer air travel than actually use it. Attitudes toward air travel, however, are a topic of some complexity and subtlety. People may be unaware of some of their attitudes or unwilling to report them.

For this reason, in some of the surveys, indirect questions about attitudes toward air travel were asked in addition to the direct questions. To obtain general emotional responses to air travel people were asked both in the 1958 and 1962 surveys to complete sentences beginning "Plane trips are . . ." In both years roughly half of the respondents gave positive comments about air travel while about 37 per cent gave negative comments:

Comments	1958	1962
Positive	50	47
Fast, quick	20	10
Nice, pleasant	13	17
Other positive comments	17	20
Negative	37	37
Dangerous, frightening	14	11
Expensive	7	9
Other negative comments	16	17
Other (don't know, no answer)	13	16
Total	100	100

Most of the positive comments are of a fairly relaxed general character, such as that air travel is pleasant, but a minority are more vigorously enthusiastic. The negative comments are of two sorts: One group mentions air trips as frightening or dangerous, while another group, almost as large, refers to them as expensive. It is interesting that the relative frequency of these two answers appears to be changing. In 1958 twice as large a proportion said "dangerous" as "expensive." In 1962 the proportions were more nearly equal. There seems to have been no change overall in the ratio of positive to negative comments about air travel, however.

In the 1955 survey, another indirect approach was taken. People were asked, "Why do you think some people travel by plane?" and "What might keep some people from traveling by plane?" The results were as follows:

Comment	Per Cent of Adults
Reasons for flying	
Speed	86
Other advantages	28
Reasons for not flying	
Expense	30
Fear	84
Other reasons	10

In this context, the advantages of air mentioned most frequently is, overwhelmingly, speed. The leading disadvantage is fear, mentioned by 84 per cent of all adults. Some of these responses are explicit. The 70 year old wife of a carpenter said, "They don't want to get that far off the ground. Our nephew offered to bring me home from Wichita in his plane, but my husband didn't want to." A house painter made a parallel observation about his wife: "They are scared, like my wife. She could have gone home lots of times if she hadn't been scared to fly." In 1955 almost everyone had in the back of his mind the idea that people might find travel by plane frightening. Expense is also mentioned by a large group, 30 per cent of the adult population. The similarity between these negative responses and those from the sentence completion is striking. Both stimuli lead to mention of fear and expense. The differences between the questions in the proportions of the population mentioning each may be explained by the phrasing of the questions.

In the same 1955 survey, a small group of respondents, those who had recently taken a trip by common carrier, were asked, "How did you happen to choose this way of traveling instead of some other?" Those who discussed plane travel gave the following responses:

Comment	Per Cent of Comments
Advantages	
Speed	40
Economy	8
Good connections	8
Other	9
Disadvantages	
Expense	9
Fear	7

(Cont'd)

Comment	Per Cent of Comments
Disadvantages (Cont'd)	
Connections, accessibility	15
Other	4
Total	100

Again speed is the advantage mentioned most commonly. For example, the wife of an electrician in an aircraft factory said, "I wanted to spend as much time with our relatives as possible." Again both expense and fear are mentioned as disadvantages, though by smaller numbers of people, and additional negative comments are made which refer to specific problems of accessibility or availability of planes for the trip being discussed. It is noteworthy that some people mention fear when the context becomes that of a particular trip and they are talking explicitly about themselves.

Finally, in the 1955 survey people were asked to report pleasant and unpleasant recollections of their last trip by air. The answers were as follows:

Recollection	Per Cent of Recollections
Pleasant	
Liked speed, saved time	40
Was comfortable, restful, less fatiguing	13
Liked physical arrangements, clean, cool	12
Liked stewardess and other personnel	8
Liked the meals	6
Is air minded; loves to fly, thrilling	10
Found it an exciting new experience	4
Enjoyed the scenery	6
Other	1
Total of pleasant recollections	100
Unpleasant	
Was too jarring; hit too many air pockets	22
Was afraid during flight; fears flying; felt unsafe	15
Became air sick	14
Take-off or landing was too rough; too rough	8
Was too cramped	6

(Cont'd) Unpleasant

Too noisy; plane vibrated too much	4
Couldn't see scenery well	2
Scheduling was bad for reasons of place; terminal inconveniently located	13
Scheduling was bad for reasons of time; coach flights badly scheduled	6
Too expensive	6
Other	4
Total of unpleasant recollections	100

In this context, also, the speed and time saving characteristics of air travel are by far the most frequently mentioned. People also comment favorably on various aspects of the comfort or the physical arrangements of the flight.

Among the unpleasant recollections, expense is not frequently mentioned though it is represented by 6 per cent. But fear and factors associated with fear are, again, surprisingly common in the replies. Fifteen per cent of the unpleasant recollections were to the effect that people were afraid. Comments that the flight was too jarring, hit too many air pockets, was too rough, or that the traveler became air sick, all suggest the presence of fear as a factor. Noise, vibration, cramping and poor view of scenery are all complaints against the plane construction. Problems of the accessibility of planes, including scheduling and terminal location, are also mentioned by a considerable minority of the air travelers. It would be instructive to know whether these replies would be different if the same questions were asked in a more recent survey, but they have not been repeated since 1955. Responses to the sentence completion item discussed above suggest there may have been changes.

Peoples' subjective estimates of changes in the safety of air travel were investigated directly in the 1962 survey by the following question: "Would you say that air travel is safer now than it was ten years ago, or not as safe, or what?" The responses follow:

Feelings About Air Safety	Per Cent of Respondents
Much safer now	6
Safer now	58
About the same	7
Not as safe now	10
Much less safe now	1
Don't know, not ascertained	18
Total	100

The question at issue, of course, is not whether air travel actually is safer now than ten years ago, but whether people have become more confident of the safety of air travel. Two thirds of the population do feel that air travel is safer, and only about 10 per cent feel that air travel is not as safe as it was.

What can be concluded about the importance of fear? The frequency with which fear of flying is mentioned depends on the context, but the subject comes up so persistently in such a variety of different contexts that it seems clear that fear looms in people's minds. How important is the fear cannot be stated from these data. The people who are most afraid may not be the ones who mention the subject most freely. Reliable measures of fear would require more elaborate research than has been undertaken.

Is fear of air travel decreasing? On this point the data, though far from conclusive, suggest an affirmative answer. The preponderance of positive replies to the question of whether air travel is safer now than 10 years ago points in that direction, as do the small observed shifts from 1958 to 1962 in response to the sentence completion item about plane travel. There is in these findings, then, some slight ground for optimism as to the future of air travel.

B. Experience With Air Travel

Up to this point, experience as an air traveler has been treated as a proxy for psychological attitudes toward air travel. It is necessary, however, to assess the attitudes more directly, especially fear of air travel. Two approaches can be taken: to show that experience is related to attitudes, and to show that experience predicts behavior. Each approach will receive some attention.

First, people who are experienced air travelers do tend to have different attitudes toward air safety than those who never have taken an air trip. They are more likely to feel that air travel is safer now than it was 10 years ago as shown by the following tabulation for the year 1962:

Feelings About Air Safety	All	Experienced	Not Experienced
Safer now	64	74	58
About the same	7	8	6
Less safe now	11	7	14
Don't know, not ascertained	18	11	22
Total	100	100	100

Differences between the groups are not large, but note that 74 per cent of the experienced air travelers feel that air travel is safer now, compared to 58 per cent of the inexperienced. Only 7 per cent of the experienced feel air travel is less safe compared to 14 per cent of the inexperienced. Thus, experience breeds assurance.

Viewed statistically, and based on many statistical investigations, experience is the most effective single variable to use as a predictor of air travel. Income, age, stage in the family life cycle, any of these variables is less useful than air experience in predicting who will fly and who will not fly. In 1962, for example, 26 per cent of adults who were experienced air travelers at the beginning of the year took an air trip, compared to only 3 per cent of the inexperienced.

The difficulty with experience as a key to people's attitudes toward air travel lies in its interpretation. Although one would like to interpret experience as a measure of preference for air travel, there are other possible interpretations. For example, it is possible that the experienced air travelers are people for whom air travel is accessible. They may live near an airport with good air service and repeatedly visit destinations easily accessible by air, family members living at a distance, perhaps. It is also possible that experienced air travelers are the experienced general travelers. They travel often by air, true, but they also travel often by all other modes.

There is, indeed, statistical evidence that the last interpretation has validity. People who are experienced air travelers are definitely more likely to travel by other modes than those without this experience. In 1962 it was found that of those who were experienced air travelers 12 per cent took a rail trip, compared to 6 per cent of those who never had taken an air trip. The relation between experience as an air traveler and use of the different modes may be summarized as follows:

Modes Used in the Twelve Month Period	Experienced Air Traveler	Not an Experienced Air Traveler
Took an air trip	26	3
Took a rail trip	12	6
Took a bus trip	10	8
Took an auto trip	75	58

People who are experienced as air travelers are much more likely to travel by air than the inexperienced, but they are also somewhat more likely to travel by rail, bus, or auto than the inexperienced.

On the basis of all the evidence now at hand, the most reasonable interpretation of experience seems to be that it does have each of these analytically separable meanings to some degree. In part, experience is a measure of preference for air, in part it is a measure of accessibility, and in part it is a measure of general attitudes toward travel. It should be used as a long run predictor of the future of air travel, therefore, only with some caution.

While *a priori* it might be argued that the magnitude of the effect of experience on air travel should decrease over the years, on the statistical record to date this decline in the effectiveness of the variable as a predictor has not taken place. Thus, it is reasonable to interpret the rise year by year in the per cent of the population who have ever taken an air trip as one factor which tends to indicate a rising demand for air travel. Changes in the level of experience, therefore, deserve attention.

The proportion of the population who are experienced as air travelers rose in the period 1955 to 1962 from 23 per cent to 36 per cent of all adults. This rise is shown in Graph 20 and in the following tabulation:

Survey Year	Per Cent Who Were Experienced
1955	23
1957	27
1958	29
1960	28
1962	36

GRAPH 20

PER CENT OF ALL ADULTS WHO WERE EXPER-
IENCED AIR TRAVELERS AT TIME OF INTERVIEW.

Per Cent

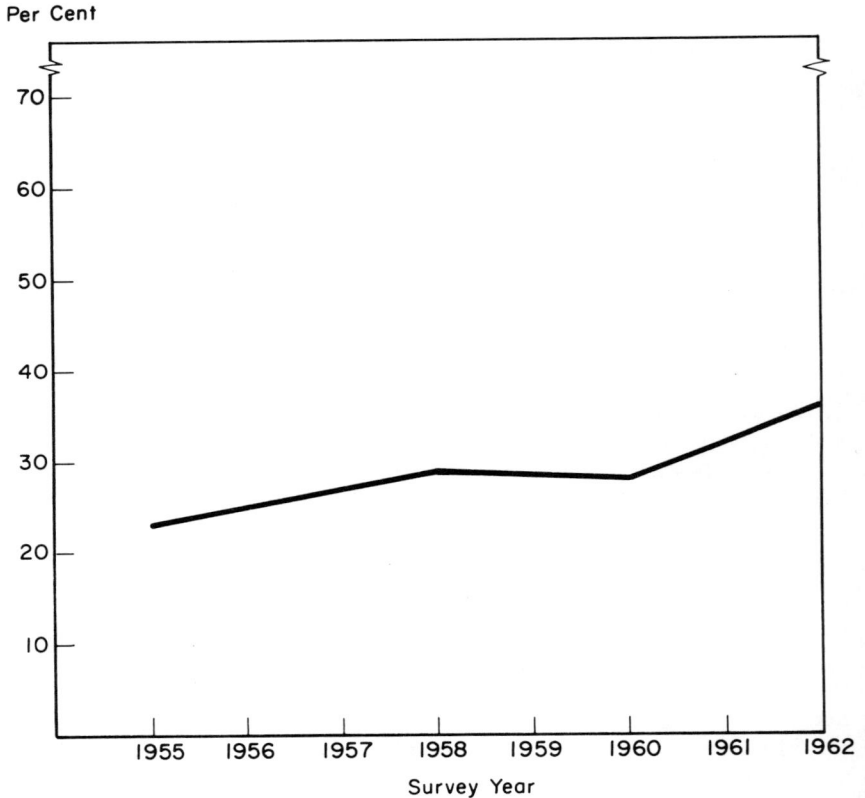

Survey Year

An alternative approach to the increase in experienced air travelers is to ask people directly in what year they first took an air trip. Responses to such a question, as asked in the 1960 survey, are shown in the tabulation (top of next page). About 2 per cent of the adult population report that they took their first air trip in 1959-1960, the year prior to the survey. Broadly speaking, this result is consistent with the slope of the line shown in Graph 20, which is increasing at the rate of about 2 per cent a year.

	Per Cent of Adults
Had ever taken an air trip	28
Year of first trip:	
Before 1940	2
1940-1945	4
1946-1949	4
1950-1955	9
1956-1958	6
1959-1960	2
Year of first trip not ascertained	1
Had never taken an air trip	72
Total	100

Information for different age groups can be used to construct retrospectively a curve showing the cumulative frequency of those in each age group who ever have taken an air trip. Such a table based on the 1957 and 1960 surveys appears in the Appendix, Table 76. Analysis suggests that the estimate of 28 per cent experienced in 1960 is probably too low, presumably a result of sampling error.

The proportion of adults who are experienced air travelers is positively associated with family income. The relation is shown in Graph 21 and in the following tabulation:

Family Income	Per Cent of Group Who Are Experienced, 1962
Under $2000	16
$2000-2999	19
$3000-3999	26
$4000-4999	26
$5000-5999	29
$6000-7499	37
$7500-9999	47
$10,000-14,999	59
$15,000 and over	59
All incomes	36

In 1962 only 16 per cent of those with incomes below $2000 were experienced air travelers, compared to 29 per cent at the income level $5000-5999 and 59 per cent at the income level $10,000 and above. In the top income groups a majority are experienced air travelers, but in the middle income groups only a minority are experienced, and at the lower end of the distribution the proportion is even less.

GRAPH   21

PER CENT OF ADULTS AT DIFFERENT INCOME
LEVELS WHO HAVE EVER TAKEN AN AIR TRIP

Per Cent

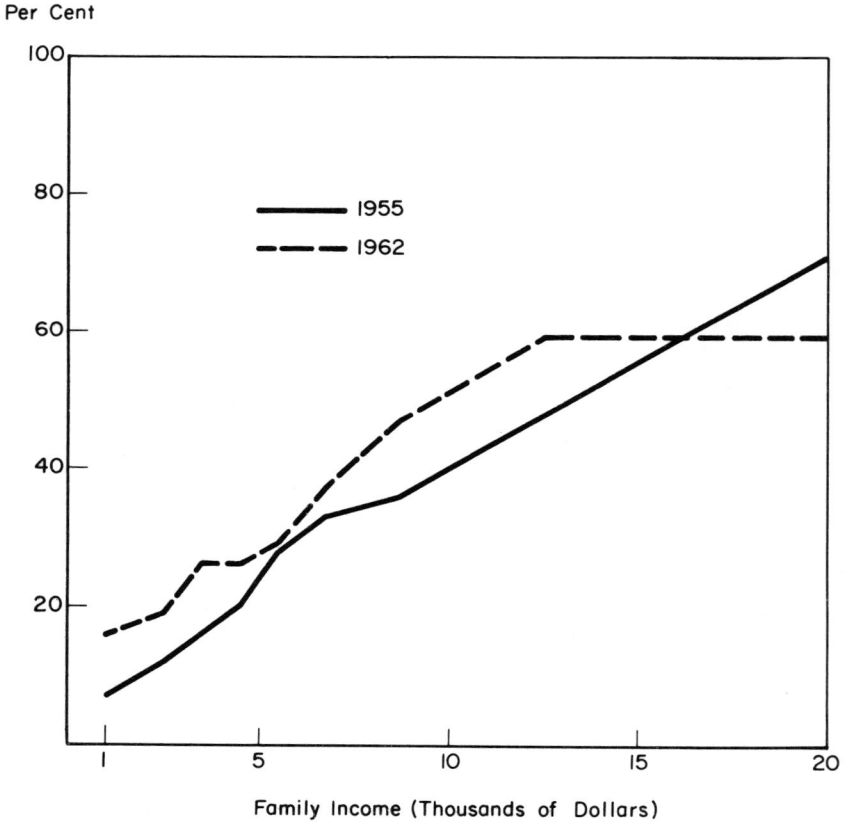

Family Income (Thousands of Dollars)

Experience as an air traveler is also associated with age. One might expect the highest level of experience among those who have had most time in which to take air trips, the oldest. However, the highest experience rate found in 1962 data is for the 25-34 age group as shown in Graph 22 and in the following tabulation:

| | Per Cent of Group Who Are Experienced, 1962 |
Age of Adult	
18-24	27
25-34	48
35-44	43
45-54	34
55-64	30
65 and over	23
All ages	36

GRAPH 22

PER CENT OF ADULTS IN DIFFERENT AGE
GROUPS WHO EVER HAVE TAKEN AN
AIR TRIP

Per Cent

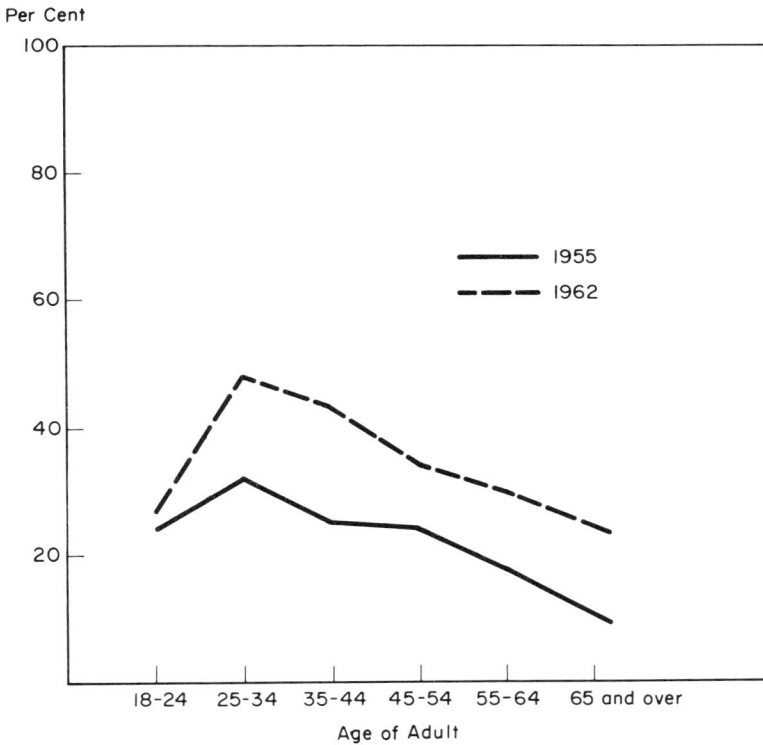

Of those aged 25-34, nearly half (48 per cent) were experienced, while of those 65 or over only a quarter (23 per cent) had taken an air trip.

These results point in an optimistic direction for the future of air travel. Experience, once gained, can hardly be lost. The proportion of experienced air travelers in the population will increase as oldsters who never have taken an air trip die off and are replaced by those now aged about 30, of whom a large proportion already are air travelers. The uncertainty as to the effect of this rise in experience on the volume of air travel has to do with whether experienced air travelers will continue to be more likely than other people to take air trips, other factors remaining constant. Two considerations point in the direction of a continued powerful effect: the continued statistical importance of experience as a variable in a multivariate context shown in Appendix I, and the evidence that experience is associated with people's attitudes toward air travel to the extent that those attitudes have been successfully measured.

C. Frequency of Travel by Air, 1955 and 1962

As has been emphasized already, people appear to overstate the number of air trips which they take in a period of a year, when asked a single question on the subject. Even allowing for overstatement, however, the data in the following tabulation (shown also in Graph 23) make it clear that a small group of people who travel repeatedly account for most of the business air travel:

GRAPH   23

PER CENT OF BUSINESS AND NON-BUSINESS
AIR TRAVELERS BY NUMBER OF AIR TRIPS
TAKEN, 1962

Per Cent

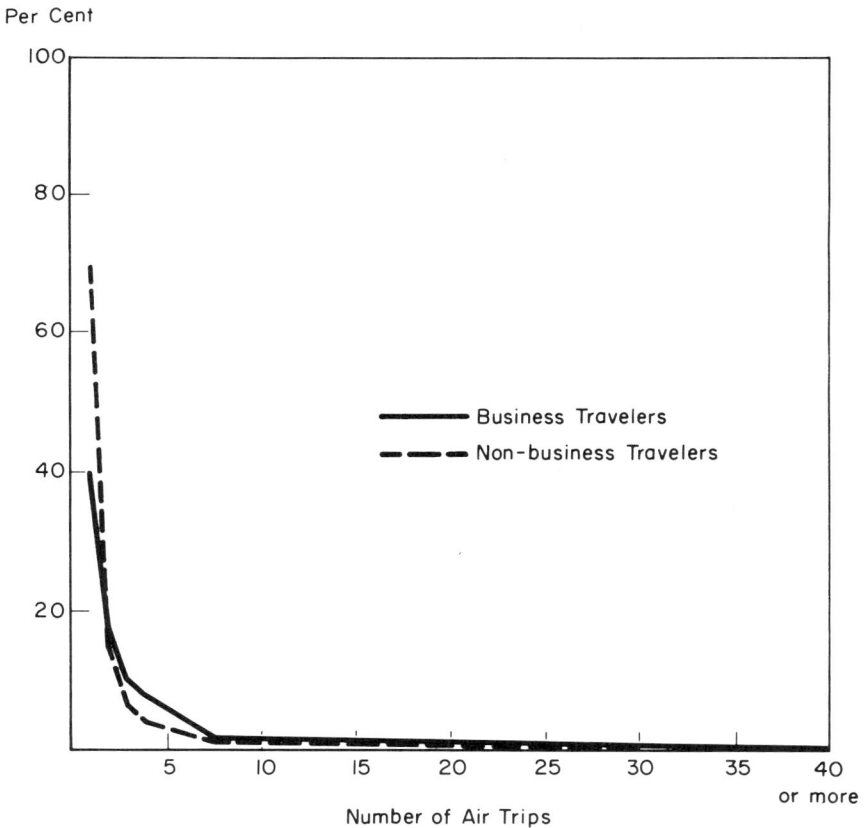

Number of Air Trips	Business Trips by Air in 1962		Non-Business Trips by Air in 1962	
	Per Cent of Travelers	Per Cent of Trips	Per Cent of Travelers	Per Cent of Trips
1	40	8	69	38
2-4	35	19	25	36
5-19	21	39	5	19
20 and over	4	34	1	7
Total	100	100	100	100

Four out of 10 business travelers report only a single trip, while almost 7 out of 10 non-business travelers are in the one-trip category. At the other end, the 5-or-more trip people on non-business trips are only 6 per cent of non-business travelers and account for only 26 per cent of such trips (probably even less, allowing for overstatement), whereas the 5-or-more business trip people constitute 25 per cent of business air travelers and chalk up two thirds or more business air trips. These frequent business travelers undoubtedly are very important in the air travel market.

Whether or not an individual takes a trip by air either for business or non-business reasons in the course of a twelve month period depends to an important extent on his income. The relation between income and the per cent of adults at different income levels who took one or more air trips is shown for 1955 and 1962 in Graph 24 and in the following tabulation:

Family Income	Per Cent Who Traveled	
	1955	1962
Under $2000	1	3
$2000-2999	2	5
$3000-3999	3	5
$4000-4999	4	6
$5000-5999	5	6
$6000-7999	9	8
$7500-9999	12	13
$10,000-14,999	22	25
$15,000 or over	40	34
All incomes	7	11

In 1962, of those with incomes below $2000 only 3 per cent took an air trip compared to 34 per cent of those with income of $15,000 or more.

GRAPH 24

PER CENT OF ADULTS AT DIFFERENT INCOME
LEVELS WHO TRAVELED BY AIR DURING THE
SURVEY YEAR

Per Cent

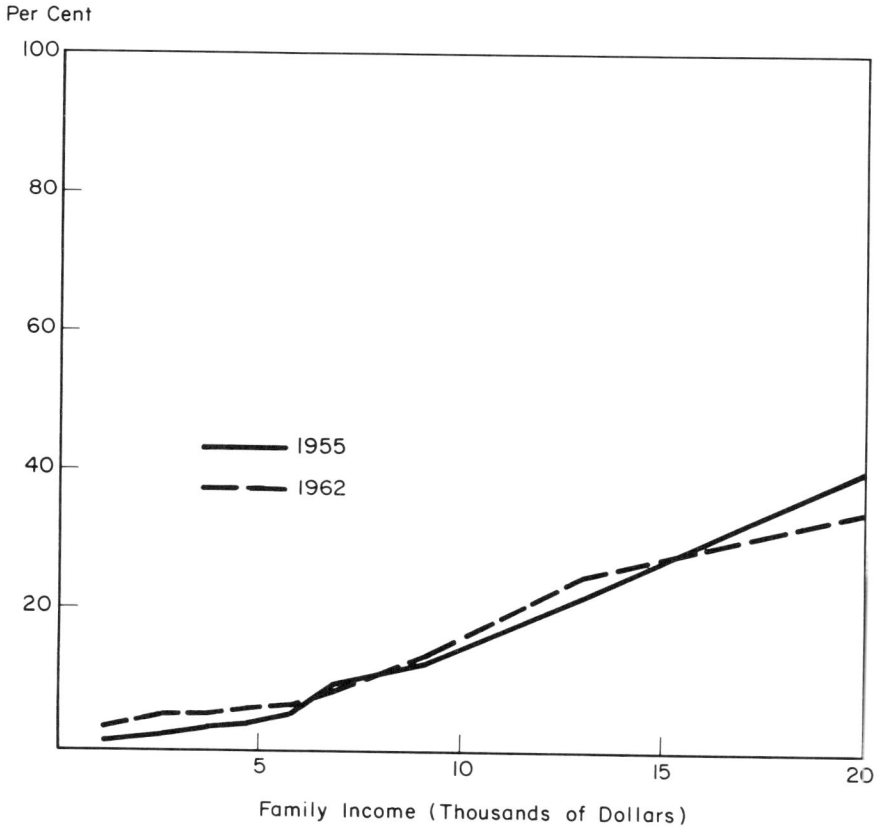

Family Income (Thousands of Dollars)

In comparing 1955 to 1962 as to effect of income on air travel, the
striking thing about Graph 24 is how little change there has been. Allowing for the sampling error of the findings, it is an open question
whether there was any change at all during this period as to the proportion of adults at each income level who took one or more air trips.
The total volume of air travel might rise also if the people who took a

single trip were more likely to take more than one trip as time went on. Comparison of the frequency distributions of the number of trips taken per year by people who took at least one trip, however, shows little evidence of an increase in the number of air trips per air traveler. Air travel did increase, but by about the amount which the upward shift in incomes might explain.

Why did air travel grow so slowly? Should not the effects of increasing experience by the population, somewhat reduced concern about air safety, not to mention improved technology, have added to the effect of rising incomes? What held back the growth of air?

One negative factor in this period has been an increased level of fares. It seems that the history of the market in this period is that the depressing effect of these fare increases about equalled the stimulating effect of favorable forces other than the increase in incomes. It is difficult to escape the conclusion that these tabulations showing the relation between income and air travel point in the direction of the more pessimistic interpretation of the future of the demand for air.

The share of the total number of air trips accounted for by adults at different income levels in 1955 and 1962 is shown in the following tabulation:

Family Income	1955		1962	
	Adults	Trips	Adults	Trips
Under $4000	44	7	28	6
$4000-5999	29	19	24	9
$6000-9999	19	24	31	25
$10,000 and over	8	50	17	60
Total	100	100	100	100

This tabulation presents the distribution of income in a manner which is parallel to the corresponding tabulation in the chapters on other modes. It shows that 44 per cent of all adults in 1955 were members of familes which had a total family income of less than $4000. According to the survey estimate, those adults with incomes below $4000 accounted for 7 per cent of all air trips in 1955. The 8 per cent of all adults with family incomes of $10,000 and over accounted for 50 per cent of all air trips in that year. In 1962 the 17 per cent of all adults associated with families in the $10,000 and over bracket accounted for 60 per cent of the air trips at that time. Thus, people in the upper income levels account for a large fraction of all air travel.

Given the relation between income and air travel, the relation between occupation and air travel is predictable. Adults in the higher status occupations are more likely to travel by air than those in the lower status occupations as shown by the following tabulation from the 1962 survey:

Occupation of Adult	Per Cent Who Took Any Air Trip	Per Cent Who Took a Business Air Trip
Professional, technical	29	19
Managerial, self-employed	27	18
Clerical, sales	15	5
Craftsmen, foremen, operatives	5	2
Laborers, service workers	3	*
Farmers, farm managers	7	2
Housewives, retired, students	7	1
All	11	4

The relation between occupation and air travel is shown also in Graph 25. The difference among occupation groups is most pronounced in business air travel. In 1962, of all professional and technical workers, 19 per cent took at least one business air trip. Of the managerial and self-employed, 18 per cent took such a trip, but of the laborers and service workers less than 1 per cent report a business air trip. The large groups of housewives, retired persons, and students, of course, include very few business travelers by air. These people are about as likely to travel for non-business reasons by air as the entire population of which they form so large a part.

In view of the relation between experience with air travel and age which has already been discussed, one would expect that there would be a relation between age at time of interview and air travel. The findings from the 1962 survey are in the following tabulation:

Age of Adult	Per Cent Who Took Any Air Trip	Per Cent Who Took Any Non-Business Air Trip
18-24	11	9
25-34	12	8
35-44	13	7
45-54	10	6
55-64	9	7
65 and over	5	5
All ages	11	8

People aged 65 and over are much less likely to travel by air than the population at large. In 1962 only 5 per cent of this age group took an air trip, compared to 11 per cent of the general population. People at this age level have been characterized as a natural market for travel

GRAPH 25

PER CENT OF ADULTS WITH DIFFERENT OCCUPA-
TIONS WHO TRAVELED BY AIR DURING THE
SURVEY YEAR

Per Cent

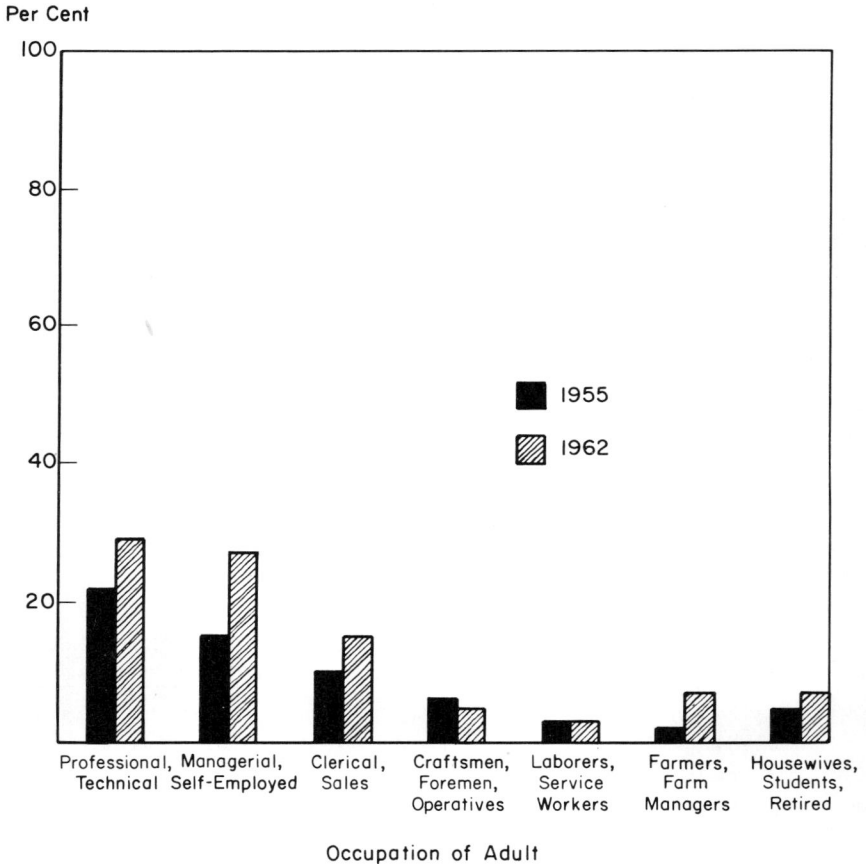

Occupation of Adult

by common carriers rather than by auto, but they do not fly. The age
group 55-64 also shows a comparatively low proportion taking an air
trip, 9 per cent in 1962 compared to 11 per cent for the population at
large. The people who travel by air are primarily those in the age
groups from about 18 to 54. These results are shown in Graph 26.

GRAPH 26

PER CENT OF ADULTS IN DIFFERENT AGE
GROUPS WHO TRAVELED BY AIR DURING THE
SURVEY YEAR

Per Cent

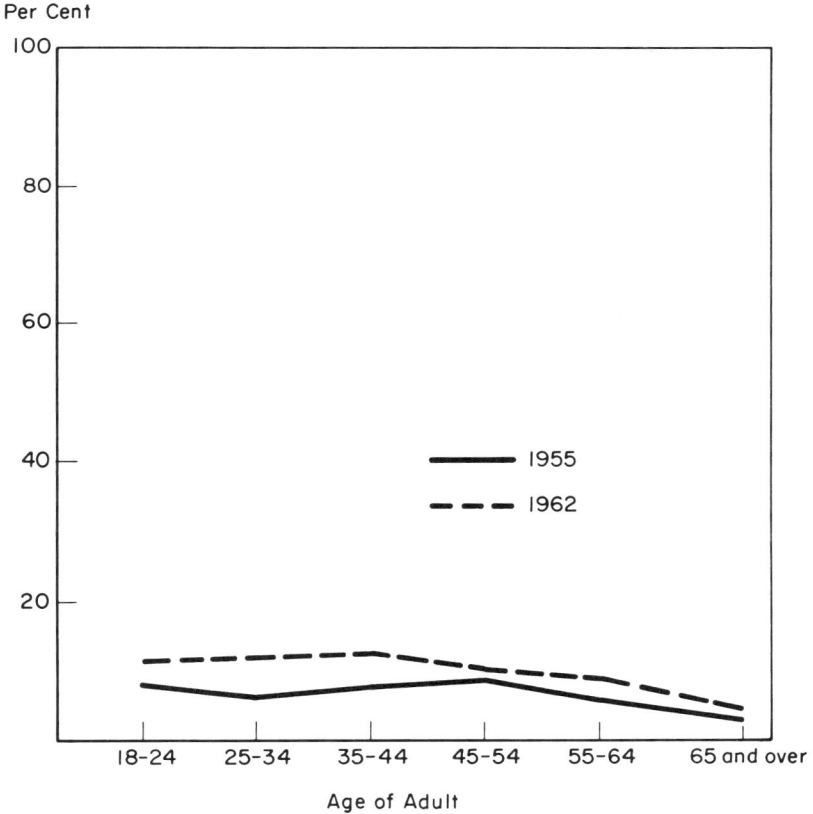

Age of Adult

One of the more interesting questions about the future of air travel is whether the young and middle aged people who now travel by air
will continue to travel frequently by air as they grow older. In this
connection it is particularly interesting that in 1955 of the age group
45-54, 9 per cent took an air trip, compared to 6 per cent of those
55-64. In 1962, however, when the people formerly aged 45-54 were 7
years older, and most fell in the age group 55-64, the proportion of air
travelers in that group was up to 9 per cent. It appears, in other words,
that these people are continuing to fly. The increase from 1955 to 1962

from 3 per cent to 5 per cent of those aged 65 and over taking an air trip points in the same direction.

Tabulations showing the relation between age and use of air travel obscure the fact that people at different stages in the family life cycle are very different with regard to their air travel. The simple relation between stage in the family life cycle and use of air is shown here for 1962:

Stage in the Family Life Cycle	Per Cent Who Took Any Air Trip	Per Cent Who Took a Non-Business Air Trip
Young, single	14	13
Under 45, married, no children	8	6
Married with children under 18	12	7
Over 45, married, no children under 18	8	6
Older, single	15	15
All stages	10	7

In 1962, 13 per cent of the young single people took a non-business air trip, but only 6 per cent of the couples with no children and 7 per cent of the married people with children took comparable trips. Of the older single people (who consist of those never married, the widowed, and the divorced), more than twice as many (15 per cent) took a non-business air trip in 1962. The difference between the older couples and single people must be explained in terms of the difference in the cost of air travel for people traveling alone and people traveling in groups. It is not old age itself which keeps to a level of 6 per cent the older couples who fly. It is expense! The importance of expense as an obstacle to air travel has already been shown in connection with discussion of choice of method of transportation for recent trips.

Few women take air trips for business reasons. If attention is restricted to non-business travel, the proportion who take an air trip in the course of a year is the same for both sexes, 7 per cent in 1962. In 1955 the proportion for both sexes was 5 per cent.

Few Negroes take air trips. The statistics may be summarized as follows:

	Per Cent Who Took an Air Trip	
Race	1955	1962
White	8	12
Negro	1	3

Only 3 per cent of Negroes took an air trip in 1962 compared to 12 per cent of whites. In the 1955 survey, even of the Negroes with incomes of $4000 or above only 2 per cent reported they had taken an air trip compared to 11 per cent of whites over $4000 income.

D. Regional Differences in Air Travel

Reference has been made already to the low proportion of adults in the New York metropolitan area and in the Northeast who take an auto trip in the course of a year. Since air is in some degree a substitute for auto, air might be expected to be used more rather than less frequently in these locations. When the country is divided into four regions the actual differences in the use of air are shown in Graph 27 and the following tabulation:

GRAPH   27

PER CENT OF ADULTS LIVING IN DIFFERENT
REGIONS WHO TRAVELED BY AIR DURING THE
SURVEY YEAR

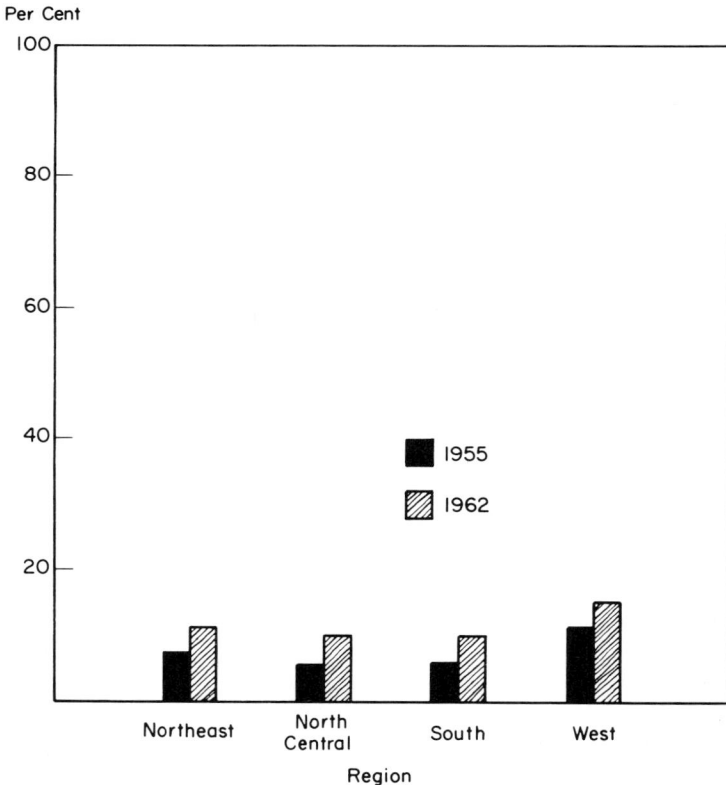

Per Cent Who Took an Air Trip

Region	1955	1962
Northeast	7	11
North Central	6	10
South	6	10
West	11	15
All regions	7	11

Among the four regions, the West, not the Northeast, stands high. It was higher than any other part of the country in both 1955 and 1962 in the per cent of adults who took any air trip. This result is reasonable in view of the greater distances between centers of population in the West and the tendency of air travel to enjoy a greater relative advantage over other means of transportation for long distances. The other three areas are about on a par with each other.

A comparison of people living in the New York metropolitan area with those who live elsewhere shows the New Yorkers more likely to take an air trip. The proportions of this tendency are shown in Graph 19 in Chapter III as well as in the following tabulation:

Per Cent Who Took an Air Trip

Year	New York	Megalopolis Excluding New York	Remainder of the Country
1955	12	8	6
1957	15	10	8
1958	14	8	9
1960	13	10	8
1962	15	14	10

The proportion who took an air trip in 1962 in New York was 15 per cent of all adults, compared to 10 per cent in the "remainder of the country." Results for earlier years also show New York with the highest proportion of air travelers. The proportion of those living outside New York but in the metropolitan corridor who took an air trip falls between the proportion for New York and that for the "remainder of the country."

Essentially the same comparison among the three areas emerges when the focus is on experience as an air traveler without regard to year of travel:

Per Cent Who Ever Had Taken an Air Trip

Year	New York	Megalopolis Excluding New York	Remainder of the Country
1955	32	24	22
1957	36	30	26
1958	36	32	28
1960	35	33	26
1962	45	42	34

Again New York is highest, and "megalopolis excluding New York" ranks second. It would appear, therefore, that the barriers to use of the auto in the New York area, combined with the availability of plane service from New York, lead to a high proportion of fliers in the metropolitan area.

The metropolitan area itself is not homogeneous. The per cent of adults who take an air trip in a year varies by sub-region in the following manner:

Sub-Divisions of the New York Area	Per Cent Who Took an Air Trip, 1962
Manhattan	28
Queens	11
Brooklyn	9
Bronx	3
Newark, Jersey City	15
Suburbs in New York	16
Suburbs in New Jersey	15
All adults in the area	15

Of the people living on Manhattan, 28 per cent took an air trip, compared to only 3 to 11 per cent in the Bronx, Queens, and Brooklyn; while the proportion who took an air trip in the suburbs was similar to that for the metropolis as a whole.

E. Response to the Introduction of Jet Powered Air Craft

Prior to the introduction of jet aircraft in scheduled domestic service in the United States, but during the period when people were talking about this development as a future event, a special effort to obtain information about people's attitudes toward jet planes was made in two surveys. Questions about the subject were asked in both the 1957 and the 1958 National Travel Market Surveys. The results were made available in the reports on those studies which have been reprinted in the two earlier volumes in the travel market series.

Now that the introduction of jet planes has been completed, one might be tempted to let these early reports quietly gather dust. But other innovations in air transportation are now being discussed, especially supersonic transport. In attempting to forecast the possible effects of future innovations it may be of value to analyze carefully the earlier experience.

In the 1957 survey, the following question was put to a cross-section of the adult population of the United States: "As you probably know, there are plans for developing jet planes for passenger service. How would you feel about traveling in a jet plane? What do you have in mind?" The following tabulation, reflecting the attitudes expressed by users of each mode, is based on the leading table in the rather extensive discussion of attitudes toward jet travel in the 1957 report:

Feelings About Jet Travel	All	Air	Rail	Bus or Auto	Took No Trip
Would like jet travel	33	67	45	38	23
Other attitudes	67	33	55	62	77
Total	100	100	100	100	100

This summary shows, first, a surprisingly high incidence of negative feelings about jet travel in the population at large. Only a third of the population said they would like to travel by jet plane. Second, there were overwhelmingly favorable attitudes toward jet travel on the part of air travelers. Of those who had taken an air trip in the year prior to the survey, 67 per cent stated clearly that they would like jet travel. Of those who had traveled by bus or auto, only 38 per cent responded favorably.

From the point of view of the aviation industry, there were two questions about jet travel. The one was, what would be the response to the jets of those already traveling by air? This tabulation suggested that the response would be favorable. The implication, of course, was that airlines that introduced jet planes would have a competitive advantage over any laggards who failed to introduce them, or introduced

them only after a time had elapsed. The other question was, would introduction of jet aircraft act generally to stimulate air travel?   The
results of the survey suggested that the response to the jets by those
not already members of the group of air travelers might not be very
favorable.

In retrospect it seems clear that the answers these different
groups gave to this question accurately foreshadowed their behavior.
Air travelers did show a preference for jets from the initial stages of
their introduction, and the earlier jets did operate with a high passenger load as a result. The general public, however, did not flock to the
jets, and the aviation industry did not experience a spurt in growth in
the years after the introduction of the jet planes. On the contrary, the
industry went through several difficult years.

Other results of the 1957 study are of some interest, though perhaps less critical. The study showed striking differences in reactions
to the idea of jet travel by people in different age groups. In order to
take into account the effect already observed of frequency of travel,
those who took no trip by any mode last year are excluded from the following tabulation of the 1957 results:

Feelings About Jet Travel	Age Groups			
	18-24	25-44	45-64	65 +
Would like jet travel	55	46	31	14
Other attitudes	45	54	69	86
Total	100	100	100	100

Of those in the age group 18-24 years in 1957, 55 per cent said that they
would like jet travel, compared to only 14 per cent of those aged 65 and
over. These results are consistent with those of other studies of innovations. Young people are generally more ready than older people to
accept new things.

There were pronounced differences, also, between men and women
in their attitudes toward jet travel, as expressed in 1957. Only men and
women who had taken at least one trip of some type in the previous
year are included in the following comparison:

Feelings About Jet Travel	Men	Women
Would like jet travel	50	28
Other attitudes	50	72
Total	100	100

The men seem equally divided pro and con. But, while 50 per cent of the men said they would like jet travel, only half as many women (28 per cent) were favorably disposed. A substantial majority of women stated that they would *not* like jet travel.

With what frame of reference did people evaluate jet planes in 1957, a year when they could have had no experience? The per cent of all travelers of each sex who gave different reasons for their attitude was as follows:

Advantages of Jet Travel	Men	Women
Faster, save time	28	16
Likes flying	8	4
Safer	7	4
More comfortable	4	2
Exciting; adventuresome	4	6
Likes new things; believes in being modern	3	1
Quieter	2	1
Other	5	3

Disadvantages of Jet Travel	Men	Women
Doesn't like flying	13	26
Too fast	8	15
"I'm afraid of jets" (personal reference)	5	13
Too new to be safe	2	2
Unsafe for other reasons	4	6
Others	4	5

In part reactions were based on general attitudes toward aviation. Eight per cent of the men stated explicitly that they tended to be positively disposed to jets because they liked flying. Twenty-six per cent of the women stated the reverse; they didn't like flying and didn't like jets. The data also indicate that some people were responding, as previously suggested, on the basis of their general feelings about something which is new.

Negative feelings about jets arising out of fear are hard to assess. It is socially more acceptable for women to admit they are afraid than men, hence, it is not safe to conclude from the data that men actually were less nervous than women about jet planes. To anyone who was already a bit nervous about air travel, the prospect of a new type of aircraft which would fly very high and very fast was not particularly reassuring.

Other investigations also have shown that people respond differently to the idea of innovations. While some people responded favorably to jets because they were new, others responded unfavorably for the same reason. While some felt jets were too new to be safe, others "believed in being modern."

As time goes on, innovations cease to be new. Attitudes toward what was once a novelty tend to be formed by forces other than general feelings about innovations. To determine present attitudes toward jet planes would require new questions specifically directed to that objective.

What can be inferred about the probable demand for travel by supersonic aircraft? The data suggest the hypothesis that the experience with jets will be repeated. That is, people accustomed to flying will respond favorably to the new supersonic planes and take every opportunity to travel by them in preference to the older jets, but people not flying in the regular planes will be even more reluctant to use the new aircraft.

There are contradictory indications, however. On the one hand, the doubtful reaction many non-fliers had to the jets suggests a similar lack of enthusiasm in the same quarter toward yet another new type of aircraft. Yet, the group of experienced air travelers is increasing. There is the possibility that people's aggregate fear of air travel is being gradually reduced. The slow response to the jet planes by people not already experienced air travelers seems to have been, at least in part, a result of underlying fear of all air travel. If this fear is reduced in broad groups in the population, then some years in the future they may respond more favorably to the introduction of the supersonic aircraft than they responded to jets. Further research would be necessary to support any prognostications.

F. Time to Reach the Airport

With the increasing speed of planes, the length of time spent get-ting to the airport to start the flight and from the terminal airport to the final destination becomes an ever larger part of the total time en route. To learn how long people spend getting to and from the airport, the 1960 survey asked for the pertinent data about their most recent air trip from those who had taken an air trip. Data were tabulated separ-ately for trips to places 1000 or more miles away and trips to destina-tions closer than 1000 miles, on the assumption that people may be will-ing to travel farther to an airport for a very long trip, than they would for a shorter trip. The results of this inquiry are summarized below for 1960:

Travel Time	All Distances	Under 1000 Miles	1000 Miles and Over
Each airport trip took less than 1/2 hour	12	18	6
At least one airport trip took 1/2 to 1 hour	32	35	30
At least one airport trip took 1 to 2 hours	34	40	30
At least one airport trip took 2 hours or more	19	6	32
Not ascertained	3	1	2
Total	100	100	100

Few people make a trip by plane without spending one or two hours time getting to and from airports. Roughly only one trip in ten con-sumes less than half an hour each way to the airport. The majority re-port that at least one of their journeys to the airport took over one hour. On outgoing trips to destinations of 1000 miles away, trips of two hours or more to the airport are reported by a third of the travelers. These results are consistent with the findings reported in Chapter II, that air is at a relative disadvantage in availability compared to other modes of travel but this disadvantage is offset by other advantages for long distances.

G. Air Trips Versus Communication Without Travel

The possibility is sometimes suggested that new communication systems, such as telephones with attached closed-circuit television screens, may compete with travel by plane. An attempt was made in the 1960 survey to obtain information about business travel to evaluate this possibility. Two questions were asked of business travelers both by air and by rail: "Were you attending a convention, or meeting with a group of people, or just talking to one person, or did you have several appointments?" and "How long did you spend at your meeting or appointments altogether? Was it less than an hour, about an hour, two or three hours, half a day, a day, or more than a day?" The information obtained about the kinds of appointments is summarized in the following tabulation:

Kinds of Appointments	Per Cent of Trips
Talked to one person	3
Attended a convention	15
Met with a group of people	39
Several appointments	33
Combination of above	10
Total	100

Length of Time Spent	Per Cent of Trips
Under 3 1/2 hours	9
3 1/2 to 6 hours	8
6 to 12 hours	20
12 hours and over	63
Total	100

Most business travelers either meet with a group of people or have several appointments. Few trips are made just to talk to a single person. Thus, the purposes of the trip could not be served by a system of communication designed for conversations between only two persons, one in each location. It is unusual for the time spent at appointments on business trips to be short. Only a minority of business travelers spend less than 6 hours with their appointments. Most spend periods of 12 hours and over. Thus, any new means of communication would have to be suitable for long periods of use in order to substitute directly for what happens on most business trips.

Considered together, the answers to these two questions suggest that business travel is not likely to be replaced by new methods of communication. An alternate possibility is that new methods of communication might complement rather than supplant business travel.

New methods might facilitate preliminary conversations prior to the business trip and follow-up conversations after it had been completed, and thus make the trip itself more useful. If a few trips become unnecessary because of new devices, others may be stimulated. It would be premature, certainly, to conclude that the future of business travel is threatened by new communication systems.

H. Use of Rented Cars on Air Trips

One of the basic advantages of automobile travel which people mention is that it may be convenient to have a car at one's destination. One way to ensure the availability of a car is to go by automobile the entire distance, but an alternative is to rent a car on arrival. It is of interest, then, in analysis of the market for air travel, to consider the extent to which people accept the rental method of meeting their needs for a car at the destination.

In the 1962 survey people were asked, in connection with their most recent trip by common carrier, whether they rented a car. Of the most recent trips by air, 11 per cent involved the use of a rented car. Only one per cent or less of the trips by rail or bus involved the use of a rented car.

The probability of renting a car is associated with the length of time that the traveler is away from home. The relation appears in the following tabulation:

Length of Time Away on the Trip	Per Cent Who Rented a Car
Back the same day	*
1-2 days	10
3-6 days	15
7-10 days	17
11 or more days	9
All lengths of time	11

Apparently, rented cars are rarely used on short one-day trips. They appear to be used with increasing frequency on trips of up to a week or 10 days duration, and less often on trips longer than that. Since these results are based on small numbers of observations, the percentages must be regarded as subject to considerable sampling error.

I. Responses to Hypothetical Changes in the Price of Air Travel

Frequent mention has been made in this report of the importance of price of travel. While it is impossible in a cross-section study to measure the effect of price directly, inferences have been made by such methods as comparing the choice of mode of travel by parties of different numbers of people. An attempt to approach the subject in another manner was made in the 1962 survey by asking: "If plane fares were half what they are now, do you think your family would take more plane trips than you do at the present time?" If the respondent said "no" to that question, he was asked: "Suppose someone were to offer you and your family a free plane trip to wherever you wanted to go, would you take it?" The responses to this pair of questions are summarized in the following tabulation:

Reaction	All	Have Taken an Air Trip	Never Have Taken an Air Trip
If plane fares were halved			
Would take more trips	28	44	20
Probably would take more trips, might take more trips	6	7	6
If plane travel were free			
Would take more trips	28	31	26
Probably would take more trips	6	4	7
Definitely would not	29	12	38
Don't know; not ascertained	3	2	3
Total	100	100	100

Thirty-four per cent of the population state that if plane fares were halved their family would take more air trips. Since only 11 per cent of the population now travel by air in any year, the implication is that the demand for air travel is price elastic. An additional 34 per cent said if they were offered a free plane trip wherever they wanted to go, they would accept. Three out of ten families would not accept free plane trips.

A 50 per cent reduction in air fares is unlikely, the cost of air service being what it is, and free plane travel is out of the question. Thus, these answers for the population as a whole must be regarded only as suggesting that there may be a considerable sensitivity of demand to reductions in the price of air travel.

An additional use of these responses is to compare attitudes of different subgroups in the population. In this way it may be possible to get some clues as to differences in the price elasticity of the demand for air travel from one group in the population to another. That there are large differences in response to this question associated with differences in air travel experience the preceding tabulation has shown. Of those who are experienced air travelers, 44 per cent say they would take more plane trips if the fares were cut in half, compared to only 20 per cent of those who never have taken an air trip. These results suggest that over the years as increasing numbers of people become experienced air travelers the price elasticity of the demand for air travel is tending to increase.

Such a shift would be consistent with what is generally believed to happen with new goods and services. The demand for a dramatically new commodity may be primarily a matter of considerations other than price. As it is introduced into the population and comes into wider use, the demand for it may become increasingly sensitive to price.

What, then, can be concluded about the argument between the optimists and the pessimists as to the future of air travel? On the optimistic side are the rising population, the upward shift in incomes, the increasing number of people who are experienced air travelers, and the possible reduction in anxiety about flying. On the pessimistic side is the failure of air travel to increase in volume except by the amount necessary to keep up with the upward shift of incomes. The most important area of uncertainty seems to be the uncertainty with regard to future prices. The data suggest that price policy will be increasingly important in determining the future volume of air travel.

As everyone concerned with the transportation of passengers is aware, the record of rail passenger transportation has been for decades a record of decline. The peak volume of rail passenger service was in 1920. From then until now, the trend has been down in railroad passenger business. The question today is the future direction of this trend. Will it continue downward? How far will it go? Are there some portions of the travel market where rail is particularly strong and where the decline might be arrested or perhaps even reversed? Or, do different parts of the market differ only in the rate of decline? Thus, the problem for study might be stated as one of searching for a place for rail travel in the travel market. Alternatively, the problem might be regarded as one of assessing the strengths and weaknesses of the market in order to assess the probable future of any proposals for the revitalization of the rail service.

Following an outline broadly similar to the treatment of other modes of transportation, this chapter will take up the following topics: people's attitudes toward rail travel, their history as rail travelers, the frequency of travel by rail in 1955 compared to 1962, and regional differences in the use of rail.

117

A. Attitudes Toward Rail Travel

The selection of topics for the National Travel Market Surveys reflects the sponsorship of the studies. Data on attitudes toward rail travel were collected in 1955-1957, but not in more recent years. The fact that these measures of attitudes are several years old is, in one sense, fortunate. They can be studied in the light of knowledge of recent events to search out answers to the question why rail travel has declined as it has. The approach to the study of attitudes toward rail in 1955-1957 was parallel to that toward air. Both direct and indirect methods of questioning were used, the latter to permit free expression of feelings which might not otherwise be revealed.

The most indirect approach relied on was to ask the following sequence, used only in 1955: "Two businessmen often travel to a city 500 miles away. One always goes by air. The other always goes by rail. What might be your idea, what kind of a person is the one who goes by air? What kind of a person is the one who goes by rail?" The answers follow:

	Per Cent of Adults
Characteristic Air Traveler	Mentioning Each Characteristic
High status (important, rich, big shot)	25
Active (busy, in a hurry, efficient)	68
Modern (progressive, modern, sophisticated)	6
Courageous (not afraid)	6
Thrifty (economical)	2
Other characteristics	11
Characteristic Rail Traveler	
Moderate status (average sort of person)	5
Less active (has time, is relaxed, takes life easier)	46
Conservative (old-fashioned, established, older person, sensible)	18
Timid (afraid to fly, cautious, afraid of air sickness)	33
Thrifty (economical, needs to save money)	13
Other characteristics	13

A pivotal point in these characterizations is time, the air passenger is saving time, the rail passenger doesn't need to. Other important points are the preference for safety and comfort attributed to rail travelers and the high status attributed to air patrons. Perhaps the best way to look at these results is to consider their emotional overtones and ask, would most businessmen rather be thought of as important, busy, efficient men or would they prefer to be thought of as men with plenty of time, old-fashioned, timid, and economical? The fact that air was believed to be the new, modern, rapid method of travel thus gave it a psychological advantage over rail apart from any calculations with a sharp pencil and paper about time and money spent.

To explore further people's attitudes toward rail travel, a cross-section of the population was asked the following questions in 1955: "Why do you think some people travel by train?" and "What might keep some people from traveling by train?" The answers are summarized in the following tabulation:

Attitudes	Per Cent of Adults Mentioning Each Attitude
Advantages of rail	
Comfortable, restful; good passenger facilities; enjoys meeting people (likes club car)	38
Avoids strain of driving; can't drive; doesn't own car	21
Safer (better in bad weather)	19
Good connections; convenient	16
Faster	11
Cheap, cheaper, reasonable	9
Enjoys seeing the scenery	4
Other	2
Disadvantages of rail	
Expensive	27
Bad connections; hard to get to a train; stations are inconveniently located	21
Slow (compared to air)	19
See less scenery	6
Dangerous (fear of train wrecks)	5
Uncomfortable (noise, sudden stops, fatiguing, monotonous)	5
Train sickness	5
Trains are dirty	3
Inconvenient not to have a car on arrival	2

Of the advantages mentioned, by far the largest group (38 per cent) had to do with the comfort and amenities of travel by rail. A substantial second group (21 per cent) refers to difficulties or handicaps in driving a car as a reason for going by train. This type of response carries with it implications that travel by automobile is the normal method of going from one place to another, and only some special groups in the population who are unable or unwilling to travel by car are likely to go

by train. One-fifth of all adults (19 per cent) mentioned that train travel is safer, some of these people referring to its advantages in bad
weather. Smaller groups refer to the train's good connections and convenience and to speed of travel. In terms of the analysis of choice of
mode in Chapter II, the advantages most stressed here have to do with
quality of service, rather than price or availability. The most frequently mentioned reasons why people might not travel by train are
cost, inconvenient availability, and slowness. Thus, important disadvantages appear in all three of the areas emphasized in Chapter II as
relevant to choice of mode.

A more direct approach to the measurement of attitudes toward
rail travel was taken in the 1957 survey by asking people in the context
of a series of questions about their most recent trip: "How did you
happen to choose this way of traveling instead of some other?" The
replies with reference to rail may be summarized as follows:

Attitude	Per Cent of All Advantages and Disadvantages of Rail
Advantages of rail	
Comfortable, restful; good passenger facilities (e.g., rest rooms, diner, club car)	19
Faster	8
Cheaper	6
Safer	4
Good (better) connections	13
Good connections; convenient, no further information	8
Trains go to more places	3
Trains go at right times	2
Trains are easy to reach; stations are conveniently located	5
Enjoy the scenery; sightseeing	3
Disadvantages	
Bad connections	10
Trains don't go to right places, enough places; are badly scheduled for reasons of destination	6
Trains don't go at right times; are badly scheduled for reasons of timing	2
Trains connect badly with one another or with other modes	1
Bad connections, no further information	1

Disadvantages (Cont'd)

Trains are slow	5
Expensive	3
Hard to get a train; stations are inconveniently located	1
Other advantages and disadvantages	23
Total	100

These evaluations of train travel are in response to why did "you" go by train or not go by train on a specific trip rather than why do "some people travel by train," as in the immediately preceding tabulation. Though the attitudes in the tabulation about "your recent trip" encompass approximately the same range as the "some people" tabulation, there is some shift in emphasis. The list of advantages for "some people" in rail travel reads in this order: comfort, avoidance of the strain of driving (a form of comfort), safety, and good connections. For "your recent trip" the list reads: comfort, good connections, faster, and cheaper. In both lists comfort is at the top. The only other advantage repeated in both lists is good connections, and it looms larger in the discussion of the specific trip than for "some people." There is close agreement on the disadvantages of rail travel. Both lists contain expense, bad connections, and slowness. Expense is the most frequently mentioned disadvantage for "some people," but for "your recent trip" it is those bad connections.

In comparing these two tabulations, it is interesting to recall that a similar pair of questions asked about air travel led in one area to divergent answers: nearly everyone thinks "some people" are afraid to fly, but many fewer persons reply that they themselves chose not to fly because of fear. In rail travel fear is occasionally imputed to "some people" (safety is an advantage, danger is mentioned as a disadvantage) but scarcely mentioned for self (safety is low on list of advantages and danger omitted entirely from disadvantages).

The last approach to the exploration of attitudes toward rail travel taken in the 1955 survey was to ask people for their recollections of their most recent rail trip. All respondents who ever had taken a rail trip of 100 miles or more were asked: "Speaking of your own last trip by *train*, we are interested in what you liked most about it and what you liked least about it. What did you like most? What did you like least?" The answers to this question are summarized in the following tabulation:

Pleasant Recollections	Per Cent of Pleasant Recollections
Was comfortable, restful	26
Liked physical arrangements, clean, roomy, cool	20
Liked dining car, meals	14
Enjoyed the scenery	11
Other pleasant recollections	29
Total	100

Unpleasant Recollections	Per Cent of Unpleasant Recollections
Uncomfortable (noise, sudden stops, fatiguing)	28
Train was dirty, unsanitary	18
Too slow	17
Bad connections	14
Other unpleasant recollections	23
Total	100

Once again, when people are requested to discuss their pleasant recollections, the most favorable comments have to do with comfort. Altogether, six out of ten of the pleasant recollections concerned comfort: 26 per cent said that the rail trip was comfortable or restful; 20 per cent liked physical arrangements such as that the train was clean, roomy, or cool; and 14 per cent liked dining car meals. The only other favorable comment mentioned with any substantial frequency was by 11 per cent who enjoyed the scenery.

Some of the emotional overtones are mirrored in these quotations. A truck driver, aged 59 and with an income of $3000-3999, said that what he liked best about his last trip by train was that he, "got waited on like a king." But what he liked least was, "I cracked my head on the upper berth. Not enough room." The wife of a farmer, income $3000-$3999, replied, "I felt safe. You can eat on the train. They have better facilities on the train than on the buses." What did she like the least? "The noise and jars and dirt." A coal miner, interestingly enough, liked the freedom of movement. "You can get up and walk around." What did he not like? "The confinement. If you went by car you could stop. But when you go by train you just have to keep riding."

In view of the preponderance of pleasant comments about comfort, it is particularly interesting to note that among the unpleasant recollections there were a large number of unfavorable comments about comfort. The most frequent, 28 per cent of all unpleasant recollections, was that the train was noisy, stopped too suddenly, or was fatiguing. Another 18 per cent said the train was dirty or unsanitary. And, in addition, 17 per cent thought the train was too slow. Thus, in brief, there was no clear concensus that trains were comfortable. The leading advantage of rail travel in 1955 was an advantage about which people were, one might say, of two minds.

B. Experience With Rail Travel

As of 1955, 68 per cent of the adult population reported that they had at some time in their lives taken a rail trip to a place 100 miles or more away. Seven years later, in 1962, the per cent was virtually unchanged, 67 per cent.

One might inquire whether this lack of change appears equally at all income levels of the population. Graph 28 and the following tabulation show the relationship between experience as a rail traveler and income in 1955 and 1962:

GRAPH 28

PER CENT OF ADULTS AT DIFFERENT INCOME LEVELS
WHO HAVE EVER TAKEN A RAIL TRIP

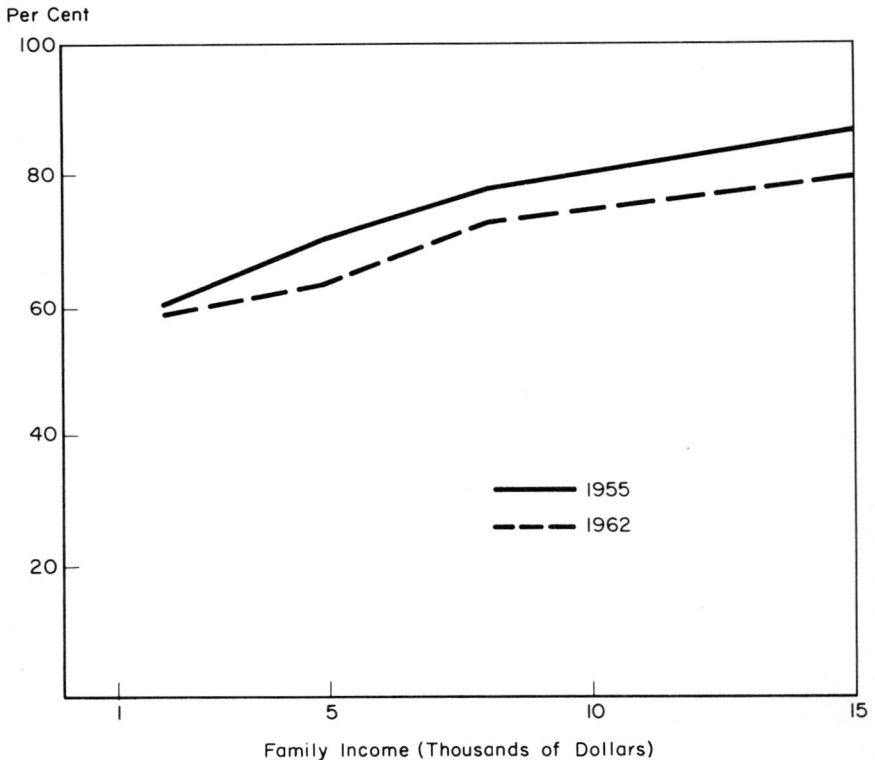

Family Income (Thousands of Dollars)

Family Income	Per Cent Who Took a Rail Trip	
	1955	1962
Under $4000	60	59
$4000-5999	70	63
$6000-9999	77	72
$10,000 and over	86	79
All incomes	68	67

If there has been a change in any income group, it has been a decline in rail travel at the top level. By 1962, persons who had reached the income level of $10,000 and over were no longer so likely to have taken a rail trip as persons at this level in 1955. Nevertheless, it remained true that nearly 8 out of 10 adults at this high income level had taken a rail trip, a higher ratio than the 6 out of 10 characteristic of those with incomes below $4000. The lack of a steep relationship between income and rail travel experience contrasts, of course, with the relation between income and air travel experience discussed in the previous chapter.

It is commonly observed that a new generation is growing up without knowledge of rail travel. The following tabulation indicates the facts of the matter:

Age	Per Cent Who Ever Had Taken a Rail Trip
18-24	43
25-34	65
35-44	74
45-54	70
55-64	70
65 and over	74
All ages	67

Here is some evidence to support the popular view. Of those in the age group 18-24, only 43 per cent have taken a rail trip, and of those 25-34 only 65 per cent have taken a rail trip, compared to 70 per cent or more at each of the higher age levels. (See Graph 29) It will be recalled that the highest level of experience with air travel, on the other hand, was in the age group 25-34. It is still true that most people have taken a rail trip at some time, but their numbers drop off rapidly among those born in the thirties and after.

In the interpretation of these results, it would be wholly unwarranted to place the same interpretation upon experience as a rail traveler as upon experience as an air traveler. There is no evidence of

GRAPH 29

PER CENT OF ADULTS IN DIFFERENT AGE
GROUPS WHO EVER HAVE TAKEN A RAIL
TRIP, 1962

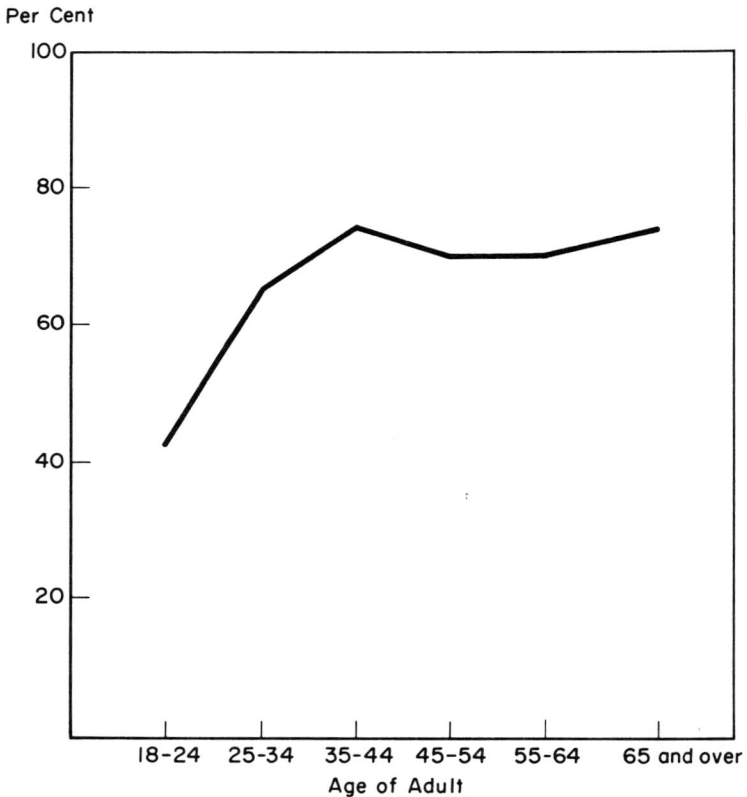

Per Cent

fear of rail travel anything like the evidence of fear of air travel, and
there is no presumption that people overcome any fear of rail travel by
taking their first rail trip. Experience as a rail traveler is simply a
straightforward measure of what people's use of trains has been. The
findings, then, are that there is a high proportion of people, even in the
lower income groups, who have at some time taken a rail trip, and that
experience with train travel decreases with youth. The relatively low
proportion of those aged 25-34 who have taken a rail trip contrasts
sharply with the relatively high proportion of this group who have taken
a trip by air.

The proportion who have ever taken a rail trip is much higher than the proportion who take a rail trip in one year, which in 1962 was only 7 per cent of all adults, and in 1955, only 10 per cent. It necessarily follows that many former rail travelers have not taken a rail trip for some time. Information on this point was obtained directly from the 1957 survey in which people were asked the year of their most recent trip:

Rail Travel History	Per Cent
Took a rail trip "last year"	11
Last rail trip was: 1954-1956	12
Last rail trip was: 1950-1953	12
Last rail trip was: 1946-1949	9
Last rail trip was: 1940-1945	9
Last rail trip was: 1939 or earlier	6
Year of last rail trip not known; can't remember	12
Never took a rail trip	29
Total	100

These figures show that one-third (35 per cent) of the adult population took a rail trip between 1950 and the time of interview in 1957. Another one-third had taken no rail trip for 7 years or more (24 per cent), or were unable to remember the year of their last rail trip (12 per cent - plus 24 equals 36 per cent). This question has not been repeated since 1957, but it is known that the number of people taking a rail trip has fallen during this interval. For an increasing proportion of the population, therefore, the memory of the most recent rail trip is receding into the past. For at least half of those who have ever traveled by rail, it must have been seven years or more since they did so. Like many others, a 52-year-old retail merchant in the seed business was stumped. "To tell you the truth, I don't know about when was the last trip I took by rail. I just can't recall."

C. Frequency of Travel by Rail, 1955 and 1962

It is the purpose of this section to discover whether the decline in rail travel from 1955 to 1962 was general or can be assigned to parts of the market. The proportion of the adult population who took a business trip by rail declined from 1955 to 1962, from 2 per cent to 1 per cent. The decline was paralleled as well by the proportion who took a rail trip for non-business reasons, from 8 to 6 per cent. The decline in business rail travel, thus, was relatively greater than the decline in non-business travel.

Were there differences between these years in the number of trips by those who took at least one rail trip? Estimates of the number of rail trips made by business and non-business travelers who have taken at least one rail trip must be based on only a limited number of observations, especially in 1962 for business travel, since a small proportion of the population taking rail trips on business means a small number of travelers in the sample. The estimates are summarized in Graph 30, and in the following tabulation:

Number of Rail Trips Taken	Per Cent of Those Who Took Business Trips		Per Cent of Those Who Took Non-Business Trips	
	1955	1962	1955	1962
1	51	63	72	72
2-4	33	24	24	23
5-19	12	13	2	5
20 or over	4	*	2	*
Total	100	100	100	100

In 1962 as in 1955 among those people who traveled by rail on business the largest group reported a single rail trip for this purpose. If anything, in 1962 more took only one trip. As far as non-business travel is concerned, in both years almost three out of four of the non-business rail travelers reported only a single non-business rail trip.

This finding is consistent with the discussion of people's year of most recent rail trip. Both sets of data point in the direction of a large number of people who occasionally take rail trips, but tend not to take very many of them. As far as non-business travel is concerned, the rail travel market in this respect resembles the air travel market. Of those who took a non-business air trip, about 70 per cent took only one trip in the last 12 months, just as is true of the rail travelers. Business travelers by air, however, tend to travel frequently by air, more frequently than business travelers by rail.

PER CENT OF BUSINESS AND NON-BUSINESS
RAIL TRAVELERS BY NUMBER OF RAIL TRIPS
TAKEN, 1962

Per Cent

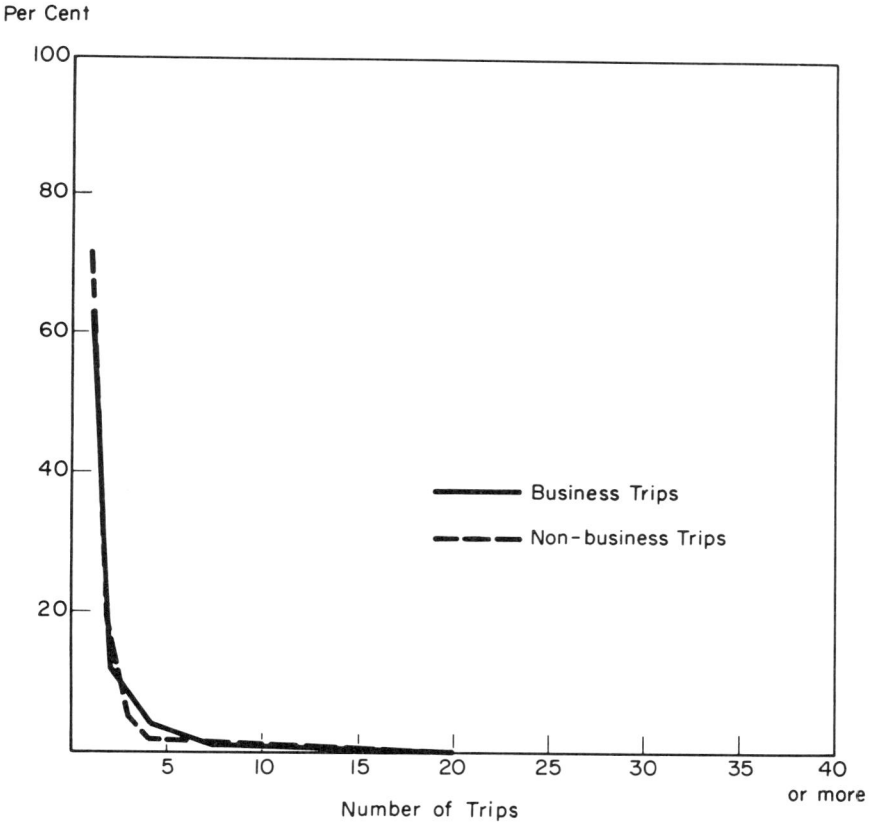

Number of Trips

When the rail travel market is broken down by income groups, the
course of events from 1955 to 1962 becomes more clear:

Family Income	Per Cent Who Traveled by Rail	
	1955	1962
Under $2000	6	5
$2000-2999	7	8
$3000-3999	8	8
$4000-4999	10	4
$5000-5999	9	6
$6000-7499	12	6
$7500-9999	16	8
$10,000-14,999	21	11
$15,000 and over	34	20
All incomes	10	7

These results are illustrated in Graph 31. Rail has lost very little in the three lowest income groups. The decline has come in the middle and upper income groups, from $4000 and up. Thus, the line showing the per cent of adults at different levels who travel by rail during the year has become much flatter in the period 1955 to 1962. Below $4000 income there has been no change, but above that income level there has been a substantial reduction in the per cent of adults who have taken a rail trip.

It remains true, nevertheless, that the per cent of adults who take a rail trip is higher in the upper income groups than it is in the middle and lower income groups. More of those with incomes over $10,000 took a rail trip in 1962 than of those with incomes under $4000. It also remains true, therefore, that people with incomes over $10,000 account for a larger proportion of all rail trips than they represent of all adults in the population as the following tabulation shows:

Family Income	1955		1962	
	Adults	Trips	Adults	Trips
Under $4000	44	29	28	24
$4000-5999	29	26	24	14
$6000-9999	19	22	31	31
$10,000 and over	8	23	17	31
Total	100	100	100	100

In 1955, 8 per cent had family incomes over $10,000; they took 23 per cent of the rail trips. By 1962, 17 per cent were in the $10,000 and over class, and they took a still higher proportion of the rail trips, 31 per cent. At the other end of the scale, those with incomes below $4000 were 44 per cent of all adults in 1955, but only 28 per cent in 1962. This reduced group still accounted for a quarter of all rail trips.

GRAPH 31

PER CENT OF ADULTS AT DIFFERENT INCOME
LEVELS WHO TRAVELED BY RAIL DURING THE
SURVEY YEAR

Per Cent

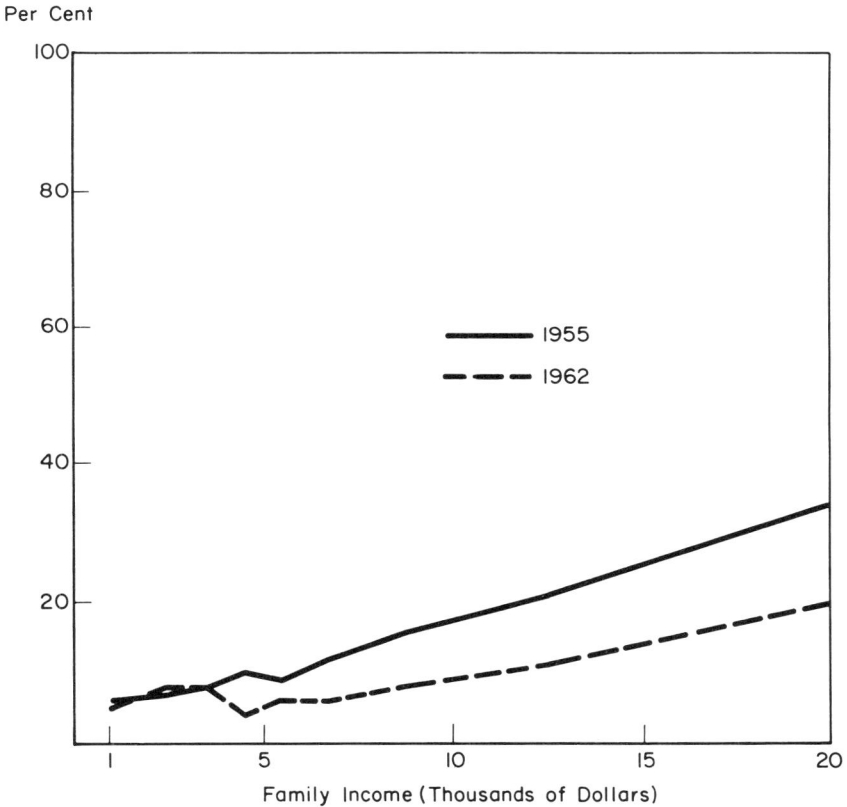

Family Income (Thousands of Dollars)

The differences in the use of rail by occupation groups are about what one might expect in view of the pattern shown by income groups. The decline in the use of rail is general, but it is especially steep among the high status occupation groups, such as the professional and technical workers:

Occupational Group	Per Cent Who Took a Rail Trip	
	1955	1962
Professional, technical	22	12
Managerial, self-employed	17	11
Clerical, sales	13	8
Craftsmen, foremen, operatives	13	5
Laborers, service workers	10	5
Housewives, retired, students	9	7
Farmers, farm managers	4	3
All occupations	10	7

This same information is shown also in Graph 32.

The table showing the relation between the respondent's age and his use of rail travel is also revealing:

Age of Adult	Per Cent Who Took a Rail Trip	
	1955	1962
18-24	12	8
25-34	8	5
35-44	10	7
45-54	13	7
55-64	11	11
65 and over	7	8
All ages	10	7

These data are also illustrated in Graph 33. The pattern shows a pivot which is similar, in a sense, to that for income. This time, however, it is the upper age groups which exhibit stability; those in the age groups over 55 were as likely to take a rail trip in 1962 as in 1955. The decline was entirely among those below 55. In each of the age groups up to 55 there was a fall. This result is consistent with that for income, as will be realized if it is recalled that the people in the age group over 65 are likely to have lower incomes than people in the peak earning years.

Some further light is shed on the matter by examining the relation between the respondent's use of rail travel and his stage in the family life cycle.

Stage in the Family Life Cycle	Per Cent Who Took a Rail Trip	
	1955	1962
Young, single	13	12
Under 45, married, no children	8	3
Married with children	9	6

Stage in the Family Life Cycle (Cont'd)	Per Cent Who Took a Rail Trip	
	1955	1962
Over 45, married, no children under 18	12	9
Older, single	11	10
All stages	10	7

This table tells a somewhat different story. The two groups who have

GRAPH 32

PER CENT OF ADULTS WITH DIFFERENT OCCUPATIONS WHO TRAVELED BY RAIL DURING THE SURVEY YEAR

Per Cent

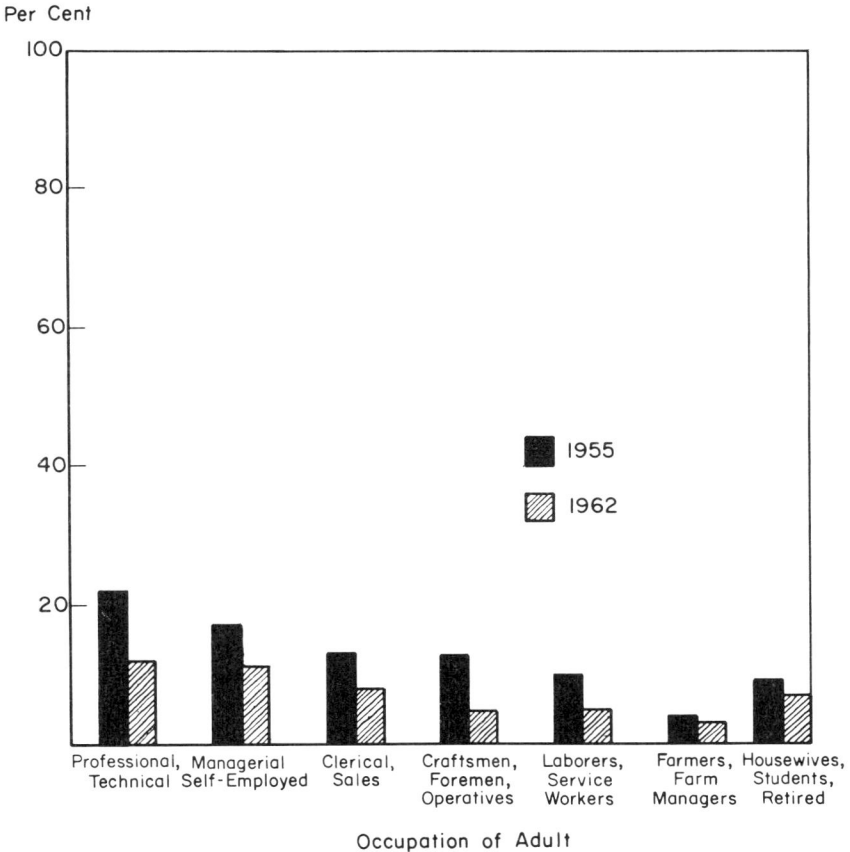

Occupation of Adult

GRAPH 33

PER CENT OF ADULTS IN DIFFERENT AGE GROUPS WHO TRAVELED BY RAIL DURING THE SURVEY YEAR

Per Cent

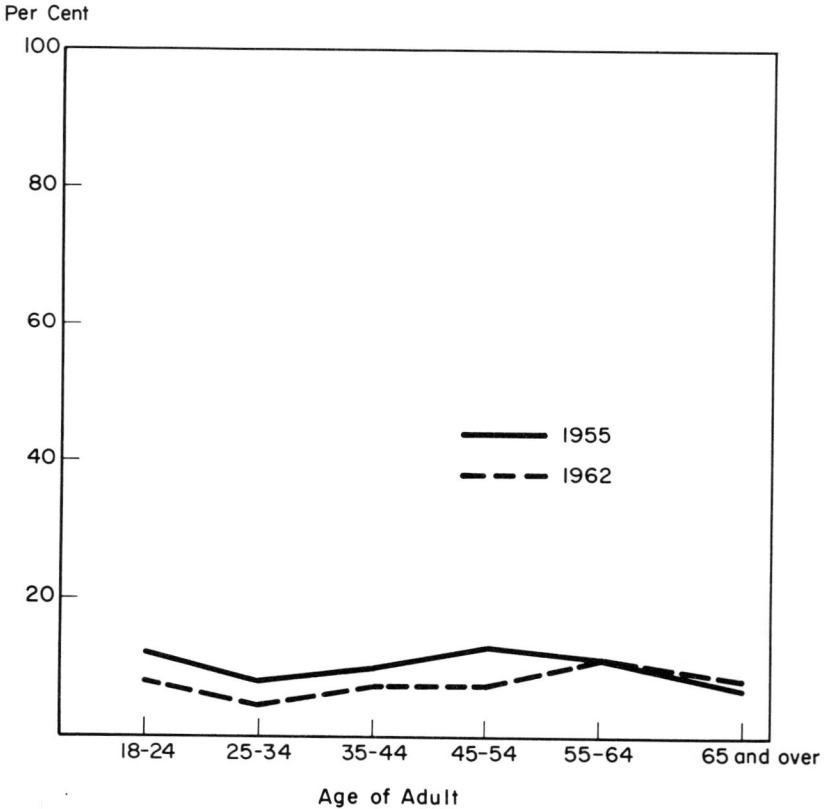

Age of Adult

almost sustained their proportionate use of rail travel from 1955 to 1962 are young single persons and single persons over 45. The biggest drop off in rail travel in those years was among the young married people without children. In this group the per cent who took a rail trip fell from 8 per cent in 1955 to 3 per cent in 1962. The other two groups of married persons curtailed their use of trains to a lesser degree, only 3 per cent.

Examination of the difference in use of rail by men or women contributes little to the picture. As shown in the appendix, the proportion who took a rail trip declined about equally for each between the two years.

In view of the finding in previous chapters that Negroes are not as likely as whites to travel by auto or by air, it is perhaps surprising to find Negroes are about as likely as whites to take rail trips, as shown below:

Race	Per Cent Who Took a Rail Trip	
	1955	1962
Negro	13	6
White	10	7

In 1955, the proportion of Negroes who took a rail trip was 13 per cent, higher than the 10 per cent proportion of whites. If attention is restricted to the income group below $4000, which includes most of the Negroes, in 1955 12 per cent of Negroes took a rail trip, compared to 6 per cent of whites. The decline in use of trains is more marked among Negroes than whites. By 1962, only 6 per cent of all Negroes took a rail trip compared to 7 per cent of all whites.

D. Regional Differences in the Use of Rail

While travel by rail is everywhere declining, the proportion taking at least one rail trip a year has remained higher in New York and the rest of "megalopolis" than in the remainder of the country. In this respect there is little or no difference between the New York metropolitan area and the rest of the corridor, as the following tabulation indicates:

Year	New York	Megalopolis Excluding New York	Remainder of the Country
1955	13	14	10
1957	15	13	10
1962	11	10	7

Even in 1962, 11 per cent of the adults living in the New York metropolitan area took a rail trip, in contrast to 7 per cent of the population in the country at large. This result is consistent with the evidence that auto travel is inhibited for people living in the center of New York. (See Table 60 in appendix for more detail.)

Within the New York area there are differences in rail travel which are broadly similar to those in air travel:

Sub-Divisions of the New York Area	Per Cent Who Took a Rail Trip
Manhattan	18
Bronx	9
Queens	5
Brooklyn	2
Suburbs in New York	15
Suburbs in New Jersey	16
Newark, Jersey City	5
All adults in the area	11

People in Manhattan or the suburbs are more likely to travel by rail than those living in the Bronx, Queens, and Brooklyn.

It remains to examine the proportion who took a rail trip in each of the four principal regions in the country. The data are summarized in Graph 34 and in the following tabulation:

Region	Per Cent Who Took a Rail Trip	
	1955	1962
Northeast	12	8
North Central	11	7
South	8	7
West	9	8
All regions	10	7

GRAPH 34

PER CENT OF ADULTS LIVING IN DIFFERENT
REGIONS WHO TRAVELED BY RAIL DURING
THE SURVEY YEAR

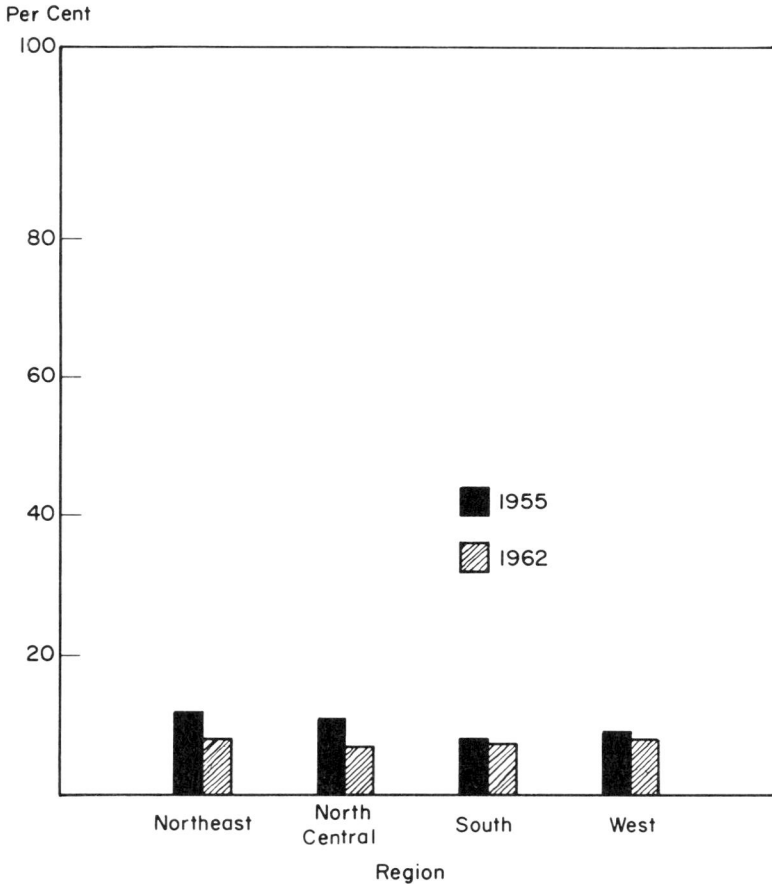

Per Cent

100

80

60

40   ■ 1955

          ▨ 1962

20

   Northeast   North   South   West
               Central

Region

For 1962, in spite of the relatively high use of rail in the New York
area, the Northeast as a whole appears little different from the rest of
the country. Over the previous seven years, the more rapid rate of decline in rail travel in the Northeast and North Central regions had
brought them to approximately the same level as the South and the

West, in which the rate was somewhat slower. These tables, it should be kept in mind, refer exclusively to round trips to places 100 miles or more away. It is quite likely that the proportion of short haul rail travel is greater in the Northeast than in the West, for example, in view of the greater density of population in the Northeast.

The future of passenger rail service will be influenced also by the trend in the relative price of travel by rail and travel by other modes, especially travel by automobile. The statistical analysis is more satisfactory with regard to air than rail, since many railroads have introduced family plans for coach travel, but the airlines had not done so in 1962. The type of reasoning developed in the previous chapter concerning the importance of the price paid by parties of two or more people, however, applies to travel by rail, as well as to travel by air.

It is possible, in sum, to say that the decline in rail travel took place in clearly defined segments of the population. Among those below $4000 annual income there was no decline, but above $4000 there was a decline. Older single people and younger single people both continue to take train trips about as in 1955, but the married couples both with and without children are much less likely to take a rail trip than they were. Business travel by rail declined faster than non-business. Geographically, the losses were small in New York.

The decline in railroad passenger service reflected increasing competitive pressure from the airlines, especially in the market for business travel. It also reflected the slow decline in the proportion of the population who own no automobile, described in Chapter III. As one might expect, and as the statistical analysis in Appendix I confirms, people who own cars are less likely to travel by train than those who have no car. The availability of service is necessarily a factor in people's choice of mode of transportation. Losses in some parts of the market must lead to reduced total offerings of rail service. The data suggest that there is a residual market for rail travel if it is possible to maintain sufficient service to satisfy that market in the face of the loss of business from other groups in the population.

During the period 1955 to 1962, a series of new developments influenced the market for bus travel. On the supply side of the market, the most dramatic development was the construction of new freeways, including the start of the system of Interstate and Defense Highways under Federal auspices. On the demand side of the market, the continuing reduction in rail service reduced the competition which the bus industry had to face from the railroads. The automobile, however, became an increasingly formidable competitor with the increase in the proportion of all families owning an automobile. The automobile, as well as the bus, benefited from the new highways. Finally, the bus, like the other common carriers, was faced with the problem of adapting to the geographical redistribution of the country's population, especially the dramatic growth around the fringes of the metropolitan areas and the decline in number of persons living at the center of the large cities.

All of these changes may be expected to continue into the future. The Interstate and Defense Highway system will not have its full impact until it has been completed. Rail passenger service is likely to continue to decline. Automobile ownership continues to rise. Cities continue to disperse into the country side.

The basic problem in understanding the market for bus travel, then, is to trace the effects of these changes on the demand for bus service. In what portions of the travel market is the demand for bus service growing stronger, and where is it growing weaker? What may be expected to be the position of the bus in the travel market in five or ten years time?

The outline of this chapter is similar to that of Chapter V, Rail. The topics to be considered include attitudes toward bus travel, experience with bus travel, frequency of travel by bus in 1955 and 1962, and regional differences in the use of bus.

A. Attitudes Toward Bus Travel

Two questions have been used to explore attitudes toward bus travel, one an indirect and one a more direct inquiry. People's general emotional responses to bus travel were obtained in the 1962 survey by the use of a sentence completion item. People were asked to complete a sentence beginning: "Bus trips are . . . ". The answers which they gave are summarized here:

Bus Trips Are	Per Cent of Adults
Positive	37
Nice, pleasant	11
All right, o.k.	10
Cheap, practical	4
Other positive comments	12
Negative	53
Dull, tiresome	16
Strong general negative comment (horrible, terrible)	13
Tiring, fatiguing	5
Other negative comments	19
Other (don't know, no answer)	10
Total	100

The most striking thing about these reactions is that they are preponderantly negative. One upper income man, the treasurer of a privately held corporation, put it succinctly: "Bus trips are...not for me!" Sixteen per cent describe bus rides as dull and tiresome, and another 13 per cent give strong general negative comments. But the typical replies are either mildly positive, neutral, or mildly negative. About one person in five gives a positive response to the idea of bus travel.

People's responses to the idea of bus travel vary with their income. Negative responses to bus travel are much more common among the high income groups than among the low income groups:

Family Income	Per Cent Who React Negatively
Under $2000	31
$2000-2999	41
$3000-3999	40
$4000-4999	50
$5000-5999	52
$6000-7499	60
$7500-9999	66
$10,000-14,999	68
$15,000 and over	70
All incomes	53

Of adults from families with income below $2000, 31 per cent reacted negatively, compared to 70 per cent of those over $15,000.

People's views about the use of bus in the context of a particular trip were obtained in the 1956 and 1957 surveys. The question asked was: "How did you happen to choose this way of traveling instead of some other?". The question brought mention of bus travel both by those who did travel by bus and by some who explained how it happened that they did not travel by bus. The responses in 1957 are summarized in the following tabulation:

Comments	Per Cent of Comments
Advantages	
Flexible schedule, better	
connections, accessibility	28
Cheaper	22
See the scenery	7
Faster	6
Safer	1
Disadvantages	
Slow	8
Fatigue, lack of comfort	7
Bad connections, poor sche-	
dule, inaccessible	4
Other advantages and dis-	
advantages	17
Total	100

The positive responses may be divided into three groups using the classification of reasons for choice of mode developed in Chapter II. The most frequent positive comments (three in ten) commend easy availability of bus service, convenient location of terminals, and other aspects of accessibility. The second kind of appeal is price; people frequently state that going by bus is cheaper. Finally, there are those who state they went by bus because of the special qualities of that mode of transportation. Within this group the most frequent advantage mentioned for bus is that it makes it possible to see the scenery.

It seems reasonable to speculate that the importance of a desire to see the scenery as a motive for travel by bus will increase as time passes. Travel by jet plane is hardly the best way to obtain a detailed view of the countryside. When rail service is not available on a particular route, someone who wishes to go by common carrier and see what the countryside is like has no alternative to travel by bus. The wife of a medical attendant in Detroit, family income $3000-3999, put it simply "Bus trips are...convenient for sightseeing."

The high frequency of the comment that bus travel was chosen because it was cheap is consistent, of course, with the more favorable attitudes toward bus travel among the lower income groups compared to upper income groups. Emphasis on the low cost of bus travel is also consistent with the data reported earlier concerning people's views about the "best way to travel." It will be recalled that only 5 per cent said in the 1962 survey that the best way to travel is by bus.

B. Experience With Bus Travel

About half the population report that they have taken a bus trip to a place 100 miles or more away at some time in their lives. Between 1955 and 1962 the proportion who were experienced increased from 46 to 52 per cent. The relation between experience with bus travel and income in 1962 is shown in Graph 35 and the following tabulation:

GRAPH 35

PER CENT OF ADULTS AT DIFFERENT INCOME LEVELS WHO EVER HAVE TAKEN A BUS TRIP

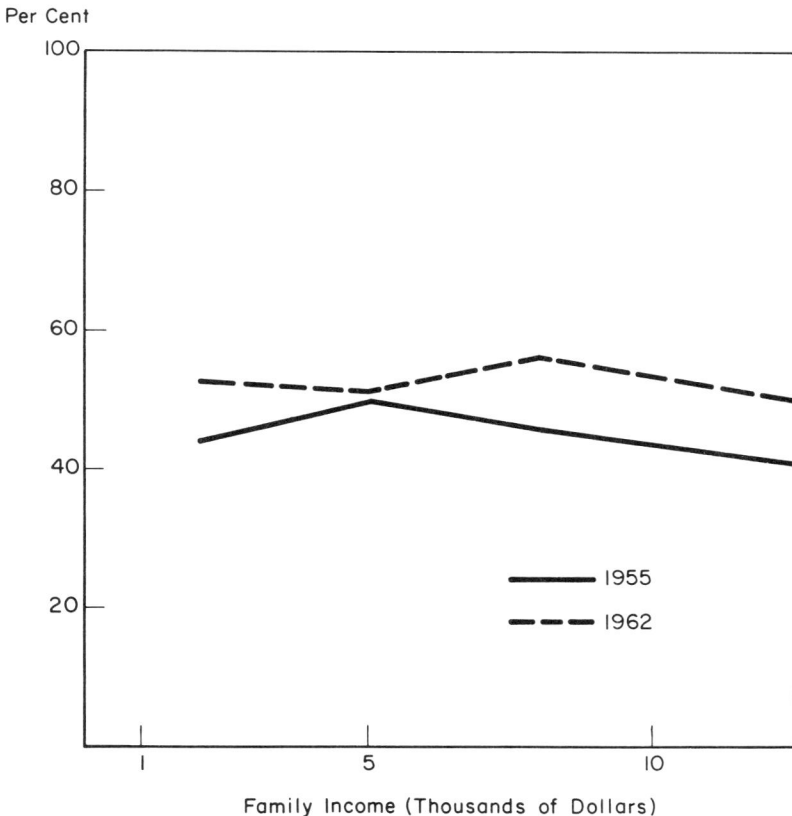

Per Cent

——— 1955

– – – 1962

Family Income (Thousands of Dollars)

Family Income	Per Cent Who Ever Have Taken a Trip by Bus
Under $4000	53
$4000-5999	51
$6000-9999	56
$10,000 and over	50
All incomes	52

There is very little difference among income groups in the proportion who have ever taken a bus trip to a place 100 miles or more away. In 1962, of those under $4000 about 53 per cent had taken a trip, while of those with incomes of $10,000 and over, 50 per cent had taken a trip. A much larger proportion of the population have taken a bus trip than an air trip (about one-third), but since two-thirds of the population have taken a rail trip, fewer people have traveled by bus than by rail.

There are differences among age groups in the proportion who ever have taken a bus trip. The peak is in the age group 25-34, of whom 60 per cent have taken a bus trip, as shown in Graph 36 and the following tabulation:

Age of Adult	Per Cent Who Ever Have Taken a Trip by Bus
18-24	46
25-34	60
35-44	56
45-54	51
55-64	48
65 and over	49
All ages	52

That peak bus travel should be among the young, 25-34 age group is interesting since it is more like the results for air travel than for rail. It may be recalled that the proportion of adults in this same age group, 25-34, who ever have taken a rail trip is lower than among the older age groups; whereas for air travel the young, 25-34 age group is highest in percentage who ever have taken an air trip. With respect to the age group at which experience reaches a peak, then, bus travel is more like what one might expect for a mode of travel whose use is increasing, than for a mode of travel whose use is on the decline. The proportion of those aged over 45 who have ever taken a bus trip appears to be slightly lower than that among those aged 35-44.

Experience with bus travel should be interpreted in a manner analagous to experience with rail travel. It is a measure of the cumulative use of bus travel by people in different segments of the population. On the whole, the evidence indicates only small differences in experience from one part of the population to another.

GRAPH 36

PER CENT OF ADULTS IN DIFFERENT AGE GROUPS WHO EVER HAVE TAKEN A BUS TRIP, 1962

Per Cent

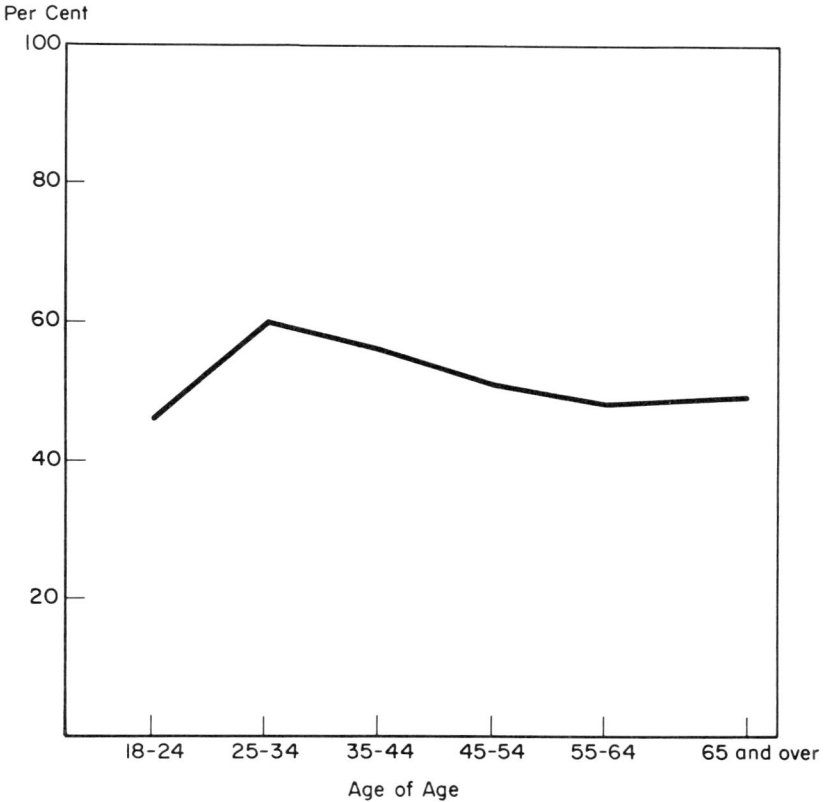

C.   Frequency of Travel by Bus, 1955 and 1962

From 1955 to 1962, the per cent of adults who took one or more bus trips in the year to a place 100 miles or more away increased from 7 to 9 per cent. As previously remarked, while this increase is contrary to what might be expected from looking at aggregate statistics on bus travel, no direct comparison is possible with statistics from other sources since none exist using the division of the market at 100 miles. In both 1955 and 1962 only about 1 per cent of all adults reported that they took a bus trip on business.

The number of bus trips per traveler taken in the prior year by those who did use the bus in 1955 and 1962 was as follows:

Number of Bus Trips Taken	Per Cent of Those Who Took Business Trips by Bus		Per Cent of Those Who Took Non-Business Trips by Bus	
	1955	1962	1955	1962
1	56	68	71	68
2-4	28	23	21	25
5-19	16	7	7	7
20 and over	*	2	1	*
Total	100	100	100	100

Of those who did travel by bus on business, the majority took a single trip only.

The results illustrate the difficulty of making estimates of counts of trips based on a sample survey. One single individual in 1962 reported more than 40 trips by bus; that individual accounted for 42 per cent of all the business trips by bus reported in that year. No other individual reported as many as 10 business trips by bus. The finding that most business travelers by bus took only a single trip, however, rests on the whole group of such travelers and is, therefore, reasonably reliable.

Most non-business bus travelers also report only a single trip, 7 out of 10 in both 1955 and 1962. Findings for non-business air and rail trips are very similar. In fact, for rail the proportion is virtually identical with that for bus travel, about 70 per cent. With respect to air travel, similarly, the proportion of non-business travelers who took only one non-business trip ranges from 72 per cent in 1955 to 69 per cent in 1962. Only for non-business automobile travel is the pattern different. The great majority of the adults who took any non-business auto trip took more than one such trip.

In 1955 there was remarkably little difference in the per cent of the adults who took one or more bus trips at different income levels. In 1962 this situation had changed. The pattern is shown in Graph 37 and below:

GRAPH 37

PER CENT OF ADULTS AT DIFFERENT INCOME
LEVELS WHO TRAVELED BY BUS DURING THE
SURVEY YEAR

Per Cent

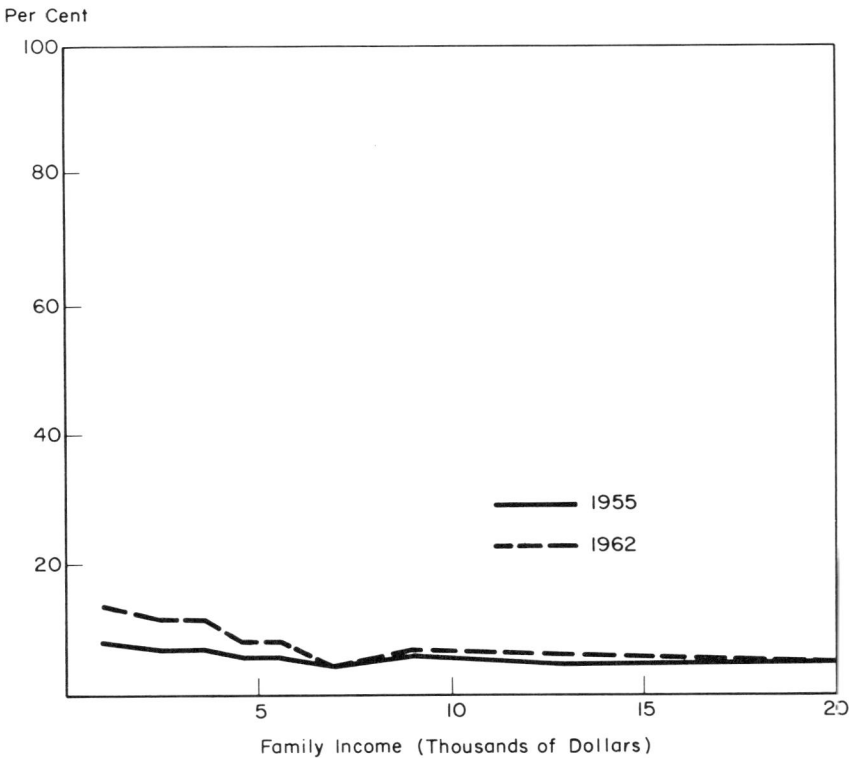

Family Income (Thousands of Dollars)

Family Income	Per Cent Who Took a Trip by Bus	
	1955	1962
Under $2000	8	14
$2000-2999	7	12
$3000-3999	7	12
$4000-4999	6	8
$5000-5999	6	5
$6000-7499	5	7
$7500-9999	6	6
$10,000-14,999	5	8
$15,000 or over	5	5
All adults	7	9

Between 1955 and 1962 there was an increase in the proportion of adults in the income groups below $4000 a year who took bus trips. Over the $4000 income level there was little change; the proportion remained on the order of 5 to 8 per cent for both years. Of those with income below $4000, however, in 1962 from 12 to 14 per cent took a bus trip, an increase of roughly 5 per cent.

It appears that the bus from 1955 to 1962 improved its position among users at the bottom of the income distribution without sacrificing its position in the higher income groups. However, it remains true that at any income level only a relatively small proportion of the population take a long distance trip by bus in any year.

There was a decrease between these two years in the proportion of adults who were in the lowest income groups, owing to the general upward shift in money incomes. The per cent of the population with family incomes below $4000 fell as the following tabulation indicates:

Family Income	Per Cent Who Took a Trip by Bus			
	1955		1962	
	Adults	Trips	Adults	Trips
Under $4000	44	48	28	47
$4000-5999	29	28	24	24
$6000-9999	19	18	31	21
$10,000 and over	8	6	17	8
Total	100	100	100	100

In 1955 the 44 per cent of all adults from families with incomes below $4000 accounted for 48 per cent of all bus trips. In 1962, 28 per cent of all adults from families with incomes below $4000 accounted for 47 per cent of all bus trips reported: in other words, a smaller group was taking about the same number of bus trips.

Broadly speaking, the differences among occupation groups in the use of the bus are about what one might expect on the basis of the differences in income. See Graph 38 and the tabulation here:

GRAPH 38

PER CENT OF ADULTS WITH DIFFERENT OCCU-
PATIONS WHO TRAVELED BY BUS DURING THE
SURVEY YEAR

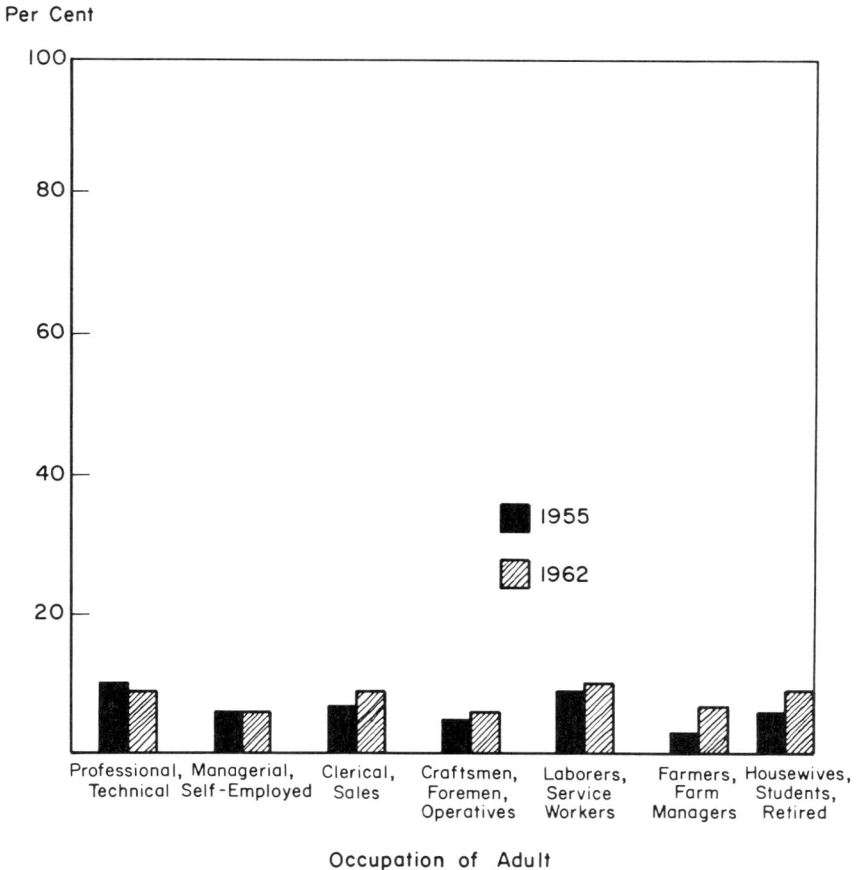

Occupation of Adult

Occupation of Adult	Per Cent Who Took Trip by Bus
Laborer, service worker	10
Professional, technical	9
Clerical, sales	9
Housewife, retired, student	9
Farmer, farm manager	7
Managerial, self-employed	6
Craftsman, foreman, operative	6
All occupations	9

In 1962 the most intensive use of bus for long trips was by laborers and service workers of whom 10 per cent took bus trips, thus giving them a very slight margin over others. It may be remarked that the professional and technical workers by 3 percentage points are more likely to travel by bus than the managerial and self-employed, even though the incomes of these two occupation groups are roughly the same. Bus travel by housewives and retired persons increased from 6 per cent in 1955 to 9 per cent in 1962 (See Graph 38). Because of the large number of people in the population who are either housewives or retired persons and the correspondingly large sample of these people in the survey, this difference is much too large to be attributable to mere sampling fluctuation. What accounts for the shift? The decline in rail service must be one important cause. As has been shown already, housewives and retired persons have a tendency to travel by common carrier rather than by automobile. Where rail schedules are no longer convenient, they are forced to travel either by air or bus, and many of them appear to be taking the bus.

The relation between age and the proportion of adults who travel by bus is shown in Graph 39 and the tabulation below:

Age	Per Cent Who Took a Trip by Bus	
	1955	1962
18-24	11	13
25-34	6	7
35-44	5	5
45-54	6	7
55-64	8	11
65 and over	8	10
All ages	7	9

In 1955 the high proportions of bus users were among the young, 18-24 group (11 per cent) and the older groups, 55 and over (8 per cent). The same relationship was true in 1962. It may be easily grasped from the shallow U-shaped curve of Graph 39.

GRAPH 39

PER CENT OF ADULTS IN DIFFERENT AGE
GROUPS WHO TRAVELED BY BUS DURING
THE SURVEY YEAR

Per Cent

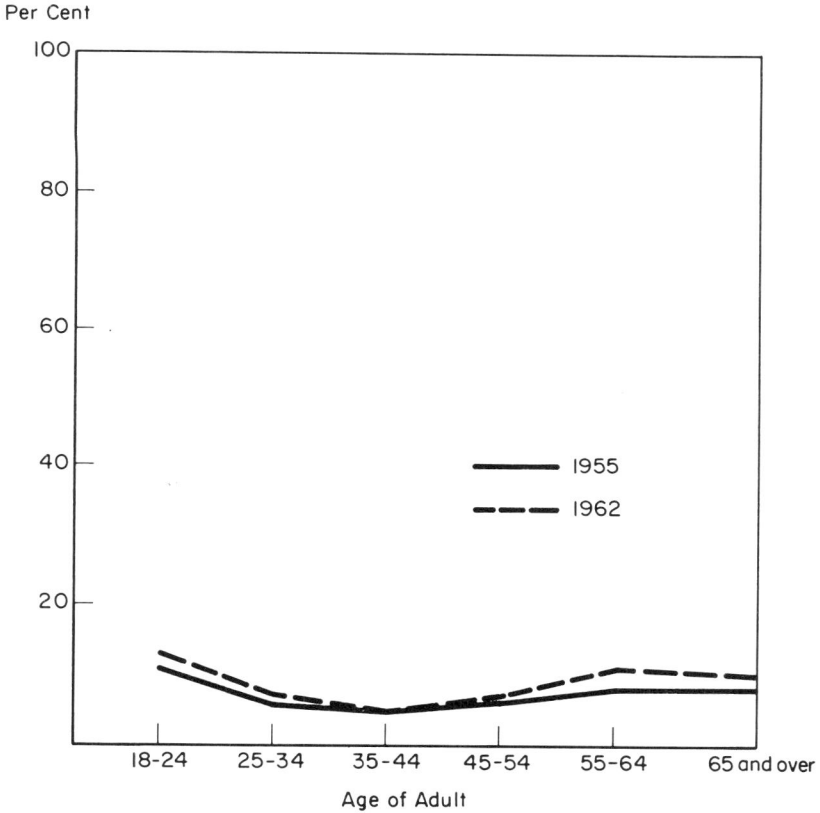

Age of Adult

   The meaning of these data become clearer when one looks at the
following relation between use of bus and the stage in the family life
cycle:

Stage in the Family Life Cycle	Per Cent Who Took a Bus Trip	
	1955	1962
Young, single	12	12
Under 45, married, no children	9	7
Married with children	5	7
Over 45, married, no children under 18	6	7
Older, single	10	15
All stages	7	9

Here in both years there would be a U-shaped curve were the data graphed. High utilizers of bus travel are single persons, both the young and the older singles. But as for change during the period, the single young have changed not at all (12 per cent both years). The only group with a substantial increase are the single older people (10 per cent to 15 per cent).

It will be recalled that Negroes are much less likely than whites to travel by either auto or air, and about equally likely to travel by rail. By bus, they have swung toward increasing likelihood of travel, as the following statistics indicate:

Race	Per Cent Who Took a Bus Trip	
	1955	1962
Negro	7	15
White	7	8

By 1962 a larger proportion of Negroes than of whites took a bus trip, 15 per cent compared to 8 per cent. Since Negroes are a minority of the population (about 10 per cent), it remains true, of course, that Negroes are a minority of bus travelers, even though the chances that a Negro will take one or more bus trips in a year are larger than the chances that a white person will do so.

In 1955 there was little difference between the proportion of men and the proportion of women who took a bus trip:

Sex of Adult	Per Cent Who Took a Bus Trip	
	1955	1962
Female	7	10
Male	6	6
All adults	7	9

By 1962 women were using the bus more, 10 per cent to only 6 per cent of men. This result, of course, is consistent with what has just been shown about the change in the market for bus travel when classified by income, occupation, age, and stage in the family life cycle. The market for bus travel is showing strength among the single people who travel alone, especially in the lower income groups, and among housewives as well as retired persons.

.

D. Regional Differences in the Use of Bus

Previous discussion has shown competitive weakness of the automobile in the New York area and corresponding strength for air. Rail, also, is competitively less weak in New York than elsewhere. Is New York also a stronghold of bus, the third common carrier?

On the contrary, bus travel has remained consistently somewhat less common in New York. In spite of the relatively frequent use of the other two common carriers in New York, the proportion of New Yorkers who take long trips by bus is on the low side. The nature of the highways in the New York area and the congestion found there may discourage bus travel as well as travel by automobile. But trip data are as follows:

		Per Cent Who Took a Bus Trip	
Year	New York	Megalopolis Excluding New York	Remainder of The Country
1955	5	6	7
1957	8	6	10
1959	7	7	9

With respect to per cent of adults who were bus travelers in the three years, New York is like the rest of "megalopolis" in being lower than the rest of the country.

Within the New York metropolitan area there are differences in the use of bus for travel, as shown below:

Sub-Division of the New York Area	Per Cent Who Took a Bus Trip, 1962
Manhattan	12
Bronx	6
Queens	5
Brooklyn	5
Newark, Jersey City	5
Suburbs in New York	5
Suburbs in New Jersey	11
All adults in the area	7

A comparatively large proportion of the population of Manhattan, 12 per cent, took a bus trip in the survey period. This finding is parallel to that for the other common carriers. All other parts of the area show a low percentage of bus travelers, 5 to 6 per cent, except the New Jersey suburbs.

These results are consistent with those showing the per cent cf bus travelers among adults in each of the four regions, as shown in Graph 40 and the following tabulation:

GRAPH   40

PER CENT OF ADULTS LIVING IN DIFFERENT REGIONS WHO TRAVELED BY BUS DURING THE SURVEY YEAR

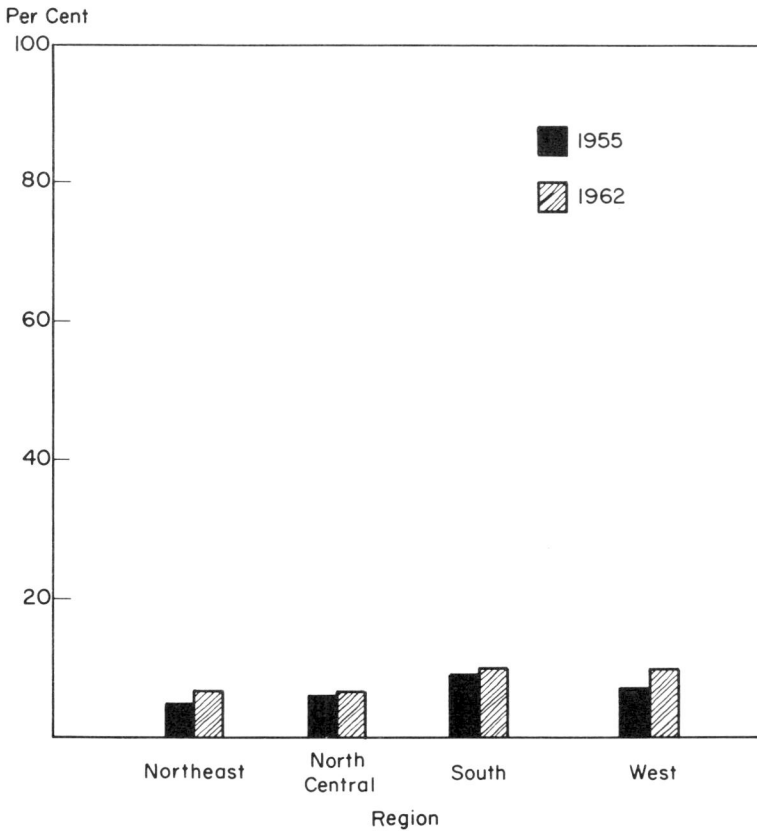

Region	Per Cent Who Took a Bus Trip	
	1955	1962
Northeast	5	7
North Central	6	7
South	9	10
West	7	10
All regions	7	9

For both years, the Northeast and North Central regions are out-rated by the South and the West in use of the bus for travel. The slight increase in bus travel during this period is evident in each region, especially the West.

But why should use of the bus be relatively stronger in the South and the West? The explanation for the two regions may not be the same. The bus may be well adapted to low density routes in the West, where relatively small numbers of people desire to be transported. In the South the advantage of the bus may be in price. Low fares may be especially attractive there because of the large proportion of the population in the low income groups.

Understanding of the travel market begins with the division between trips on business and trips for non-business purposes. In the market as a whole non-business travel is much the more important, but business travelers do account for a large part of all air travel, and there is also a substantial volume of business travel by auto, especially for shorter distances. While the underlying purposes of business travel never have been analyzed in detail, most business travelers either meet with several people in a group or have a series of appointments which altogether last six hours or more.

From the point of view of the people involved there are powerful motives for taking non-business trips and also important barriers to travel. The way in which people resolve the resulting conflicts, given the supply of transportation available to them, decides the number of trips which they take and the modes of travel which they select. The motives for non-business travel are diverse. Some trips are taken by people in connection with their personal affairs - going to school, moving to a new home, seeking medical attention. The motives for travel are in part social - people want to see relatives and friends who live at a distance. In part the motivation arises from social pressure in another sense - it is the expected thing to do, it is a type of activity associated with upper socio-economic status. People also derive satisfaction of a more personal sort from getting away from the home environment and from good times seeing the sights or doing other things they enjoy on trips.

The list of major barriers to travel must begin with lack of money. A great many people would travel more if expense were not a consideration. Old age and poor health are major obstacles for some. It may be hard to get away from home or job. Others find that it is difficult and expensive to travel with children. Some people feel less strongly the desire to travel, or are ambivalent about venturing into strange places or trusting to unaccustomed methods of transportation.

The importance of the financial barrier is shown in many ways. The amount of money people spend on vacation travel rises rapidly with income, in fact, the per cent of income spent for this purpose increases as income increases. Income is closely associated with air travel and overseas travel. The effect of price on choice of mode also reflects the importance of lack of money as an obstacle to travel. People who want to travel and cannot easily afford it look for the most economical means to achieve their goal. The results appear in the tendency of families to go together by car and in the tendency of better educated single people to travel by bus.

Old age and poor health force some people to stay home. Old people who do travel tend to avoid the strain of driving and travel by common carrier. The new, high speed freeways are not attractive to widows, for example, who may own no car or never have learned to drive.

People who have trouble finding time to travel also may be forced to stay at home. If they can afford it, they are likely to travel by the fastest mode, air, so that they can take long trips even if their free time is measured in days. Retired people usually have enough time, but they travel less than the active population. For most old people lower incomes and lower physical capacity more than offset the gain in available time.

The presence of young children in a family deters travel just as old age does. The problems are in part financial - it costs more to travel with more people and there are more competing claims on the budget - and in part physical - it is hard on active children to confine them in a vehicle for long periods, and also hard on the adults in the vehicle with them. People with young children tend to stay home or to travel by car, not by common carrier. For them automobile travel is likely to be the cheapest.

Absense of the desire to travel or ambivalence about travel also may lead people to stay at home. If they do travel, they tend to avoid those destinations or methods of transportation which create anxiety or make them feel too strange or uncomfortable.

On the other side of the market are the available means of transportation. The most important development in recent decades has been the increasing availability of automobile transportation. The automobile is so familiar a vehicle that it is easy to forget that the United States has yet to complete a national system of highways designed for use by modern automobiles. The effects of the automobile are revealed indirectly by study of areas where the automobile is not readily available, the principal such area being the congested central portion of New York City. People who live there are less likely to own cars and more likely to take rail trips and air trips than people who live in less congested areas, such as the suburbs of New York.

The automobile offers remarkable advantages in accessibility of service to those who own cars. They can leave from their own doorsteps, at the exact hour of the day or night they prefer, and travel by the route of their choice to their exact destination. For parties of several people and especially for short distances the cost of travel by car compares favorably with the cost of other modes of travel.

People's attitudes toward travel by automobile are reasonably favorable. For most people of high status and for frequent travelers the auto is not the "best way to travel", but for others it is the preferred method.

In competition with automobile travel the advantages of air travel have to do primarily with quality of service - speed, comfort, the amenities of travel - rather than price or accessibility. Many people do think of air as the "best way to travel", but there is evidence of ambivalence in people's feelings, especially concern about safety. However, air travel with the passage of time is becoming less of an innovation. It started as a high status form of travel patronized by relatively few people. Price policy, particularly price policy for families, now is likely to be the key to the extent to which air becomes a mass means of transportation.

The new network of modern highways for the automobile is equally a new network for the bus. The motivations for bus travel seem to be mixed. In part people travel by bus because much of the country is poorly served by the other common carriers. Air never has reached the small towns, and rail passenger service is leaving them or already has disappeared. People who do not wish to travel by car - old people, for example, or people traveling alone may have no choice but bus. In part, however, people travel by bus because it is cheap. This mixed motivation leads to a diverse clientele.

Rail, originally the dominant mode of transportation, has lost business in all directions, to the automobiles, airlines, and buses. Barring any revolutions in railroad technology, the question for the future of rail passenger service is whether there is enough of a residual market so that the downward trend can be stopped at a level of patronage that will cover costs. It is already clear that the residual market must be the inverse of the automobile market. The people involved are likely to be non-business travelers, old people, single people traveling alone, residents of areas where auto service is poor, such as the center of New York, and residents of those areas where rail service is accessible. A major uncertainty, as with air travel, has to do with the question of whether the railroads can develop a price structure which will permit them to compete with the automobile for travel by married couples and families with children.

MULTIVARIATE ANALYSIS
APPENDIX I

Throughout this volume many factors taken separately have been shown to have an effect on travel decisions. These factors really operate simultaneously. Whether a person decides to take a trip depends upon a wide variety of personal characteristics of the traveler at a given moment of time. Each of these characteristics (income, education, and the like) can be shown to have a discernible impact on travel. Yet, if travel were predicted by adding up the results obtained by relating each separate variable to travel the total would likely be overstated, or certainly misstated. What we attempt to do in this Appendix is to show whether each characteristic (or independent variable) that is used to explain travel has any remaining impact on travel (which in this case is the dependent variable) after the effects of all of the other independent variables simultaneously have been taken into account! The methods of statistical analysis employed are multiple discriminant analysis and multiple regression.

As suggested in Chapter I there are two approaches to explaining the total volume of travel. The first approach requires two stages, first, explaining the total volume of travel without regard to specific modes, and, second, evaluating reasons for choice of specific modes. The second approach proceeds directly to the explanation of a given type of travel.

In this Appendix we first present findings of a multivariate analysis of frequency of total travel accompanied by direct estimates of the determinants of non-business travel by mode. There follows a multivariate analysis of factors affecting three significant mode choices:

1. Choice between air and auto for business purposes.
2. Choice between air and auto for non-business purposes.
3. Choice between all common carriers combined and auto for non-business travel.

---

[1] This Appendix is based on research reported in an unpublished doctoral dissertation in economics submitted to the University of Michigan in 1963 by Dwight M. Blood entitled "A Cross-Section Analysis of the Domestic Intercity Travel Market." Considerably more details are found in the dissertation concerning travel by all modes than are presented here. Microfilm and positive copies of the entire dissertation may be obtained from University Microfilms, Inc., 313 North First St., Ann Arbor, Michigan

A. Frequency of Travel

In this section we make use of data from the fall wave of the 1955
National Travel Market Survey and from the entire 1962 National Travel Market Survey. The 1955 data represent travel information on all
modes for 4,210 adults and the 1962 data provide information for 5,329
adults. By applying a comparable statistical analysis to data for these
two years, it is possible to assess the extent of changes over time in
the relative impact of the various explanatory variables. Thus, we can
not only determine which variables are the most important predictors
of travel, but we can also determine whether the variables that were of
greatest importance in 1955 were still the principal predictors of travel in 1962.

Developing a scale for trip frequency: If we are to predict
"travel", how shall travel be specified for purposes of prediction? A
prediction could be made of whether an adult with known characteristics is a likely prospect to take at least *one* trip a year. Alternatively
the *number* of trips that an adult is likely to take might be predicted.

Differences may exist between reasons impelling an individual to
move over the threshold from zero trips to one trip as compared with
taking an additional trip after having already taken many trips. If total
number of trips is to be predicted, a few extreme cases - such as adults
who take more than 100 trips - will distort the final results. Moreover,
the problem of response error must be faced. If adults systematically
overreport, then errors will be compounded by predicting total travel
on the basis of reported count of trips.

In order to circumvent these problems, a scale for the dependent
variable (travel) was sought in this analysis which would give more
weight to frequent travelers than would be the case in simply predicting
whether people travel and yet avoid the errors that would result from
predicting exact trip numbers as reported.

The method used was to divide all adults into groups based on the
number of trips they took and weight those in the high-frequency categories more than those who took only one or two trips. The following
scale of values was used as dependent variable in the regression equations on total travel:

Trip Frequency	Scale of Frequency of Travel - Total Travel
0 trips	0.0
1 trip	1.0
2-4 trips	1.6

(Cont'd)

Trip Frequency	Scale of Frequency of Travel - Total Travel
5-15 trips	2.4
16 or more trips	3.2
Number of trips not ascertained	1.6

Thus, those who took 1 trip received a score of 1, while those who took 16 or more trips received a score of 3.2.

The procedure used in developing the scale is known as multiple discriminant analysis. Essentially, this scale is estimated from the explanatory variables that are set forth in the following section of the Appendix. The scale has the property that, when it is used as the dependent variable in regression analysis, the amount of variation in total travel which can be explained by the regression analysis is maximized. Those readers interested in further details concerning the computation of the scale should consult the study from which these findings are taken, as cited in the footnote on the first page of Appendix I, and a textbook on statistics that deals with multiple discriminant analysis.

The same type of calculation was made for non-business travel by each of the four modes. The scales developed are as follows:

	Scale of Frequency of Travel		
Trip Frequency	Non-Business Air	Non-Business Rail	Non-Business Bus
0 trips	0.0	0.0	0.0
1 trip	1.0	1.0	1.0
2 or more trips	1.4	1.3	1.2
Number not ascertained	0.0	0.2	0.8

The similarity of the scales for 2 or more trips emerged from the calculations; it was in no way imposed by the assumptions made. For auto travel the data permitted the following more detailed scale:

Trip Frequency	Scale of Frequency of Travel Non-Business Auto
0 trips	0.0
1 trip	1.0
2-4 trips	1.4
5-15 trips	1.7
16 or more trips	2.0
Number not ascertained	1.0

All of the computations in this study were made on an International Business Machines 7090 computer at the University of Michigan

Computing Center. The regression equations were estimated by a program entitled "Multivariate Statistical Program" written by R. A. Hoodes of the Littauer Statistical Laboratory, Harvard University, and adapted to the University of Michigan computer system by W. H. Locke Anderson of the Michigan Research Seminar in Quantitative Economics. The program used for estimating the multiple discriminant function scale for the dependent variable was written by the staff of the Research Seminar in Quantitative Economics.

Definition of variables: The independent variables which are used in the regression analysis are defined in Table A-1. As is apparent from Table A-1, the variables selected for the regression equations are scaled in the form of categorical classifications according to whether an adult possesses a particular attribute. The adult is assigned the value of one if he or she possesses the particular attribute or characteristic and zero otherwise. The use and interpretation of categorical variables, called "dummy variables", have been discussed elsewhere by Suits.[1] The only comment that needs to be made here is that where the population is divided up into several groups on the basis of a given characteristic (age, education, etc.), it is necessary to leave one variable out of the computations in order to achieve a determinate solution. For example, if we have three income groups, 0-$5000, $5000-10,000, and $10,000 or over, we include variables for only two out of the three income groups. Whether any individual is a member of the third group could be determined from knowledge of whether he is a member of the two groups.

Stratification of data by stage in the family life cycle: The way in which income level affects certain travel decisions is known to depend on the particular stage in the family life cycle in which an adult belongs. Hence, regressions based on the entire population would tend to obscure the real effects of income upon travel decisions. Accordingly, rather than estimate one combined regression for the whole population, five separate regressions were estimated, one for each of the following five stages in the family life cycle:

1. Single adults under the age of 45. (Single adults include all those not married at the date of interview.)
2. Married adults under the age of 45 without children.
3. All married adults with children under 18.

---

[1] Daniel B. Suits, "Use of Dummy Variables in Regression Equations," *Journal of the American Statistical Association*, Vol. 52 (December 1958), and "Interpreting Regressions Containing Dummy Variables," Technical Paper, Research Seminar in Quantitative Economics, the University of Michigan, May 1962 (mimeographed).

    4. Married adults over the age of 45 without children under 18.

    5. Single adults over the age of 45.

The merit of the detailed breakdown into the above groups was shown in preliminary work which demonstrated different results for different stages in the life cycle.

Results of the regression analysis: The results of the multivariate regression analysis, stratified by stage in the family life cycle, are shown in Tables A-2 through A-6. The data are there presented in the standard format for showing the results of regression analysis. While some readers may prefer to study the data in this form, we prefer to convert some of these regression coefficients into a different format, which has been done in Table A-7 and the accompanying graphs. Before turning to these results we may note that a principal merit of the format of Tables A-2 to A-6 is that it includes a measure of the reliability of each regression coefficient.

How reliable are the coefficients in Tables A-2 to A-6? The National Travel Market Surveys, as discussed in detail in Appendix II, are not simple random surveys. Thus the usual formulas for estimating reliability are no longer valid. One method of allowing for the peculiarities of the sample from which these data are drawn in assessing reliability of statistical estimates is to accept as reliable at the .05 level only those coefficients that are three times their own standard errors instead of twice their standard error. This method is based on some estimations made by Leslie Kish.[2] In Tables A-2 - A-6, those coefficients three times their own standard error are indicated by a double asterisk, and those coefficients twice their own standard error are specified by a single asterisk.

The format in which the results of the multivariate analysis are shown in Table A-7 for total travel is known as multiple classification analysis.[3] In multiple classification analysis the mean of the dependent variable is taken as a first approximation of the magnitude that is being estimated; here, level of travel. The mean of the dependent variable is then adjusted according to whether the adult possesses a particular

---

[2] Leslie Kish, "Confidence Intervals for Clustered Samples," *American Sociological Review,* Vol. XXII (April, 1957).

[3] See T. P. Hill, "An Analysis of the Distribution of Wages and Salaries in Great Britain," *Econometrica,* Vol. 27 (July, 1959), pp. 335-381; James N. Morgan, et. al., *Income and Welfare in the United States* (New York: McGraw Hill, 1962), p. 33; pp. 508-511.)

attribute or belongs to a particular group. For instance, a person who does not own an automobile can be expected to take fewer trips than one who does own an automobile; therefore, classification into the group of non-owners would produce a negative deviation from the mean of the dependent variable in estimating travel. The value in multiple classification analysis is especially evident where one variable (for example, income) is divided into several classes. In such cases the effect of being assigned to particular income classes upon level of travel is represented directly by positive and negative deviations from the mean of the dependent variable.

There is one further advantage to using multiple classification analysis that will be of interest to those who have used regression analysis. The constant term in an ordinary regression equation usually indicates the level of the dependent variable that can be expected at a zero level of the explanatory variables. The constant term in regressions which make use of dummy variables can no longer be interpreted in such a straightforward way; rather, the constant terms from such equations reflect the trends in the effects of all groups for which the regression coefficients have been constrained to zero (such as the income group under $3000 in the regressions shown in Table A-2) as well as trends in the mean. Accordingly, it is more relevant to consider changes in the mean of the dependent variable and the effect on the value of the mean that results from being classified into various population subclasses by the use of multiple classification analysis than it is to consider changes in the constant term in the regression analysis.

The most important relationships are shown in Graphs A-1 through A-4. The discussion in the text will be restricted to the variables shown in these graphs.

Income: The relation between income and frequency of total travel is shown in the first section of Graph A-1. For each stage in the family life cycle, the mean level of travel shown in Table A-7 was adjusted by the deviations which result from assignment into each category and the results plotted. For example, the mean level of travel in 1962 for single adults under the age of 45 is 1.23. A negative deviation of -.10 is subtracted from this value which yields an estimated travel level of 1.13 for adults in this life cycle stage with incomes of less than $3000 for income level A. All of the other points in the first part of Graph A-1 were obtained from Table A-3 in the same way.

Two major conclusions with respect to the relationship between travel and income emerge from this part of the graph: first, travel, generally speaking, increases with rising income levels. Second, the

GRAPH A-I

EFFECT OF INCOME ON FREQUENCY
OF TRAVEL FOR ADULTS IN DIFFERENT
LIFE CYCLE GROUPS, 1962

Scale of Frequency of Travel

Income Groups
A. Under $ 3,000   C. $ 6,000-9,999
B. $ 3,000-5,999   D. $ 10,000 and over

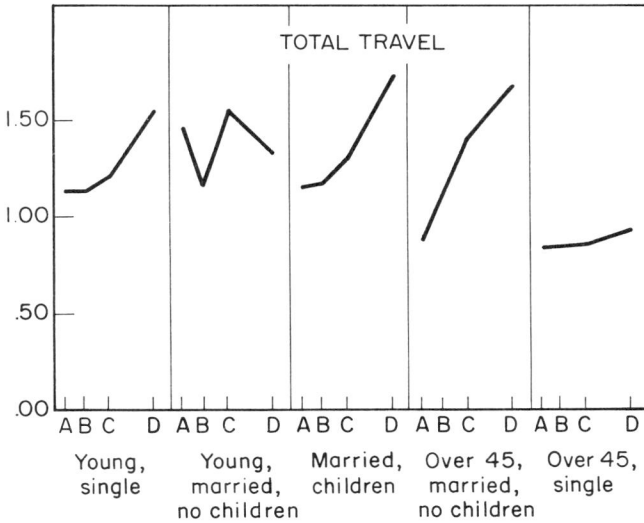

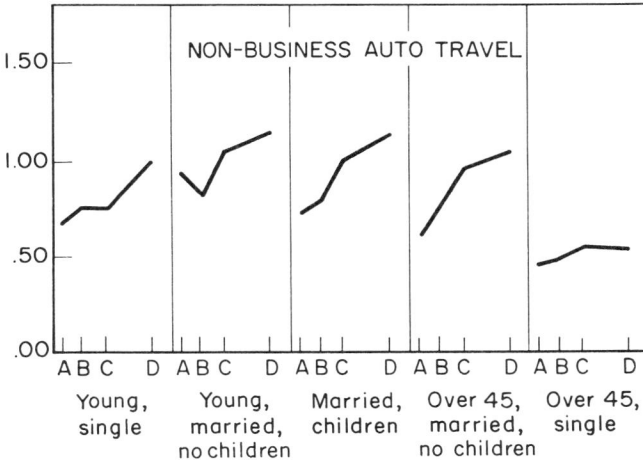

GRAPH A-I (CONT.)

Scale of
Frequency
of Travel

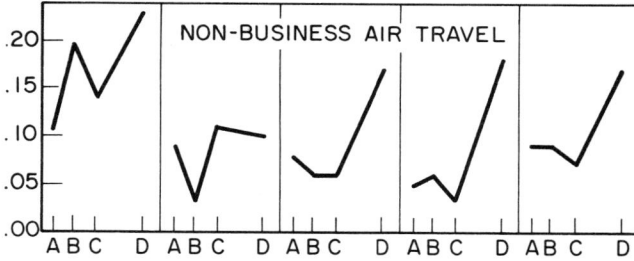

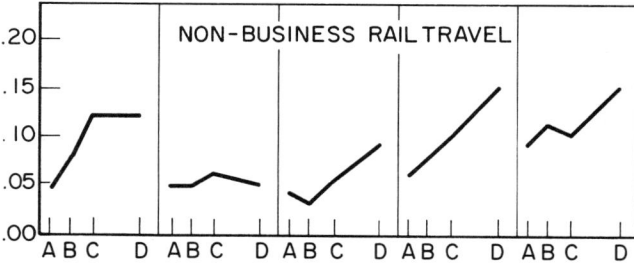

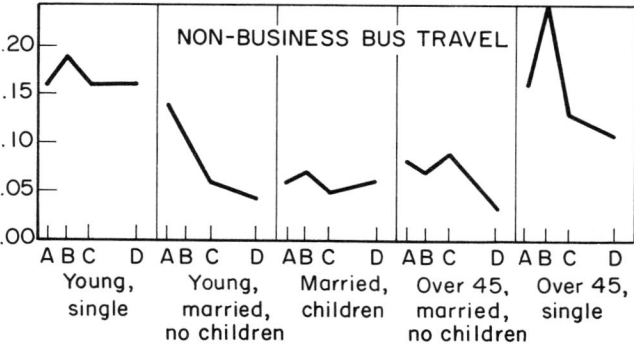

NON-BUSINESS AIR TRAVEL

NON-BUSINESS RAIL TRAVEL

NON-BUSINESS BUS TRAVEL

Young, single   Young, married, no children   Married, children   Over 45, married, no children   Over 45, single

GRAPH A-2

EFFECT OF EDUCATION ON FREQUENCY
OF TRAVEL FOR ADULTS IN DIFFERENT
LIFE CYCLE GROUPS, 1962

Scale of
Frequency
of Travel

■ Less than a high school graduate
▨ High school graduate or more

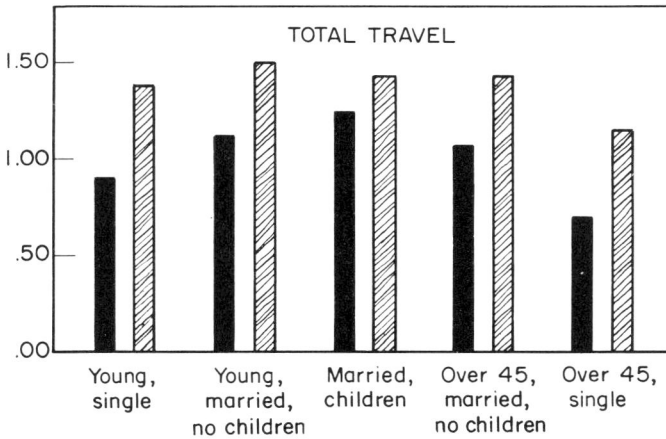

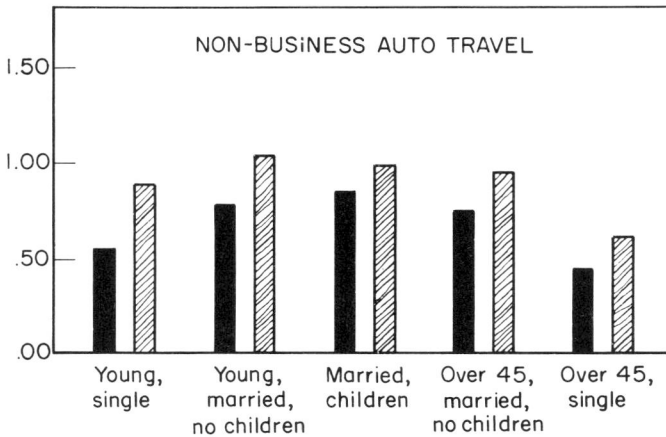

TOTAL TRAVEL

1.50 —

1.00 —

.50 —

.00

Young,
single

Young,
married,
no children

Married,
children

Over 45,
married,
no children

Over 45,
single

NON-BUSiNESS AUTO TRAVEL

1.50 —

1.00 —

.50 —

.00

Young,
single

Young,
married,
no children

Married,
children

Over 45,
married,
no children

Over 45,
single

GRAPH A-2 (CONT.)

Scale of
Frequency
of Travel

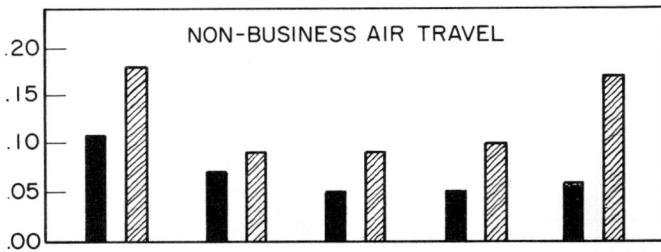

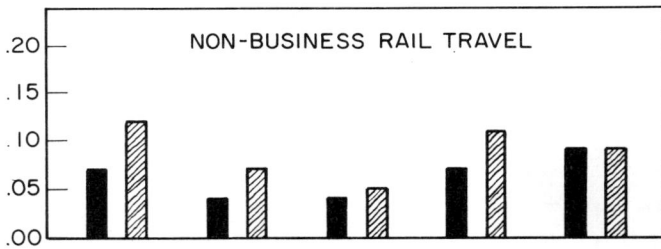

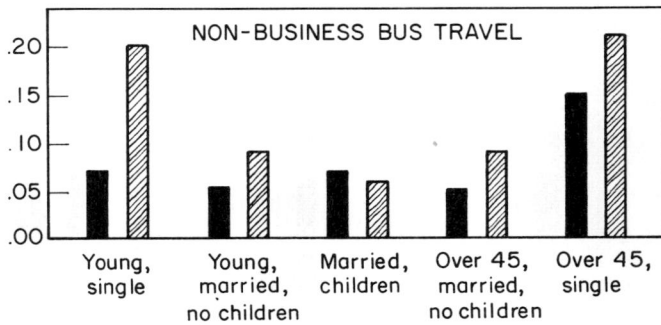

impact of rising income on frequency of travel depends on stage of the
family life cycle.

People who are over 45 and single do not travel very much regardless of the level of their income. As discussed in Chapter I, old age
is a major barrier to travel. For people in the earlier stages of the life
cycle, frequency of total travel does depend on income. The erratic income relationship for the second life cycle group, young married people
without children, does not appear in the data for 1955 (see Table A-2)
and may be the result of chance fluctuation in the 1962 data. For the
other stages in the family life cycle the effect of rising income is
clearly powerful.

The succeeding sections of Graph A-1 refer to non-business travel by auto, air, rail, and bus, respectively. They were constructed in
the same manner as the first section, and rest fundamentally on the
accompanying regression equations. It should be kept in mind that for
the common carriers the dependent variable is scored differently and
is plotted on an enlarged scale.

Note especially that frequency of non-business travel by bus falls
with income while frequency of travel by all other modes increases.
This result, however, must be interpreted in the light of the discussion
in Chapter VI, *Bus*. It was there shown that there was little relation between income and frequency of bus travel in 1955 but by 1962 there had
been an increase in bus travel in the low income groups with no change
in bus travel by the more prosperous. In other words, the income effect
has been shifting. This shift also appears in Table A-5 but the reliability of the coefficients is low. It would be incautious to assume that
the relation between income and bus travel found to exist in 1962 will
persist without further change in the years to come.

Note also the sharp increase in non-business air travel as income
rises to the level of $10,000 and over. The regression results show that
the effect of income on air travel also was important in 1955; it was, in
fact, much more pronounced at that time.

Comparisons in Graph A-1 can also be made for the same life
cycle group across modes of travel. For example, the widows, widow-
ers, and others over 45 and not currently married travel by automobile
about equally often regardless of income. Increasing the income of
people in this group increases the frequency with which they travel by
air or rail but decreases travel by bus.

Education: The relationship between education and travel is shown
in Graph A-2. Adults with a high school education travel more at all

stages in the life cycle than other adults. Education is especially important in predicting travel for single people. For them, education tends
to take the place of income and occupation as a discriminator or an in-
dicator of status. Single adults tend either to be young and have not yet
worked their way up the income scale, or older women who are living
on fixed sources of income. Though their incomes may not be too high
viewed as family incomes, they may still be reasonably high on a *per
capita* basis. Whether they will choose to spend money on travel depends on their education. Education has its smallest effect on travel by
married adults with children. Here it may logically be expected that
increased income levels will substitute for education in explaining travel, and education no longer must serve as a proxy for income.

People with a high school education or better travel more in general, and also take more non-business trips by each mode considered
separately. They take more bus trips than people with less education as
well as more trips by air, rail and auto.

Graph A-2 also shows visually the relation between stage in the
life cycle and choice of mode. For each of the common carriers the
relation between life cycle and frequency of travel is U-shaped, but for
auto travel the relation is an inverted U. Married couples tend to drive,
while single persons tend to travel by common carrier.

Automobile ownership: The results of the regression equations
show, as might be expected, that those who own an auto are more likely
to travel than those who do not. It is also not surprising that automobile
ownership has an effect on frequency of non-business auto travel, as
shown in Graph A-3. In fact, one might reasonably have expected an
even stronger relationship. People must travel frequently in automobiles owned by someone outside their immediate family.

People who do not own a car are more likely to take non-business
rail and bus trips than those who do own one. The effect of owning a car
is particularly important for single people. These people are likely to
travel by rail or bus if they don't own a car, while married couples do
not travel by these modes very frequently regardless of whether they
own cars. Owning a car is shown in the regression equations to have
little or no effect on frequency of non-business air travel. Why the depressing effect of auto ownership should be restricted to rail and bus
travel is not obvious. It may be that the car is a closer substitute for
rail and bus trips than it is for air trips for single people.

Place of residence: Graph A-4 shows that adults who live in one
of the twelve largest metropolitan areas are less likely to travel than
adults living elsewhere. The deterrent effect of living in one of the

GRAPH A-3

EFFECT OF AUTOMOBILE OWNERSHIP ON
FREQUENCY OF TRAVEL FOR ADULTS IN
DIFFERENT LIFE CYCLE GROUPS, 1962

Scale of
Frequency
of Travel

■ Family does not own a car
▨ Family owns a car

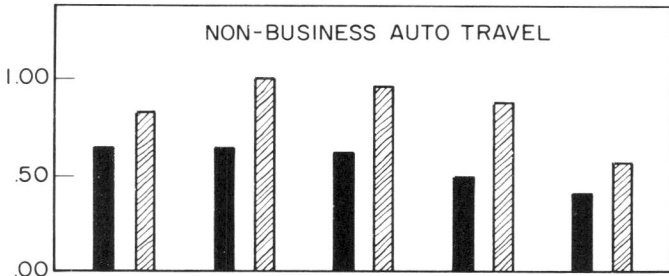

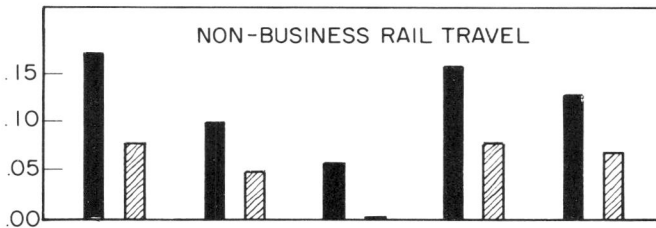

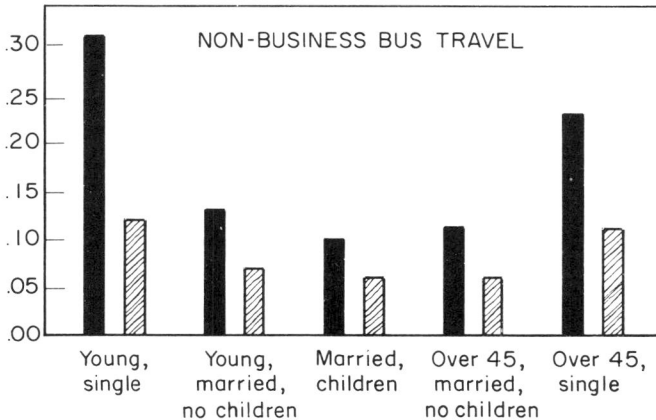

GRAPH A-4

EFFECT OF LIVING IN ONE OF THE TWELVE
LARGEST METROPOLITAN AREAS ON
FREQUENCY OF TRAVEL FOR ADULTS IN
DIFFERENT LIFE CYCLE GROUPS, 1962

Scale of
Frequency
of Travel

Live in one of the 12 largest
metropolitan areas
Live elsewhere

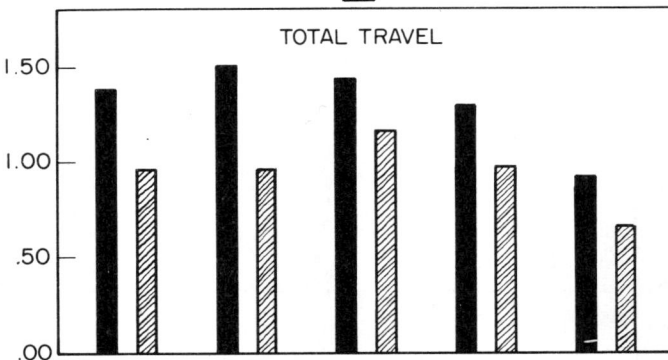

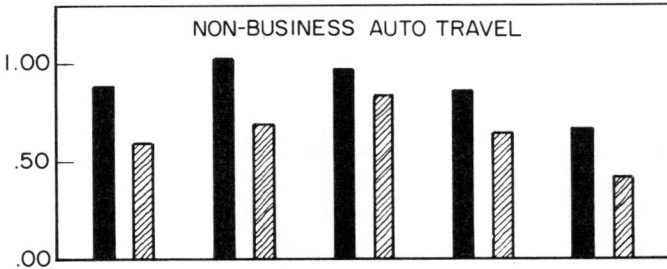

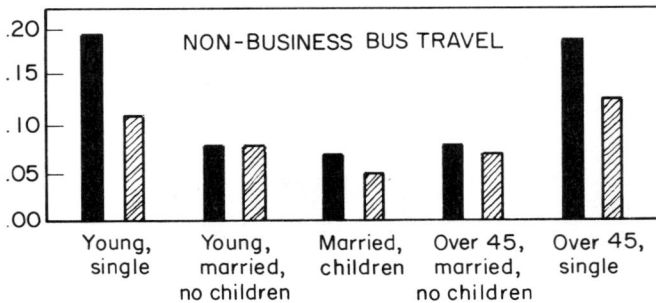

TOTAL TRAVEL

1.50

1.00

.50

.00

NON-BUSINESS AUTO TRAVEL

1.00

.50

.00

NON-BUSINESS BUS TRAVEL

.20

.15

.10

.05

.00

Young,
single

Young,
married,
no children

Married,
children

Over 45,
married,
no children

Over 45,
single

largest metropolitan areas is especially evident for young, single people and young married couples without children. Much of the negative effect of place of residence on travel is due to the low rates of auto ownership in central cities, but this effect has been taken into account by the inclusion of automobile ownership in the multiple regression equations. The effect illustrated in Graph A-4 is the incremental effect on travel of living in a large metropolitan area. This effect may be taken as a rough measure of the depressing effect of urban congestion on auto and bus travel. There is little depressing effect on auto or bus travel by families with children, who live typically in suburban areas where access to intercity highways is easy.

In summary, the findings in the multivariate statistical analysis reported in this Appendix support and reinforce the main findings reported earlier concerning the determinants of the frequency of travel. In addition, it has been shown that the effects of many variables upon total travel depend on the stage in the family life cycle. Even after simultaneous consideration of all other factors, income, education, auto ownership, and place of residence are shown to have important effects upon the market for travel.

B.   Choice of Mode

We present here the results of a multivariate analysis designed to provide insight into the complex array of factors that influence the choice of mode in intercity travel.   The choices to be considered are: the choice between air and auto for business purposes; the same choice for non-business purposes; and the choice between all common carriers combined and auto for non-business purposes.

The goal is to allow for the simultaneous effects of all of the relevant variables in explaining choice.   The method of estimation used is multiple least-squares regression.   The regression results are again converted to a multiple classification format to facilitate explanation of the findings.

The data were obtained from information provided by each respondent in the 1962 National Travel Market Survey concerning the details of the most recent common carrier trip and the most recent automobile trip taken by any member of the respondent's family.   Many of the principal findings from these same data were presented in detail in Chapter II in the form of two-way tables.

A set of "either-or" choices was simulated in the multivariate analysis of mode choice by assembling all of the relevant data for each trip on one data-processing card along with information about the characteristics of the trip-taker.   The numbers of trips for each of the pairs of modes to be considered are:

Pairs of Modes	Number of trips
Business air or business auto	348
Non-business air or non-business auto	1602
Non-business common carrier or non-business auto	1880

For each of the three pairs of modes to be considered, all of the cards in the pair were selected.   A dichotomous dependent variable was then obtained by assigning all of the cards for one of the modes in the pair the value of 1, and all of the cards for the other mode the value of zero.   For example, in the choice between non-business air and non-business auto, all of the auto trips and all of the air trips were selected; the air trips then arbitrarily received the value of 1 and the auto trips the value zero.   The analysis then became a search for the best arrangement of independent variables to discriminate between these two groups.

Since the dependent variable is a "zero-one" variable, the findings may be interpreted roughly as estimated probabilities. Basically, the greater the computed probability, the greater the likelihood of choosing the mode with the predetermined value of 1 for the dependent variable.

Specification of the model: The independent variables used in the analysis of the various mode pairs, which are listed in Table A-8, are completely specified in terms of dummy variables.

In order to simplify the discussion, the independent variables were classified into the following six groups:

1. Variables reflecting travel tastes and experience.
2. Variables reflecting distance of trip.
3. Variables reflecting supply of travel.
4. Variables reflecting income.
5. Variables reflecting price.
6. Variables reflecting demographic characteristics.

Since the variables have been discussed extensively in other parts of this report, the reasons for including them need not be reviewed here.

Choice between air and auto for business trips: The two principal modes of business travel are air travel and automobile travel. Business air trips accounted for about three-fifths of all air trips reported in both the 1955 and 1962 National Travel Market Surveys, and business auto trips accounted for about one-fourth of all automobile trips. Because of the predominance of air and auto for business travel purposes, considerations related to the choice of bus and rail for business trips are not discussed here.

The results of the calculations appear in Tables A-9 and A-1C. The regression coefficients from Table A-9 are converted to the multiple classification format in Table A-10. The effect on choice of mode cf possessing any one or any combination of the characteristics listed in Table A-10 may be ascertained by adjusting the "mean" of the dependent variable (.47) by the amount of the deviation for the characteristic. The mean of the dependent variable is not meaningful in this context. It indicates only the ratio of the number of air trips to auto trips which happened to be available for analysis. It is the magnitude of the adjusted deviations which is of interest.

According to Table A-10, people who travel for business purposes are more likely to use air rather than auto as the trip distance increases. Business air trips are associated with shorter stays away from home than business automobile trips, indicating that speed is an important factor on long trips in minimizing time away from home.

Trips involving distances of less than 300 miles, or involving 11 or more days away from home, are more likely to be taken by auto than by air.

High levels of family income (about $10,000) are more likely to be associated with business air trips than with business auto trips. Family income levels below $5000 are associated more with business auto trips than with business air trips.

One would expect that price considerations would be less important in selecting a mode for business travel than for non-business travel. The fare is a smaller part of the total cost of trips for business purposes. The deviation in Table A-10 for cheapness as a perceived attitude, however, is .26, second in importance of the variables investigated in predicting a choice of air over auto.

Those who mention danger of air travel appear to be more likely to fly than to drive! The regression coefficient on which the positive deviation of .07 for air danger in Table A-10 is based has a large standard error attached to it, however, so this finding is of questionable validity. The possibility that fear may be positively associated with air travel was also raised in an earlier study. [1]

In the analysis presented in this chapter, mentioning danger of air travel is positively associated with business air travel and negatively associated with non-business air travel. A possible hypothesis to explain the differences in the effect of air danger on both business and non-business air travel is that business travelers who travel more frequently than non-business air travelers become more ready to talk about what they regard as the dangers involved in air travel.

As far as supply variables are concerned, it appears that those few non-automobile owners who travel on business are more likely to travel by air than by automobile. The relationship here is not entirely straightforward, however, people who drive company-owned cars on both business and personal affairs may not own an automobile of their own.

---

[1] John B. Lansing and Dwight M. Blood, "A Cross-Section Analysis of Non-Business Air Travel," *Journal of the American Statistical Association*, December 1958. See p. 942.

Adults who live in the Northeast are more likely to take their business trips by air than adults living in the other three geographic areas of the country.

To summarize: A business trip is more likely to be taken by air than by auto if the trip is over 300 miles in length, if the family income of the adult is over $5000, if the adult has air travel experience and positive feelings toward air travel, if the trip lasts less than eleven days, if the traveler does not own a car, and if he lives in an area well provided with air service.

Choice between air travel and automobile travel for non-business purposes: The results of the regression analysis of the choice of air over auto for non-business travel are listed in Table A-11. The interpretation of these results is facilitated by conversion of the regression coefficients to the multiple classification format, which is shown in Table A-12.

Price considerations are a major factor in deciding whether to travel by air or by auto. There are two measures of price in Table A-12, and both show large effects. Only a small minority of trips studied were taken by adults who said air is the cheapest mode, but those who did say air was cheapest were much more likely to travel in this manner. The adjusted deviation for parties of one is .18 even when reported cheapness is taken into account. (The two-way correlation coefficient between perceived air cheapness and number who went is -.19, confirming that air is less likely to be the cheapest mode if two or more go on the trip.)

The distance variables (time away and length of trip) may also be interpreted in part as price variables. Cost of travel is partly a function of trip distance and partly a function of time away, since the cost of meals, hotel rooms, etc., increases with each day away from home. There is likely to be substantial pressure to minimize actual travel costs for trips involving lengthy stays away from home. (Perceived cheapness of air has a two-way correlation coefficient of .27 with distance of over 1000 miles, and a coefficient of .21 with being gone over 11 days.)

Automobile travel appears to have a clear edge over air travel for trips of 100-299 miles, and air is more likely to be chosen over auto for trips of 1000 miles or more.

The choice between air and auto for non-business trips is also influenced by income and by preference variables.

Choice between common carrier and automobile for non-business trips: In this section of the analysis, attention is turned to the general question of why people travel by any common carrier rather than by automobile. All common carrier trips for non-business purposes by air, rail, and bus were lumped together and paired against non-business automobile travel. The dependent variable was assigned the value 1 for common carrier trips and the value zero for automobile trips. Table A-13 contains the regression estimates and Table A-14 presents the regression coefficients converted to the form of multiple classification analysis.

Of the variables reflecting supply of travel services (auto ownership, place of residence, region) only auto ownership was important in discriminating auto travelers from air travelers. Length of time away had no separate effect on the choice decision after other factors had been accounted for in the regression.

Travelers go by common carrier if they feel that the particular mode they choose is cheaper than going by automobile, if they travel alone, if they do not own an automobile, if they are going on a trip that is more than 1000 miles in length, and if they are in the younger stages of the life cycle. Frequent travelers, those who have air travel experience, and those who have family incomes of more than $10,000 are more likely to travel by common carrier.

Common carrier competition with the automobile must meet the issue of price. The evidence presented in this analysis suggests that price-related factors stand collectively as the biggest single obstacle to travel by common carrier. Better evidence is not likely to change the conclusion that price is a major determinant of choice of mode for non-business travel.

SURVEY METHODOLOGY
APPENDIX II

A. Description of Methods

Sampling methods: The National Travel Market Surveys are based on a series of successive samples of the population of the United States. The samples are probability samples in which every member of the universe studied has a known chance of selection. The samples are multi-stage samples in which the first step is the selection of primary sample units, which are metropolitan areas, and, outside of metropolitan areas, individual counties, or, in some situations, groups of counties. Within primary sample units there may be two or more additional stages of selection. Methods designed to provide exact knowledge of the probability of selection are used at every stage in the process.

The universe studied in these surveys may be defined as all families in the United States exclusive of inmates of institutions (such as hospitals and prisons) and those living on military reservations. Single people living alone are considered as families for purposes of these surveys. The method of obtaining the sample of families is to select a sample of occupied dwelling units and to interview families found in the dwelling units selected. Single family homes, multiple family homes, apartments, trailers, and residential quarters in commercial structures are considered as dwelling units.

When a family has been designated for inclusion in the survey, it remains to designate the person within the family who is to respond. In single person families there is no choice; in families where there are two or more adults the respondent is designated on a random basis as the head or wife of the head of the family. This procedure is used on the presumption that these two individuals are most likely to be informed about the affairs of the family as a whole. Since other adults such as grown children living at home have no chance to be interviewed, they have no chance to be included in tabulations which show information for respondents only. In the travel surveys the most important type of information obtained from respondents only is the information about people's attitudes and motives. It is believed that the distributions of replies are not greatly influenced by the omission since the extra adults are a small fraction of the population. Information was obtained in the 1955 and 1962 surveys from respondents about the trips taken by all adults in the family and the resulting tabulations concerning frequency of travel include the travel of all adults aged 18 or over.

The travel surveys have been conducted as sections of the Omnibus Economic Surveys of the Survey Research Center in which questions are asked in a single interview about a variety of topics.

Interviewing methods: The travel surveys have been based on personal interviews conducted by the national field staff maintained by the Survey Research Center. Interviewers are residents of the areas in which they interview. They are hired, trained, and periodically visited by a staff of supervisors who report to the central staff in Ann Arbor. An exception to these generalizations is that a successful reinterview by telephone with a small sample was taken in 1962, the results of which are shown in the report on that survey.

The methods used in the conduct of the interviews are intended to interest the respondent in the survey, and to motivate him to cooperate with the interviewer. In the design of the questionnaires the attempt is made to translate the objectives of the researcher into questions which will fit the psychological world of the respondent.

The types of questions are varied according to the purpose. Simple factual questions are ordinarily "closed." The interviewer asks, for example, "Have you ever rented a 'drive-it-yourself' automobile?" and checks a box to indicate "yes" or "no." Attitudinal questions may be "open," that is, the respondent will answer in his own words which the interviewer records more or less verbatim. For example, in 1958 the question was asked: "As you probably know, there are plans for regular use of jet planes for passenger service. How would you feel about traveling in a jet plane?" Such a question may yield information both about whether the person is positively or negatively disposed and about the frame of reference within which he makes this evaluation. When the subject matter is likely to be threatening to the respondent in some way, indirect methods of questioning may be used. For example, respondents may be asked to fill out incomplete sentences with the first answer which comes to their minds. A more complete discussion of interviewing may be found in *The Dynamics of Interviewing* by Robert L. Kahn and Charles F. Cannell, (New York: John Wiley and Sons, 1957).

B. Expansion of Number of Air Trips

One method of checking the accuracy of the results of sample surveys is to compare estimates of such quantities as the total volume of travel by a given means of transportation based on expansions of survey results with total counts obtained by other methods such as reports of total sales of tickets. In the field of passenger travel the best available body of statistics which can be used to compare with the survey results is in the field of air travel. There seem to be no reliable statistics of travel by other modes which can be adjusted to give estimates of the number of trips to destinations 100 miles or more away. An attempt in this direction with regard to automobile travel is reported elsewhere.[1] The principal result of that analysis is to raise questions about the accuracy of some of the widely used statistics of auto travel.

The statistics of air travel are much better adapted to the purpose, and an attempted reconciliation was included in the report on the 1955 survey. Subsequently attempts at reconciliation have been prepared and circulated by Nathan S. Simat, of Systems Analysis and Research Corporation. Like other comparisons of survey data and aggregate statistics the purpose essentially is to check the accuracy of the survey estimate of the mean number of air trips. The comparison is complicated by a series of differences in concept between the survey results and the non-survey data.

The survey data from the 1962 Survey were obtained by the following sequence of questions asked with reference to each adult in the family:

T5. Have (you) ever taken a trip to a place 100 miles or more away by *air?*		
(If Yes)	T5a. During the last two years have (you) taken any trips by commercial airline to places 100 miles away?	YES / NO
	T5b. Did (you) take your first air trip in the last 12 months?	YES / NO
	T5c Thinking of (your) most recent air trip, what *month* and *year* was that?	

[1] *Papers - Fourth Annual Meeting, Transportation Research Forum,* December 26-28, 1963, pp. 85-91, "Some Inconsistencies in Statistics of Intercity Automobile Travel," By Dwight M. Blood.

(If Yes)	T5d. What *month* and *year* did (you) take the trip before that?
	_____
	(IF TWO TRIPS IN LAST 12 MONTHS - in T5c and T5d)
	T5e. Altogether, how many trips did (you) take *in* the last 12 *months,* counting a round trip as one trip?
	_____

No special effort was made to make clear to the respondent what was meant by a "commercial airline," but the term is obviously rather broad. An attempted reconciliation between the responses to this sequence and the industry statistics follows:

Comparison of Total Air Trips
Estimated from Survey Data and from Industry Sources

Survey Estimate

1.	Estimated total number of adults in the civilian population, mid-1962	118,755,000
2.	Adults in sample	5,329
3.	Expansion factor	22,285
4.	Reported number of round trips by air	1,728
5.	Expanded estimate of number of round trips by air	38,500,000
6.	Estimated number of one-way trips by commercial airline by adult Americans to points 100 miles or more away	77,000,000

Estimate from Industry Sources

1.	Domestic scheduled service:	
	a. Revenue passenger miles in domestic scheduled service (000)	33,125,528
	b. Mean trip length (miles)	687
	c. Estimated number of scheduled domestic trips, one-way	48,217,000
2.	Domestic operations of unscheduled airlines:	
	a. Revenue passenger originations	421,000
3.	International scheduled service:	
	a. Revenue passenger miles in international scheduled service, United States airlines (000)	8,769,000

Estimate from Industry Sources - (Cont'd)

      b. Average airline passenger trip
         length (miles)   1,539
      c. Estimated number of scheduled
         international trips   5,698,000
4. Approximate total number of trips   54,000,000
5. a. Approximate discrepancy   23,000,000
      b. Ratio of survey estimate to
         industry estimate   142

Sources for Industry Estimates

1. a. *Air Carrier Traffic Statistics,* C.A.B., 12 months
     ended August 31, 1962.
  b. *Handbook of Airline Statistics,* 1962 edition
     page 421. (From origin-destination survey for
     1961.)
  c. Line 1a divided by line 1b.
2. a. *Air Carrier Traffic Statistics,* C.A.B., 12 months
     ended August 31, 1962.
3. a. *Handbook of Airline Statistics,* 1962 edition,
     page 47. (Date for 1961.)
  b. Ibid, page 82.
  c. Line 3a divided by line 3b.
4. Sum of lines 1c, 2a, and 3c.
5. a. Line 6 above minus line 4.
  b. Line 6 above divided by line 4.

It is possible to carry a comparison of this sort to a degree of refinement which the underlying data hardly justify. For example, while in principle trips to places 90 miles away should not be counted, no stress was laid on this point in the interview, and some respondents may have included them. If he had been absolutely precise, the respondent would have left out those trips for which the total distance from point of origin to point of destination including the trip to the airport at one end and the trip from the airport at the other end was under 100 miles. Again, trips by Americans on Canadian airlines ought to be included in the industry estimate, but trips by Canadians on American airlines ought to be left out. In principle the following adjustments should be made:

Adjustments which Theoretically Should be Made but Have
Not Been Carried Out:

1. The following should be *added* to the industry estimate:
  a. Trips by Americans on Canadian and other foreign airlines including international trips on foreign airlines.

(Cont'd)

      b. Trips by Americans on international operations of do-
         mestic non-scheduled airlines. However, only trips by
         the non-institutional population should be added.
   2. The following should be *deducted* from the industry estimate:
      a. Trips by foreigners on American airlines, both domestic
         and international.
      b. Trips on domestic airlines by military personnel living
         on military bases.
      c. The air component of trips totaling under 100 miles.
      d. Trips by those aged under 18.

However these adjustments are handled, the main conclusion is clear:
people tend to report too many air trips. As a first approximation they
report about 40 to 50 per cent more trips than they should.

    This result is taken into account in the interpretation of the find-
ings. It also has led to an attempt to reconsider the method of data
collection. Systematic experimentation with alternative methods of data
collection is expensive. Results may be disappointing, especially if the
experiments are not based on preliminary studies of the errors, and
such preliminary studies also are expensive and difficult to conduct.
A program of research into the problems of measuring travel behavior
has been beyond the means of the travel surveys.

    Work on response errors in surveys in other content areas led to
the development of hypotheses about the air travel data. The most probable source of the difficulty appeared to be memory error. As argued
in the text (Chapter I), there is no reason to believe frequent travelers
can recall all of their trips individually. But it is also possible that
people will tend to recall air travel as more recent than it really is.
People generally value air travel positively, and there is a tendency for
people to err in the direction of bringing positively valued experiences
closer to them in time while they push negatively valued experiences
into the past. Since the error was too many reported air trips, the
hypothesis was foreshortening.

    To reduce this tendency a revised sequence about air travel was
introduced without preliminary experimentation in 1962. The strategy
was to ask about air travel over a two year period. People thus were
given the opportunity to characterize themselves as air travelers by
saying they had taken a trip by air within two years. The two year
question was intended only to lead up to questions which asked the
specific month and year of the two most recent air trips. Whether these
trips were within 12 months was inferred rather than asked directly.

The hypothesis was that, if foreshortening was the problem, the results would show a reduced percentage of air travelers. The exact sequence of questions in 1962 is shown above. The 1960 sequence, for comparison, was as follows:

T7.	Have you (he) ever taken a trip to a place *100* or more miles away by *AIR?*	YES NO
T8.	In about what year did you (he) first take an air trip?	_____ Year
T9.	During the last twelve months, did you (he) take any air trips to places *100* miles or more away on *COMMERCIAL OR PUBLIC AIRLINES?*	YES NO
T10.	How many air trips on commercial airlines did you (he) take during the last twelve months - *COUNTING A ROUND TRIP AS ONE TRIP?*	_____ (Number of trips)

The per cent of adults traveling by air was estimated to be as follows:

Year of Survey	Per Cent of Adults Traveling by Air
1955	6.7
1956	7.2
1957	8.8
1958	9.0
1960	9.6
1962	10.7

Lacking a controlled experiment one cannot be precise about the effect of the changed questions. The 1960 survey is only roughly a "control group." But the observed increase from 1960 to 1962 is of a magnitude which can be easily explained by the known increase in air travel. The changed questions, as a first approximation, made no difference. Thus, these results fail to confirm the hypothesis that foreshortening of the date of the most recent trip by air is the cause of the observed over-report of air travel. The most probable interpretation is that the error is not in an excess proportion of adults taking one or more trips but in an excess number of trips reported per air traveler.

There is one more bit of evidence which points in the same direction. Also in the 1962 survey, as noted above, there was a telephone

reinterview. The families selected for reinterview were those reporting in the spring wave of interviews ten or more trips by any mode of
transportation in the preceding twelve months. The reinterview by
phone asked for complete details on all trips by all family members
over the ensuing three months. The 224 families who were successfully reinterviewed reported (in detail) 950 man-trips for the three
month period covered by the reinterview, implying roughly 3800 trips a
year. The same 224 families in the first interview reported 6,463 man-
trips for the preceding 12 months. The annual rate from the reinter-
views was thus about 60 per cent of that from the original report. It is
possible that these families actually did not travel during the period
covered by the reinterview as much as they had earlier. One might say
that their trips were completed, and therefore, they stayed home. It is
also possible, however, that the reported rate of travel in the summer
was lower because the method of interviewing required detailed recall
and covered a shorter period and thus prevented exaggerated estimates
of frequency of travel. Thus, these results are at least consistent with
the interpretation that people exaggerate the number of trips they take
when asked to report for a full year.

C. Sampling Errors

Properly conducted sample interview surveys yield useful estimates but they do not yield exact values. Errors arise from several sources: sampling, non-response, reporting and processing. Each source of error may be important in evaluating the accuracy of information. The present discussion is limited to sampling errors.

Sample statistics reflect the random variations arising from interviewing only a fraction of the population. The distribution of individuals selected for a sample will usually differ by an unknown amount from that of the population from which the sample is drawn. The value which would have been obtained if the entire population had been interviewed by the same survey procedures will be referred to as the population value. If different samples were used under the same survey conditions, some of the estimates would be larger than the population value and some would be smaller. The sampling error is a measure of the chance deviation of a sample statistic from the corresponding population value. The sampling error does not measure the actual error of a particular sample estimate; rather it leads to statements in terms of confidence intervals that are correct in a specified proportion of cases in the long run.

"Sampling error" as used here is to be interpreted as two standard errors; it is the range, on either side of the sample estimate, chosen frequently in social research in order to obtain the 95 per cent "level of confidence." If one requires a greater degree of confidence than this, a wider range than two standard errors should be used. On the other hand, most of the time the actual error of sampling will be less than the sampling error defined above; in about 68 cases of every 100 the population value can be expected to lie within a range of one-half the sampling error (one standard error) of the sample estimates.

Sampling errors themselves are products of the sampling processes and are subject to the effects of random fluctuations. Therefore, a range, rather than a single value, has been used in the tables which follow. The upper limits are based on computations of data from earlier travel surveys. They are not averages but values on the high or conservative side. The smaller values were computed by use of the formula for simple random samples which can be viewed as the lower bound to the Survey's sampling errors.

Appendix Table S-I shows approximate sampling errors of percentages on a per adult basis when individual percentages are considered separately. Appendix Table S-II shows approximate sampling

errors of differences between two percentages derived from two different subgroups of the study population. The sampling errors of differences indicate the range in which the "true" differences between the
population values of the two compared classes can be expected to fall
95 out of 100 times. Appendix Table S-III and S-IV show approximate
sampling errors on a per interview basis.

LIST OF PUBLICATIONS
APPENDIX III

The Travel Market 1955, 1956, 1957. John B. Lansing and Ernest Lilienstein. Available from the Publications Clerk, Institute for Social Research as a combined reprint, bound in cloth, $10.00.

The Travel Market 1958, 1959-1960, 1961-1962. John B. Lansing, Eva Mueller, Thomas Lorimer, William Ladd, and Nancy Barth. Available from the Publications Clerk, Institute for Social Research, as a combined reprint, bound in cloth, $10.00.

A Cross-Section Analysis of the Domestic Intercity Travel Market. Dwight M. Blood. Unpublished doctoral dissertation in economics, University of Michigan, 1963. Microfilm and positive copies available from University Microfilms, Inc., 313 N. First Street, Ann Arbor.

1962 Survey of Consumer Finances. G. Katona, C. L. Lininger, R. F. Kosobud. 1963. Available from the Publications Clerk, Institute for Social Research. $4.00 (paperbound), $6.00 (cloth).

"A Cross-Section Analysis of Non-Business Air Travel," *Journal of the American Statistical Association.* John B. Lansing and Dwight M. Blood. Vol. LIII (December, 1958), pp. 928-947.

"An Analysis of Interurban Air Travel," *The Quarterly Journal of Economics.* John B. Lansing, Jung-Chao Liu, and Daniel B. Suits. Vol. LXXV (February, 1961), pp. 87-95.

"An Analysis of Non-Business Rail Travel," *Land Economics.* Herbert E. Neil, Jr. and John B. Lansing. Vol. XXXV (May, 1959), pp. 139-148.

An Analysis of the Demand for Non- Business Bus Travel. Ernest Oksanen. Unpublished master's thesis in economics, University of Michigan, 1959.

TABLES AND GRAPHS
APPENDIX IV

A. List of Tables

Table   Page

1   Shares of all Trips by Mode and Purpose of Travel, 1955 and 1962 205

2   Purpose of Most Recent Trip, 1955 206

3   People Who Travel A Lot, 1962. 207

4   Sentence Completions on Going to Europe, 1958 208

5   Are There Any Trips That You Have Thought You Would Like to Take but you Haven't Been Able to, 1956 209

6   Trips People Would Like to Take by Purpose of Trip, 1956 210

7   Sentence Completion on What People Would Like to do in Europe, 1958.. 211

8   Sentence Completions on Traveling in the United States and in Foreign Countries, 1958 212

9   Reasons Why People Don't Go on the Trips They Would Like to Take, 1958 213

10   Reasons for Not Accepting an Expense-Free Tour of the United States, 1962............................... 214

11   Socio-Economic Characteristics of the Population: Age, Stage in the Family Life Cycle, Occupation, Family Income, and Region, 1955 and 1962 215

12   Frequency of Travel by All Modes by Family Income, 1955 and 1962 217

13   Frequency of Travel by All Modes Last Year by Age of Adult, 1955 and 1962............................. 218

14   Frequency of Travel by Sex of Adult, 1956 and 1962 219

15   Frequency of Travel by Region, 1955 and 1962 220

16   Frequency of Travel by Whether Now Living in the New York Area, 1955 and 1962 221

17   Frequency of Travel Within the New York Metro Area, 1962. 222

18   Total Number of Trips Taken in Last 12 Months, 1962 ... 223

19   Socio-Economic Characteristics of Frequent Travelers, 1962 224

Table   Page

20   The Importance of Call-Backs in Determining Air Travel
      Experience, 1960 226

21   Experience With Vacation Travel to a Place 100 Miles
      Away, 1958 227

22   Amount Spent on Vacation Trips by Income in 1961 228

23   Mean Expenditure on Vacation Trips by Income in
      1961. 229

24   Number of Vacation Trips Taken by Income in 1961 230

25   Overseas Travel by Family Income, 1959-1960 231

26   Experience with Overseas Travel by Stage in the Family
      Life Cycle, 1959-1960. 231

27   Overseas Travel by Prior Experience with Overseas
      Travel, 1959-1960 232

28   Overseas Travel History by Age, 1959-1960 232

29   The Proportion Taking Trips by Air, Rail, Bus and Auto,
      1955 and 1962 233

30   Frequency of Travel by Each Mode for Business and Non-
      Business Reasons, 1955 and 1962 234

31   Per Cent of Passenger Miles Accounted for by Each Mode
      of Travel by Distance to Destination 235

32   Advantages and Disadvantages of Automobile Travel,
      1955. 236

33   Advantages and Disadvantages of Different Modes for
      Respondent's Most Recent Trip by Common Carrier,
      1957. 237

34   Could You Have Gotten Where You Wanted to Go Con-
      veniently by Other Modes on Most Recent Trip, 1962 238

35   Best Way to Travel by Frequency of Travel Last Year,
      1962. 240

36   Attitudes Toward Long-Distance Auto Trips, 1960 241

37   Sentence Completions on Automobile Trips, 1958 and
      1962. 242

38   Preferred Mode of Travel if Cost Had Been the Same,
      1962. 243

Table   Page

39 Modes Spontaneously Mentioned by Adults in Discussing
    Their Choice of Mode for Their Most Recent Trip,
    1956. 244

40 Use of Air, Rail, Bus, Auto, and Mixed Modes on Most
    Recent Business and Non-Business Trips by Distance,
    1962. 245

41 Determinants of Choice of Mode on Most Recent Trip,
    1955. 246

42 Determinants of Choice of Mode for Vacation and Pleasure
    Trips Only, 1956 247

43 Total Number of People Who Went on Most Recent Long
    Distance Trip by Air or Auto, 1962 248

44 Use of Air, Rail, Bus, Auto, and Mixed Modes on Most
    Recent Non-Business Trip by Distance and Whether
    Traveled Alone, 1962 249

45 Selection of Mode on Long Distance Air and Auto Trips
    by Experience as an Air Traveler, 1962............. 250

46 Preferred Mode if Cost Had Been the Same, 1962. 251

47 Experience as an Auto Traveler by Family Income, 1955
    and 1962. 252

48 Experience as an Auto Traveler by Age, 1962 253

49 Number of Business and Non-Business Auto Trips, 1962. . 254

50 Use of Auto by Family Income, 1955 and 1962 255

51 Per Cent of All Auto Trips Taken by Adults in Specified
    Income Groups, 1955 and 1962 256

52 Use of Auto by Occupation of Adult, 1955 and 1962 257

53 Use of Auto by Age of Adult, 1955 and 1962. 258

54 Use of Auto by Stage in the Family Life Cycle, 1955 and
    1962. 259

55 Use of Auto by Sex of Adult, 1955 and 1962 260

56 Use of Auto by Race and Income, 1955 261

57 Use of Auto by Race, 1955 and 1962................. 262

58 Use of Auto by Region, 1955 and 1962. 263

59 Auto Ownership by Region, 1955 and 1962............. 264

Table   Page

60   Use of Air, Rail, Bus, and Auto by Whether Living in the
     New York Area, 1955, 1957, and 1962. 265

61   Auto Ownership in the New York Metropolitan Area, Spring
     of 1962. 267

62   Auto Ownership Within the New York Metropolitan Area by
     Boroughs, 1962 268

63   Auto Ownership in the New York Metropolitan Area and the
     Next Eleven Largest Metropolitan Areas, 1958-1959. 269

64   Type of Neighborhood in the New York Metropolitan Area
     by Use of Auto, 1962. 270

65   Use of Auto Within the New York Metropolitan Area,
     1962. 271

66   Use of Superhighways by Sex and Age, 1962. 272

67   Positive Feelings About Driving Fast by Sex and Age,
     1962. 272

68   Sentence Completions on Plane Trips, 1958 and 1962 273

69   General Advantages and Disadvantages of Air Travel,
     1955. 274

70   Advantages and Disadvantages of Air for the Respondent's
     Most Recent Trip, 1955. 275

71   Pleasant Recollections of the Most Recent Air Trip,
     1955. 276

72   Unpleasant Recollections of the Most Recent Air Trip,
     1955. 277

73   Feelings About Whether Air Travel is Safer Now Than Ten
     Years Ago by Experience as an Air Travelers, 1962. 278

74   Use of Rail, Bus and Auto by Experience as an Air Traveler,
     1955 and 1962 279

75   Per Cent of Experienced Air Travelers by Whether Living
     in the New York Area, 1955-1962 281

76   Year of First Air Trip by Age of Adult, 1957 and 1960 . . . 282

77   Experience as an Air Traveler by Family Income, 1955
     and 1962. 283

78   Experience as an Air Traveler by Age of Adult, 1955
     and 1962. 284

Table   Page

79   Per Cent of Adults in Specified Income Groups by Stage in
     the Family Life Cycle and by Whether Experienced or In-
     experienced Air Travelers, 1955. 285

80   Number of Business and Non-Business Air Trips, 1955,
     1960 and 1962 286

81   Use of Air by Family Income, 1955 and 1962. 287

82   Per Cent of all Air Trips Taken by Adults in Specified In-
     come Groups, 1955 and 1962. 288

83   Use of Air by Occupation of Adult, 1955 and 1962 289

84   Use of Air by Age of Adult, 1955 and 1962. 290

85   Use of Air by Stage in the Family Life Cycle, 1955 and
     1962. 291

86   Use of Air by Sex of Adult, 1955 and 1962. 292

87   Use of Air by Race and Income, 1955. 293

88   Use of Air by Race, 1955 and 1962. 294

89   Use of Air by Region, 1955 and 1962 295

90   Per Cent Taking and Air Trip in Year by Whether Living
     in the New York Area, 1955-1962 296

91   Use of Air Within the New York Metro Area, 1962 297

92   Attitudes Toward Jet Travel by Modes of Travel Used Last
     Year, 1957 298

93   Attitudes Toward Jet Travel by Age of People Who Took a
     Trip Last Year, 1957 299

94   Attitudes Toward Jet Travel by Sex of People Who Took a
     Trip Last Year, 1957 300

95   Reasons for Attitudes Toward Jet Travel by Sex for People
     Who Took a Trip Last Year, 1957 301

96   Time Required for Airport Trips by Distance of Trip,
     1960. 302

97   Kinds of Appointments on Most Recent Business Trip,
     1960. 303

98   Whether Rented an Automobile on Most Recent Air Trip by
     Length of Time Away, 1962 304

Table   Page

99   Reactions to Reduced Fares and Free Plane Trips by
      Experience as an Air Traveler, 1962 305

100   Perceived Characteristics of Air Travelers, 1955 306

101   Perceived Characteristics of Rail Travelers, 1955 307

102   General Advantages and Disadvantages of Rail Travel,
      1955. 308

103   Advantages and Disadvantages of Rail for the Most Recent
      Trip, 1957. 309

104   Pleasant Recollections of the Last Rail Trip, 1955 310

105   Unpleasant Recollections of the Last Rail Trip, 1955 311

106   Experience as a Rail Traveler by Family Income, 1955
      and 1962. 312

107   Experience as a Rail Traveler by Age of Adult, 1962 313

108   Rail Travel History by Age of Adult, 1957. 314

109   Number of Business and Non-Business Rail Trips, 1955
      and 1962. 315

110   Use of Rail by Family Income, 1955 and 1962 316

111   Per Cent of all Rail Trips Taken by Adults in Specified
      Income Groups, 1955 and 1962 317

112   Use of Rail by Occupation of Adult, 1955 and 1962 318

113   Use of Rail by Age of Adult, 1955 and 1962 319

114   Use of Rail by Stage in the Family Life Cycle, 1955 and
      1962. 320

115   Use of Rail by Sex of Adult, 1955 and 1962 321

116   Use of Rail by Race and Income, 1955 322

117   Use of Rail by Race, 1955 and 1962 323

118   Use of Rail by Region, 1955 and 1962. 324

119   Use of Rail Within the New York Metro Area, 1962. 325

120   Reactions to Trips by Bus, 1962 326

121   Reactions to Bus Travel by Family Income. 327

122   Advantages and Disadvantages of Bus for the Most Recent
      Trip, 1957. 328

Table		Page
123	Experience as a Bus Traveler by Family Income, 1955 and 1962	329
124	Experience as a Bus Traveler by Age of Adult, 1962	330
125	Number of Business and Non-Business Bus Trips, 1955 and 1962	331
126	Use of Bus by Family Income, 1955 and 1962	332
127	Per Cent of all Bus Trips Taken by Adults in Specified Income Groups, 1955 and 1962	333
128	Use of Bus by Occupation, 1955 and 1962	334
129	Use of Bus by Age of Adult, 1955 and 1962	335
130	Use of Bus by Stage in the Family Life Cycle, 1955 and 1962	336
131	Use of Bus by Sex of Adult, 1955 and 1962	337
132	Use of Bus by Race, 1955 and 1962	338
133	Use of Bus by Region, 1955 and 1962	339
134	Use of Bus Within the New York Metro Area, 1962	340
A-1	Definition of Independent Variables Used for Estimation of Multiple Discriminant Function Scales and for Multiple Regression Analyses	341
A-2	Estimates of Regression Equations for Total Non-Business Travel Stratified by Life Cycle for Years 1955 and 1962	342
A-3	Estimates of Regression Equations for Non-Business Air Travel Stratified by Life Cycle for Years 1955 and 1962	343
A-4	Estimates of Regression Equations for Non-Business Rail Travel Stratified by Life Cycle for Years 1955 and 1962	344
A-5	Estimates of Regression Equations for Non-Business Bus Travel Stratified by Life Cycle for Years 1955 and 1962	345
A-6	Estimates of Regression Equations for Non-Business Auto Travel Stratified by Life Cycle for Years 1955 and 1962	346
A-7	A Multiple Classification Analysis of Major Factors Affecting Total Non-Business and Business Travel by all Modes Combined for Years 1955 and 1962	347
A-8	Definition of Dependent and Independent Variables Used for Estimation of Regression Equations	349

Table   Page

A-9   Estimate of Regression Equation for Factors Affecting the
       Choice of Business Air Travel Over Business Automobile
       Travel 352

A-10   Multiple Classification Analysis of Major Factors Affecting
       Choice of Business Air Travel Over Business Automobile
       Travel 353

A-11   Estimate of Regression Equation for Factors Affecting the
       Choice of Business Air Travel Over Business Automobile
       Travel 355

A-12   Multiple Classification Analysis of Major Factors Affecting
       Choice of Non-Business Automobile Travel. 356

A-13   Estimate of Regression Equation for Factors Affecting the
       Choice of Non-Business Common Carrier Travel Over
       Non-Business Automobile Travel 357

A-14   Multiple Classification Analysis of Major Factors Affecting
       Choice of Non-Business Common Carrier Travel Over
       Non-Business Automobile Travel 358

S-I   Approximate Sampling Errors of Percentages for "Per
       Adult" Responses. 360

S-II   Sampling Errors of Differences for "Per Adult" Re-
       ponses 361

S-III Approximate Sampling Errors of Percentages for "Per
       Interview" Responses 363

S-IV   Sampling Errors of Differences for "Per Interview" Re-
       sponses 364

B. List of Graphs

Graph   Page

1   Per Cent of Adults at Different Income Levels Who Took
     5 or More Trips by any Mode During the Survey Year. . . .   15

2   Per Cent of Adults at Different Income Levels Who Took
     No Trips by any Mode During the Survey Year   16

3   Per Cent of Adults in Different Age Groups Who Took No
     Trips by any Mode During the Survey Year   18

4   Per Cent of Adults Living in Different Regions Who Took
     5 or More Trips by any Mode During the Survey Year. . . .   19

5   Per Cent of Travelers by Number of Trips Taken, 1962 . .   25

6   Per Cent of Adults at Different Income Levels Who Took
     a Vacation Trip, 1961   30

7   Per Cent of Adults Traveling by Each Mode During the
     Survey Year   37

8   Per Cent of Passenger Miles Accounted for by Each Mode
     of Travel by Distance to Destination   40

9   Per Cent of Most Recent Business and Non-Business Trips
     at Different Distances Accounted for by Air, Rail, Bus,
     and Auto, 1962   51

10   Per Cent of Most Recent Trips by Each Mode Taken by
     People at Different Income Levels, 1955   52

11   Per Cent of Pleasure and Vacation Trips Accounted for by
     Air, Rail, and Bus at Different Levels of Income and Dis-
     tance, 1956   54

12   Per Cent of Most Recent Long Distance Trips Taken by
     Air or Auto by the Number of People Who Went, 1962   56

13   Per Cent of Adults at Different Income Levels Who Have
     Ever Traveled by Auto   60

14   Per Cent of Adults in Different Age Groups Who Have Ever
     Traveled by Auto, 1962   63

15   Per Cent of Adults at Different Income Levels Who Traveled
     by Auto During the Survey Year   65

16   Per Cent of Adults With Different Occupations Who Traveled
     by Auto During the Survey Year   68

17   Per Cent of Adults in Different Age Groups Who Traveled
     by Auto During the Survey Year   69

Graph   Page

18   Per Cent of Adults Living in Different Regions Who
      Traveled by Auto During the Survey Year   73

19   Per Cent of Adults Traveling by Air and Auto in the Survey
      Year by Whether Now Living in the New York Area, 1955,
      1957, and 1962   75

20   Per Cent of all Adults Who Were Experienced Air Travel-
      ers at Time of Interview   90

21   Per Cent of Adults at Different Income Levels Who Have
      Ever Taken an Air Trip   92

22   Per Cent of Adults in Different Age Groups Who Ever Have
      Taken an Air Trip   93

23   Per Cent of Business and Non-Business Air Travelers by
      Number of Air Trips Taken, 1962   95

24   Per Cent of Adults With Different Occupations Who
      Traveled by Air During the Survey Year   97

25   Per Cent of Adults With Different Occupations Who
      Traveled by Air During the Survey Year 100

26   Per Cent of Adults in Different Age Groups Who Traveled
      by Air During the Survey Year 101

27   Per Cent of Adults Living in Different Regions Who
      Traveled by Air During the Survey Year 104

28   Per Cent of Adults at Different Income Levels Who Have
      Ever Taken a Rail Trip 124

29   Per Cent of Adults in Different Age Groups Who Ever Have
      Taken a Rail Trip, 1962 126

30   Per Cent of Business and Non-Business Rail Travelers by
      Number of Rail Trips Taken, 1962 129

31   Per Cent of Adults at Different Income Levels Who
      Traveled by Rail During the Survey Year 131

32   Per Cent of Adults With Different Occupations Who Traveled
      by Rail During the Survey Year 133

33   Per Cent of Adults in Different Age Groups Who Traveled
      by Rail During the Survey Year 134

Graph   Page

34   Per Cent of Adults Living in Different Regions Who
          Traveled by Rail During the Survey Year 137

35   Per Cent of Adults at Different Income Levels Who Ever
          Have Taken a Bus Trip 143

36   Per Cent of Adults in Different Age Groups Who Ever
          Have Taken a Bus Trip, 1962 145

37   Per Cent of Adults at Different Income Levels Who
          Traveled by Bus During the Survey Year. 147

38   Per Cent of Adults With Different Occupations Who
          Traveled by Bus During the Survey Year 149

39   Per Cent of Adults in Different Age Groups Who Traveled
          by Bus During the Survey Year 151

40   Per Cent of Adults in Different Regions Who Traveled by
          Bus During the Survey Year 155

A-1   Effect of Income on Frequency of Travel for Adults in
          Different Life Cycle Groups, 1962 167

A-2   Effect of Education on Frequency of Travel for Adults in
          Different Life Cycle Groups, 1962 169

A-3   Effect of Automobile Ownership on Frequency of Travel for
          Adults in Different Life Cycle Groups, 1962 173

A-4   Effect of Living in One of the Twelve Largest Metropolitan
          Areas on Frequency of Travel for Adults in Different Life
          Cycle Groups, 1962 174

TABLE 1

SHARES OF ALL TRIPS BY MODE AND PURPOSE OF TRAVEL, 1955 AND 1962
(Percentage distribution of all trips in the last 12 months)

Mode and Purpose of Trips	1955	1962
Air	6	7
Business	4	4
Non-business	2	3
Rail	7	3
Business	2	1
Non-business	5	2
Bus	5	4
Business	1	1
Non-business	4	3
Auto	82	86
Business	17	21
Non-business	65	65
All modes	100	100
Business	24	27
Non-business	76	73
Number of trips	30,638[a]	24,032
Number of adults	8485	5329

[a] Revised, trips by very frequent travelers are included in the revised
estimate.

TABLE 2

PURPOSE OF MOST RECENT TRIP, 1955
(Weighted percentage distribution of adults
who took a trip in the last 12 months)

Purpose	All Adults Who Took a Trip
Vacation and pleasure travel	64
To visit friends, relatives	25
To attend organized sports events, concert, other special event	2
No further information; other recreation; sightseeing; honeymoon	35
To attend wedding	1
To attend convention (non-business)	1
Business travel	18
For employer (business, government)	8
By self-employed (business or professional man)	7
Convention or meeting	3
Personal affairs	17
Shopping trip	*
Emergency, illness, death, to visit doctor or hospital	7
To and from school	*
Moving to new home	2
Escort or drive someone	3
Other personal affairs	5
Purpose not ascertained	1
Total	100
Number of adults	2510

* Less than one-half of one per cent.

TABLE 3

PEOPLE WHO TRAVEL A LOT, 1962[a]

(Percentage distribution of respondents)

People who travel a lot are:	Per Cent of Respondents
Wealthy, can afford to travel	14
Well-informed	11
Interesting	3
Lucky; happy	28
Restless; nervous	4
Unfortunate; unhappy	2
Crazy; stupid	3
Other (tourists)	23
Don't know, no answer	12
Total	100
Number of respondents	2651

[a] The question was: "People who travel a lot are ... "

TABLE 4

SENTENCE COMPLETIONS ON GOING TO EUROPE, 1958

(Percentage distribution of respondents)

"Mr. and Mrs. Smith went to Europe because:"		"Mr. and Mrs. Brown were offered an expense-free trip to Europe, but they don't want to go because:"	
To go sight-seeing; to travel around	23	Obstacles other than money prevent them	38
To see the World's Fair in Brussels	2	They are in poor health	5
To see historic places	1	They are too old, feeble	3
To see how other people live	2	Someone in the family is sick, old	4
To see Europe, or a particular country in Europe	2	They have children they don't want to leave or take	11
Visit friends, relatives	8	They have family they don't want to leave or take	4
Visit someone in the service; see where their boy fought	1	They have other obligations at home	7
To see where their own ancestors lived	1	They do not have the time	2
		Mr. Brown might lose his job	2
Other people go; the Joneses went	3	They don't want to go	31
They can afford it (want to show they can); they have the money	6	They don't like to leave home for various reasons	20
Have a good time, have a vacation	13	They are afraid of the sea, of flying	7
They like to travel, take long trips	8	It is too far from home	2
		They want to see the U.S. first	2
Travel is broadening, educational, interesting	2	They are crazy, nuts, silly	6
They have never been there	9	Other comments	17
Other comments	14		
Not ascertained	5	Not ascertained	8
Total	100	Total	100
Number of respondents	1456	Number of respondents	1456

TABLE 5

ARE THERE ANY TRIPS THAT YOU HAVE THOUGHT YOU WOULD LIKE TO TAKE
BUT THAT YOU HAVEN'T BEEN ABLE TO?, 1956[a]

(Percentage distribution of respondents)

Attitude toward taking trips	Per Cent of Respondents
Yes, there are trips I would like to take	66
No, there are no trips I would like to take	33
Not ascertained	1
Total	100
Number of respondents	1732

[a] This question was asked in April 1956 only.

TABLE 6

TRIPS PEOPLE WOULD LIKE TO TAKE BY PURPOSE OF TRIP, 1956[a]

(Percentage distribution of respondents)

Purposes of Trips People Would Like to Take	Per Cent of Respondents Who Report Trips They Would Like to Take	Per Cent of Respondents Who Specify Purpose of Trip
Vacation and pleasure	62	99
To visit friends or relatives	22	35
To attend a special event	1	2
Sightseeing, touring	19	30
To visit a resort	1	2
Vacation, no further purpose	19	30
Personal affairs	1	1
Business	*	*
No purpose mentioned	36	*
Not ascertained	1	*
Total	100	100
Number of respondents	1142	710

* Less than one-half of one per cent.

[a] People were asked: "Are there any trips that you have thought you would like to take but that you haven't been able to?" "What sort of trip were you thinking about?"

TABLE 7

SENTENCE COMPLETION ON WHAT PEOPLE WOULD LIKE TO DO
IN EUROPE, 1958

(Percentage distribution of respondents)

"If I Were in Europe the Thing I'd Like Most To Do Is:"	Per Cent of Responders
Go sight-seeing, travel around..................................	<u>25</u>
See something in particular....................................	<u>16</u>
See the World's Fair...	2
See historic places...	2
See a specific sight (Eiffel Tower, museums, cathedrals, etc.)...	6
Go to concerts, festivals, other events (be a spectator at some activity)...	1
See how other people live.....................................	1
Visit friends, relatives......................................	2
See where my own ancestors lived..............................	1
Have a good time, learn a language, attend school, visit someone now in the service, see where my boy fought (died)..............	1
See particular countries (or parts of countries)................	<u>29</u>
France...	10
Italy..	6
Switzerland..	4
Great Britain..	3
Germany..	2
Spain, Austria...	*
Europe in general; other parts of Europe......................	4
Don't know what I'd want to do.................................	<u>3</u>
Return home, hurry back to the good old U.S.A..................	<u>9</u>
Other comments..	<u>9</u>
Not ascertained...	<u>9</u>
Total	100
Number of respondents	1456

* Less than one-half of one per cent.

TABLE 8

SENTENCE COMPLETIONS ON TRAVELING IN THE UNITED STATES
AND IN FOREIGN COUNTRIES, 1958

(Percentage distribution of respondents)

"Traveling in the United States Is:"		"Traveling in Foreign Countries Is:"	
Total positive comments........	81	Total positive comments........	61
Fascinating, interesting.......	11	Fascinating, interesting.......	14
Stimulating, exciting, adventurous....................	2	Stimulating, exciting, adventurous....................	7
Entertaining, fun..............	9	Entertaining, fun..............	5
A new experience, different....	1	A new experience, different....	4
Educational, broadening........	9	Educational, broadening........	13
Cheaper........................	1	Cheaper........................	1
Comfortable, easy, convenient..	4	Comfortable, easy, convenient..	*
Seeing what your homeland is like, best place to travel.....	2	Seeing what your homeland is like, best place to travel.....	*
Wonderful, nice, pleasant, a joy	29	Wonderful, nice, pleasant, a joy	13
Is for me, is what I've done...	1	Other positive comments........	4
The thing to do first..........	1		
OK, all right, good (lukewarm reaction)....................	3	Total negative comments........	29
Other positive comments........	8	Expensive......................	9
		Difficult......................	5
Total negative comments........	13	Tiresome, dull, fatiguing......	1
Expensive......................	6	Dangerous......................	5
Difficult......................	1	Dangerous because of language difficulties..................	1
Tiresome.......................	2	For other people, not for me...	2
Dangerous......................	1	Other negative comments........	6
Other negative comments........	3		
Not ascertained................	6	Not ascertained................	10
Total........................	100	Total........................	100
Number of respondents..........	1456	Number of respondents..........	1456

* Less than one-half of one per cent.

TABLE 9

REASONS WHY PEOPLE DON'T GO ON THE TRIPS
THEY WOULD LIKE TO TAKE, 1958

(Percentage distribution of respondents)

Reason	Per Cent of Respondents Who Report Trips They Would Like to Take
Too expensive	62
Can't leave business or job	18
Lacks time; too busy; refers to activity other than his job	7
Too busy, not clear whether refers to job or other activities	6
Children or other dependents	12
Respondent or other member of family doesn't like to travel	17
Health reasons	4
Our car is too old	2
We are too old	2
Other	7
Total	a
Number of respondents	1142

a Does not add to 100 because some respondents mentioned more than one
reason.

TABLE 10

REASONS FOR NOT ACCEPTING AN EXPENSE-FREE TOUR
OF THE UNITED STATES, 1962[a]
(Percentage distribution of respondents)

Reasons	Per Cent of Respondents
<u>Obstacles to travel other than expense</u>	<u>42</u>
Poor health	8
They are too old	8
They have children whom they don't want either to leave or to take	11
Cannot get away from job	5
Cannot get away for non-job reasons; they have other plans	10
<u>Lack of desire to travel</u>	<u>26</u>
Rather stay home	6
Do not like travel	9
Afraid to go far, not adventurous	3
Crazy, nuts, silly, stupid	8
<u>Other</u>	<u>16</u>
<u>Don't know, no answer, not ascertained</u>	<u>16</u>
Total	100
Number of respondents [b]	1299

[a] The question was: "Mr. and Mrs. Brown were offered an expense-free tour of the United States but they don't want to go because..."

[b] Based on the spring, 1962 wave of interviews.

TABLE 11

SOCIO-ECONOMIC CHARACTERISTICS OF THE POPULATION: AGE, STAGE IN
FAMILY LIFE CYCLE, OCCUPATION, FAMILY INCOME, AND REGION, 1955 AND 1962
(Distribution of adults)

	1955		1962	
Age of adult	Number	Per Cent	Number	Per Cent
18-24	1009	12.0	720	13.6
25-34	1882	22.4	1048	19.7
35-44	1802	21.5	1149	21.6
45-54	1509	18.0	990	18.7
55-64	1188	14.2	708	13.4
65 and over	998	11.9	691	13.0
Total	8388	100.0	5306	100.0
Stage in family life cycle				
Under 45, single	868	10.5	275	10.3
Under 45, married, no children	685	8.3	455	5.8
Married, children	3896	47.3	1248	47.0
45 or over, married, no children	1952	23.7	710	26.7
45 or over, single	837	10.2	270	10.2
Total	8238	100.0	2958	100.0
Occupation of adult				
Professional, technical	476	5.8	405	7.8
Managerial, self-employed	637	7.7	402	7.8
Clerical, sales	787	9.4	507	9.8
Craftsmen, foremen, operatives	1564	18.9	820	15.9
Laborers, service workers	887	10.7	435	8.4
Farmers, farm managers	320	3.9	109	2.1
Housewives, retired, students	3606	43.6	2489	48.2
Total	8277	100.0	5167	100.0

(Continued on next page)

Table 11

SOCIO-ECONOMIC CHARACTERISTICS OF THE POPULATION: AGE, STAGE IN
FAMILY LIVE CYCLE, OCCUPATION, FAMILY INCOME, AND REGION, 1955 AND 1962 continued

	1955		1962	
Family income	Number	Per Cent	Number	Per Cent
Under $2000	1271	15.4	573	11.2
$2000-2999	981	11.9	407	8.0
$3000-3999	1364	16.5	438	8.6
$4000-4999	1294	15.7	566	11.1
$5000-5999	1094	13.2	662	13.0
$6000-7499	896	10.9	800	15.7
$7500-9999	709	8.6	764	15.0
$10,000-14,999	389	4.7	600	11.8
$15,000 or over	257	3.1	284	5.6
Total	8255	100.0	5094	100.0
Region [a]				
Northeast	2339	27.6	1182	22.2
North Central	2689	31.7	1549	29.1
South	2300	27.1	1796	33.7
West	1156	13.6	801	15.0
Total	8484	100.0	5328	100.0

[a] For the definition of the different regions see Table 15.

TABLE 12

FREQUENCY OF TRAVEL BY ALL MODES BY FAMILY INCOME, 1955 AND 1962
(Percentage distribution of adults)

Family Income

Number of trips	All Adults 1955	All Adults 1962	Under $2000 1955	Under $2000 1962	$2000-2999 1955	$2000-2999 1962	$3000-3999 1955	$3000-3999 1962	$4000-4999 1955	$4000-4999 1962
No trips	39	34	63	55	52	49	44	44	38	43
1 trip	21	18	17	19	21	17	23	19	24	19
2 - 4 trips	22	23	14	16	17	18	20	22	22	21
5 - 15 trips	14	19	5	8	8	13	12	12	13	13
16 or more trips	4	6	1	2	2	3	1	3	3	4
Total	100	100	100	100	100	100	100	100	100	100
Number of adults	8485	5329	1255	573	967	407	1366	438	1290	566

Number of trips	$5000-5999 1955	$5000-5999 1962	$6000-7499 1955	$6000-7499 1962	$7500-9999 1955	$7500-9999 1962	$10,000-14,999 1955	$10,000-14,999 1962	$15,000 or More 1955	$15,000 or More 1962
No trips	29	32	28	27	22	23	20	19	14	14
1 trip	23	20	21	20	18	17	16	14	15	8
2 - 4 trips	24	27	29	25	29	27	25	24	27	30
5 - 15 trips	17	16	18	20	23	26	28	31	29	32
16 or more trips	7	5	4	8	8	7	11	12	15	16
Total	100	100	100	100	100	100	100	100	100	100
Number of adults	1084	662	908	800	706	764	389	600	259	284

TABLE 13

FREQUENCY OF TRAVEL BY ALL MODES LAST YEAR BY AGE OF ADULT, 1955 AND 1962

(Percentage distribution of adults)

Number of trips	All Adults		18 - 24		25 - 34		35 - 44		45 - 54		55 - 64		65 +	
	1955	1962	1955	1962	1955	1962	1955	1962	1955	1962	1955	1962	1955	1962
No trips	39	34	34	34	34	31	34	26	40	32	44	36	59	51
1 trip	21	18	22	17	21	17	22	19	20	17	21	18	20	17
2 - 4 trips	22	23	26	24	23	24	24	26	19	24	22	23	14	18
5 - 15 trips	14	19	13	19	17	21	16	20	16	20	10	17	6	13
16 or more trips	4	6	5	6	5	7	4	9	5	7	3	6	1	1
Total	100	100	100	100	100	100	100	100	100	100	100	100	100	100
Number of adults	8485	5329	1005	720	1895	1048	1789	1149	1502	990	1175	708	981	691

TABLE 14

FREQUENCY OF TRAVEL BY SEX OF ADULT, 1955 AND 1962

(Percentage distribution of adults)

| Number of trips | All Adults | | Sex of Adult | | | |
| | | | Male | | Female | |
	1955	1962	1955	1962	1955	1962
No trips	39	34	37	33	42	35
1 trip	21	18	20	16	21	19
2 - 4 trips	22	23	22	22	22	25
5 - 15 trips	14	19	15	20	12	17
16 or more trips	4	6	6	9	3	4
Total	100	100	100	100	100	100
Number of adults	8485	5329	3921	2516	4523	2808

TABLE 15

FREQUENCY OF TRAVEL BY REGION, 1955 AND 1962
(Percentage distribution of adults)

| Number of trips | All Adults | | Region [a] | | | | | | | |
| | | | Northeast | | North Central | | South | | West | |
	1955	1962	1955	1962	1955	1962	1955	1962	1955	1962
No trips	39	34	48	39	36	32	41	34	29	31
1 trip	21	18	20	18	22	18	18	18	24	15
2 - 4 trips	22	23	18	23	23	25	21	22	26	24
5 - 15 trips	14	19	11	16	15	18	15	20	17	21
16 or more trips	4	6	3	4	4	7	5	6	4	9
Total	100	100	100	100	100	100	100	100	100	100
Number of adults	8485	5328	2342	1182	2670	1549	2295	1796	1150	801

[a] The regions are defined as follows:

Northeast: Conn., Dela., Me., Mass., N.H., N.J., N.Y., Penna., R.I., Vt.
North Central: Ill., Ind., Ia., Kans., Mich., Minn., Mo., Nebr., N.D., Ohio, S.D., Wis.
South: Ala., Ark., D.C., Fla., Ga., Ky., La., Md., Miss., N.C., Okla., S.C., Tenn., Tex.,
Va., W.Va.
West: Ariz., Calif., Colo., Idaho, Mont., Nev., N.M., Ore., Utah, Wash., Wyo.

TABLE 16

FREQUENCY OF TRAVEL BY WHETHER NOW LIVING IN THE NEW YORK AREA, 1955 AND 1962
(Percentage distribution of adults)

Number of trips	All Adults		New York Metropolitan Area		Megalopolis (Excluding N.Y. Metro Area)		Remainder of Country	
	1955	1962	1955	1962	1955	1962	1955	1962
No trips	39	34	50	46	48	33	38	33
1 trip	21	18	18	15	19	18	21	18
2 - 4 trips	22	23	17	22	21	24	22	23
5 - 15 trips	14	19	11	12	9	21	15	19
16 or more trips	4	6	4	5	3	4	4	7
Total	100	100	100	100	100	100	100	100
Number of adults	8485	5329	705	380	1169	552	6583	4397

TABLE 17

FREQUENCY OF TRAVEL WITHIN THE NEW YORK METRO AREA, 1962
(Percentage distribution of adults
in the New York Metro area)

Number of trips	Entire Metro Area	New York Metro Area						
		Bronx	Queens	Brooklyn	Manhattan	Jersey City, Newark	New York Suburbs	New Jersey Suburbs
No trips	46	58	50	69	47	70	40	29
1 trip	16	7	21	24	16	10	17	11
2 - 4 trips	22	14	29	5	10	20	22	34
5 - 15 trips	12	*	*	2	21	*	18	18
16 or more trips	4	21	*	*	4	*	*	8
Not ascertained	*	*	*	*	2	*	3	*
Total	100	100	100	100	100	100	100	100
Number of adults	380	29	56	42	49	20	74	110

*Less than one - half of one per cent.

TABLE 18

TOTAL NUMBER OF TRIPS TAKEN IN LAST 12 MONTHS, 1962

(Percentage distribution of trips and travelers)

Number of trips taken	Per Cent of Travelers	Per Cent of Trips
1	27	4
2	15	5
3	12	5
4	8	5
5-9	18	17
10-19	12	22
20-29	4	12
30-39	2	8
40 and over	2	22
Total	100	100
Number of travelers	3526	
Number of trips		23,838

TABLE 19

SOCIO-ECONOMIC CHARACTERISTICS OF FREQUENT TRAVELERS, 1962[a]

(Percentage distribution of frequent travelers)

	Per Cent of Adults Who Are Frequent Travelers
Family income	
Under $2000	3
$2000-2999	4
$3000-3999	4
$4000-4999	7
$5000-5999	10
$6000-7499	20
$7500-9999	16
$10,000-14,999	22
$15,000 or more	14
Education of adult	
None; grade school	8
Some high school	7
Some high school plus non-academic	5
Completed high school	21
Completed high school plus non-academic	12
Some college	23
Have college degree	24
Age of adult	
18-24	13
25-34	23
35-44	30
45-54	20
55-64	12
65 and over	2
Size of Place of Residence	
Twelve largest metropolitan areas	
Central cities	5
Suburbs 50,000 and over	4
Suburbs 2500-49,999 and other urban	11
All other suburbs	*

(continued on next page)

TABLE 19 continued   SOCIO-ECONOMIC CHARACTERISTICS OF FREQUENT TRAVELERS, 1962

	Per Cent of Adults Who Are Frequent Travelers
Other areas	
Cities 50,000 and over	28
Other urban parts of metro areas	16
Places 2500-49,999 not in metro areas	12
Places under 2500 not in metro areas	4
Rural parts of metro areas	3
Other rural areas	17
Region [b]	
Northeast	14
North Central	33
South	32
West	21
Number of adults	336

* Less than one-half of one per cent.

[a] Frequent travelers are those adults who took 16 or more trips in the survey year.

[b] For the definition of different regions see Table 15.

TABLE 20

THE IMPORTANCE OF CALL-BACKS IN DETERMINING AIR TRAVEL EXPERIENCE, 1960[a]

(Percentage distribution of adults)

Air travel experience	All Adults	Number of Calls Made by Interviewer Before Interview Was Taken							
		One	Two	Three	Four	Five	Six	Seven or More	Not Recorded
Have taken an air trip	29	25	27	35	36	39	35	32	24
Have never taken an air trip	71	75	73	65	64	61	65	68	76
Total	100	100	100	100	100	100	100	100	100
Number of adults	5520	1897	1748	840	535	240	103	71	86

[a] This table is based on data from the 1960 Survey of Consumer Finances.

TABLE 21

EXPERIENCE WITH VACATION TRAVEL TO A PLACE 100 MILES AWAY, 1958
(Percentage distribution of respondents)

Experience with vacation travel	All Respondents	Family Income			
		Under $3000	$3000-4999	$5000-7499	$7500 and Over
Have taken a vacation trip	77	60	74	88	93
Never have taken a vacation trip	23	40	25	12	7
Not ascertained	*	*	1	*	*
Total	100	100	100	100	100
Number of respondents	1456	384	376	350	288

* Less than one-half of one per cent.

a The question was: "Have you ever taken a vacation trip to a place 100 miles or more away?"

TABLE 22

AMOUNT SPENT ON VACATION TRIPS BY INCOME IN 1961[a]

(Percentage distribution of spending units)

Amount spent on vacation trips in 1961	All Spending Units	Under $1000	$1000 -1999	$2000 -2999	$3000 -3999	$4000 -4999	$5000 -5999	$6000 -7499	$7500 -9999	$10,000 -14,999	$15,000 or more
Zero or under $100	73	95	93	86	86	75	81	70	52	41	23
$100 - 199	9	1	4	6	9	10	7	13	17	11	3
$200 - 299	5	1	1	3	3	7	3	7	12	8	8
$300 - 399	6	1	1	1	1	3	5	4	8	23	14
$400 - 499	2	1	*	*	*	2	1	2	4	3	9
$500 - 749	3	1	1	2	*	1	2	4	5	7	10
$750 - 999	*	*	*	*	*	*	*	*	*	2	4
$1000 or more	2	*	*	2	1	1	1	*	2	4	29
Amount not ascertained	*	*	*	*	*	1	1	*	*	1	*
Total	100	100	100	100	100	100	100	100	100	100	100

* Less than one-half of one per cent.

a This table is taken from 1962 Survey of Consumer Finances, p. 150.

TABLE 23

MEAN EXPENDITURE ON VACATION TRIPS BY INCOME IN 1961[a]

(Percentage distribution of spending units)

Income in 1961	All Spending Units	
	Per Cent	Mean Expenditure
Under $3000	28	$ 30
$3000 - 4999	21	60
$5000 - 7499	26	70
$7500 - 9999	12	150
$10,000 - 14,999	9	260
$15,000 or more	4	610
Total	100	
Grand mean		$100

[a] This table is taken from 1962 Survey of Consumer Finances, p. 152.

TABLE 24

NUMBER OF VACATION TRIPS TAKEN BY INCOME IN 1961[a]

(Percentage distribution of spending units)

Income in 1961	Total	None	One	Two	Three	Four or More
				Number of Vacation Trips		
All	100	73	20	5	1	1
Under $3000	100	91	6	2	1	*
$3000 - 4999	100	80	16	3	1	*
$5000 - 7499	100	75	20	3	1	1
$7500 - 9999	100	51	39	8	1	1
$10,000 - 14,999	100	41	35	15	6	3
$15,000 or more	100	24	41	17	6	12
Number of spending units	2117					

* Less than one-half of one per cent.

[a] This table is taken from 1962 Survey of Consumer Finances, p. 154.

TABLE 25

OVERSEAS TRAVEL BY FAMILY INCOME, 1959-1960

(Percentage distribution of adults)

Overseas travel	All Adults	Family Income					
		Under $3000	$3000 -4999	$5000 -7499	$7500 -9999	$10,000 -14,999	$15,000 and Over
Took an overseas trip	1	*	*	1	1	2	8
Did not take an overseas trip[a]	99	100	100	99	99	98	92
Total	100	100	100	100	100	100	100
Number of adults	8329	1773	1732	2309	1093	919	399

* Less than one-half of one per cent.

[a] Includes a few adults for whom it was not ascertained whether they took an overseas trip.

TABLE 26

EXPERIENCE WITH OVERSEAS TRAVEL BY STAGE IN THE FAMILY LIFE CYCLE, 1959-1960

(Percentage distribution of adults)

Overseas travel	All Adults	Stage in the Family Life Cycle					
		Young, Single	Young, Married, No Children	Young, Married, Children	Older, Married, Children	Older, Married, No Children	Older, Single
Took an overseas trip	1	1	2	*	1	2	1
Did not take an overseas trip[a]	99	99	98	100	99	98	99
Total	100	100	100	100	100	100	100
Number of adults	8329	870	528	2396	1653	1788	918

* Less than one-half of one per cent.

[a] Includes a few adults for whom it was not ascertained whether they took an overseas trip.

TABLE 27

OVERSEAS TRAVEL BY PRIOR EXPERIENCE WITH OVERSEAS TRAVEL,
1959-1960

(Percentage distribution of adults)

| Overseas travel | All Adults | Prior Experience with Overseas Travel | |
		Had Taken an Overseas Trip	Had Not Taken an Overseas Trip
Took an overseas trip	1	12	*
Did not take an overseas trip[a]	99	88	100
Total	100	100	100
Number of adults	8329	487	7848

* Less than one-half of one per cent.

[a] Includes a few adults for whom it was not ascertained whether they took an overseas trip.

TABLE 28

OVERSEAS TRAVEL HISTORY BY AGE, 1959-1960

(Percentage distribution of adults)

| Whether have ever taken an overseas trip | All Adults | Age of Adult | | | | | |
		18-24	25-34	35-44	45-54	55-64	65 and Over
Have taken an overseas trip	6	2	6	5	7	9	7
Have never taken an overseas trip	94	98	94	95	93	91	93
Total	100	100	100	100	100	100	100
Number of adults	8329	969	1767	1837	1636	1030	1037

* Less than one-half of one per cent.

TABLE 29

THE PROPORTION TAKING TRIPS BY AIR, RAIL, BUS AND AUTO, 1955 AND 1962

(Percentage distribution of adults)

Use of Mode	Auto		Air		Rail		Bus	
	1955	1962	1955	1962	1955	1962	1955	1962
Took one or more trips last year	55	64	7	11	10	7	7	9
For business reasons	2	3	2	3	2	1	1	1
For non-business reasons	48	54	5	7	8	6	6	8
For both business and non-business reasons	5	7	*	1	*	*	*	*
Did not take a trip last year by this mode	45	36	93	89	90	93	93	91
Total	100	100	100	100	100	100	100	100
Number of adults	8485	5329	8485	5329	8485	5329	8485	5329

* Less than one-half of one per cent.

TABLE 30

FREQUENCY OF TRAVEL BY EACH MODE FOR BUSINESS AND NON-BUSINESS REASONS, 1955 AND 1962

(Percentage distribution of adults who took trip)

Non-Business Trips

Number of trips	Mode Used							
	Auto		Air		Rail		Bus	
	1955	1962	1955	1962	1955	1962	1955	1962
1	36	32	69	69	71	72	70	68
2	19	16	17	16	17	16	18	14
3	11	13	5	6	7	5	3	6
4	8	8	5	4	3	2	2	5
5 or more	26	31	4	5	2	5	7	7
Total	100	100	100	100	100	100	100	100
Number of adults	2325	3250	209	397	376	336	275	428

Business Trips

Number of trips	Mode Used							
	Auto		Air		Rail		Bus	
	1955	1962	1955	1962	1955	1962	1955	1962
1	28	32	38	40	53	63	59	68
2	18	15	19	17	19	13	12	16
3	8	9	8	10	8	8	8	9
4	8	5	9	7	4	4	2	*
5 or more	38	39	26	26	16	12	19	7
Total	100	100	100	100	100	100	100	100
Number of adults	289	569	99	215	81	77	44	47

* Less than one-half of one per cent.

TABLE 31

PER CENT OF PASSENGER MILES ACCOUNTED FOR
BY EACH MODE OF TRAVEL BY DISTANCE TO DESTINATION

(Weighted percentage distribution of passenger miles: 1955, 1956, and 1957 data combined)

Mode used	Airline Distance to Destination (miles) [a]						
	100-199	200-299	300-499	500-699	700-999	1000-1499	1500 and Over
Air	1	4	9	10	16	18	38
Rail	3	4	7	9	10	7	14
Bus	3	3	2	4	4	4	6
Auto	93	89	82	77	70	71	42
Total	100	100	100	100	100	100	100
Per cent of all passenger miles	27.4	14.4	14.6	10.8	9.2	12.9	10.8

[a] This table is based on data for automobile travel for 1955 and common carrier travel from the 1955, 1956, and 1957 surveys. The basic data consisted of information on the most recent trip by common carrier in 1955-1957 and the most recent trip by auto in 1955. Only trips within twelve months of the survey are considered. Each trip was weighted by the total number of trips by the adult involved in the year in which he took that trip. The overall relative frequency of travel by auto and by common carrier was estimated at 81 per cent auto and 19 per cent for common carrier on the basis of the 1955 survey. Estimates of distance refer to airline distance to the farthest point reached. Trips outside continental North America are excluded.

TABLE 32

ADVANTAGES AND DISADVANTAGES OF AUTOMOBILE TRAVEL, 1955
(Percentage distribution of advantages and disadvantages)[a]

Advantages of auto	Per Cent of All Advantages and Disadvantages of Auto
"More of us could go"; "free ride at someone else's expense"; chose auto for reasons of companionship	7
Cheaper	24
Faster	5
No schedule; one can time one's trip as one pleases (can start and stop when one wishes); can choose one's own route	19
Easier with children (babies) or with old (sick) people	4
Car is available upon arrival	5
Car goes door-to-door, avoid changing modes or going to and from terminals; personal belongings more easily carried	5
Enjoy the scenery	7
No good connections by other modes; "only way you could get there"; car is better for short distances	5
Convenient	11
Disadvantages of auto	
Fatigue ("it's hard to drive so far"); doesn't like to drive; can't drive; didn't have car; roads may be bad (ice, snow, construction)	1
Other advantages and disadvantages of auto	7
Total	100
Number of respondents who discussed auto	1044

[a] The question was: "How did you happen to choose this way of traveling instead of some other?"

TABLE 33

ADVANTAGES AND DISADVANTAGES OF DIFFERENT MODES FOR
RESPONDENT'S MOST RECENT TRIP BY COMMON CARRIER, 1957[a]

(Percentage distribution of selected advantages and disadvantages)

Factors Influencing Choice of Mode	All Modes	Air	Rail	Bus	Auto
Availability	10.4	1.0	3.8	3.0	2.6
Mentioned as available (goes right to destination)	5.0	0.1	1.4	2.7	0.8
Mentioned as not available (does not own a car; does not go to right place)	5.4	0.9	2.4	0.3	1.8
Convenience of arrival and departure	20.3	5.6	8.0	6.1	0.6
Convenient times of day	3.0	0.2	0.8	1.7	0.3
Inconvenient times of day	1.6	0.3	1.0	0.3	*
Actual time of arrival is uncertain (may be delayed by bad weather)	1.7	1.7	*	*	*
Terminals conveniently located	2.7	*	2.1	0.5	0.1
Terminals inconveniently located	1.9	1.3	0.3	0.3	*
"Convenient" ("good connections") (no further information)	8.7	1.7	3.5	3.3	0.2
"Inconvenient" ("bad connections") (no further information)	0.7	0.4	0.3	*	*
Price	15.6	4.5	3.2	7.0	0.9
Inexpensive, cheap	13.0	2.9	2.5	7.0	0.6
Expensive	2.6	1.6	0.7	*	0.3
Speed	26.7	16.5	5.3	4.2	0.7
Fast, faster	21.7	16.5	3.3	1.8	0.1
Slow, slower	5.0	*	2.0	2.4	0.6
Safety	5.2	3.1	1.5	0.3	0.3
Safe, safer	2.5	0.7	1.5	0.3	*
Unsafe, people are afraid	2.7	2.4	*	*	0.3
Comfort	17.2	3.6	9.0	2.0	2.6
Comfortable (restful, easy with children, good meals)	11.7	3.6	8.1	*	*
Not comfortable (rough, noisy, tiring)	5.5	*	0.9	2.0	2.6
Varied experience	4.6	0.8	1.5	2.2	0.1
Interesting (scenery, new people, new way to travel)	4.6	0.8	1.5	2.2	0.1
Uninteresting	*	*	*	*	*
Total	100.0	35.1	32.3	24.8	7.8
Number of respondents	707	220	220	179	88

*Less than one-half of one per cent.

[a]The question was: "How did you happen to choose this way of traveling instead of some other?"

TABLE 34

COULD YOU HAVE GOTTEN WHERE YOU WANTED TO GO CONVENIENTLY BY OTHER MODES ON MOST RECENT TRIP, 1962[a]

(Percentage distribution of most recent trips)

Convenience of alternative modes	Most Recent Trip							
	Auto		Air		Rail		Bus	
	Business	Non-Business	Business	Non-Business	Business	Non-Business	Business	Non-Business
Could have reached destination conveniently by air	45	40	-	-	64	60	52	47
Could not have reached destination conveniently by air	54	57			29	38	48	46
Not ascertained	1	3			7	2	*	7
Total	100	100			100	100	100	100
Could have reached destination conveniently by rail	45	44	60	56	-	-	45	55
Could not have reached destination conveniently by rail	53	53	37	38			52	37
Not ascertained	2	3	3	6			3	8
Total	100	100	100	100			100	100

TABLE 34 continued – COULD YOU HAVE GOTTEN WHERE YOU WANTED TO GO CONVENIENTLY
BY OTHER MODES ON MOST RECENT TRIP?

Convenience of alternative modes	Most Recent Trip							
	Auto		Air		Rail		Bus	
	Business	Non-Business	Business	Non-Business	Business	Non-Business	Business	Non-business
Could have reached destination conveniently by bus	65	65	60	58	71	79	–	–
Could not have reached destination conveniently by bus	33	32	35	35	29	18		
Not ascertained	2	3	5	7	*	3		
Total	100	100	100	100	100	100		
Number of trips	266	1555	169	168	24	111	31	175

* Less than one-half of one per cent.

a The question was: "Could you have gotten where you wanted to go conveniently: by air? by rail? by bus?

TABLE 35

BEST WAY TO TRAVEL BY FREQUENCY OF TRAVEL LAST YEAR, 1962[a]

(Percentage distribution of respondents)

Best way to travel	All Respondents	Number of Trips in Last Year				
		No Trips	1 Trip	2-4 Trips	5-15 Trips	16 or More Trips
Air	28	20	26	30	35	43
Rail	14	20	11	13	9	8
Bus	5	9	6	3	2	1
Ship	1	2	2	*	1	2
Auto	40	35	44	44	42	35
Other	2	5	3	2	1	3
Don't know, not ascertained	10	9	8	8	10	8
Total	100	100	100	100	100	100
Number of respondents	2651	783	473	625	525	182

* Less than one-half of one per cent.

[a] The question was: "The best way to travel is . . ."

TABLE 36

ATTITUDES TOWARD LONG-DISTANCE AUTO TRIPS, 1960
(Percentage distribution of respondents who have ever taken an
auto trip to a place 500 miles or more away)

Attitudes toward long auto trips	Per Cent of All Long-Distance Auto Travelers
Likes long auto trips	47
Qualified liking for long auto trips	15
Uncertain; depends	5
Qualified disliking for long auto trips	4
Dislikes long auto trips	23
Not ascertained	6
Total	100
Number of respondents	878

TABLE 37

SENTENCE COMPLETIONS ON AUTOMOBILE TRIPS, 1958 AND 1962
(Percentage distribution of respondents)

Auto Trips Are:	1958	1962
Positive, enthusiastic	58	59
Fascinating, educational, interesting	2	4
Exciting, adventurous, stimulating	1	*
Fun, entertaining	7	10
Convenient, easy	3	1
Comfortable, relaxing	2	1
Nice, pleasant	26	31
All right, o.k.	4	5
Cheap, practical	2	1
Fast, quick	*	*
Other positive comments	11	6
Negative comments	39	37
Dull, boring, tiresome	20	16
Dangerous	6	4
Expensive	6	10
Other negative comments	7	7
Other (don't know, no answer)	3	4
Total	100	100
Number of respondents	1456	2651

* Less than one-half of one per cent.

TABLE 38

PREFERRED MODE OF TRAVEL IF COST HAD BEEN THE SAME, 1962[a]

(Percentage distribution of most recent trips)

Preferred mode	Most Recent Trip by Auto	Most Recent Trip by Common Carrier		
		Air	Rail	Bus
Air	14	93	24	1⁷
Rail	3	*	63	8
Bus	2	*	1	55
Auto	80	3	11	16
Not ascertained	1	4	1	4
Total	100	100	100	100
Number of trips	1821	337	135	206

* Less than one-half of one per cent.

[a] The question was: "If the cost had been the same no matter how you went, what kind of transportation would you have taken on this trip?"

TABLE 39

MODES SPONTANEOUSLY MENTIONED BY ADULTS IN DISCUSSING THEIR
CHOICE OF MODE FOR THEIR MOST RECENT TRIP, 1956[a]

(Percentage distribution of most recent trips)

| Mode | Modes Spontaneously Mentioned, But Not Used | | | |
	Air	Rail	Bus	Auto[b]
Air		37	15	19
Rail	82		85	53
Bus	18	63	___	28
Total	100	100	100	100
Number of trips	136	106	86	139

[a] The question was: "How did you happen to choose this way of traveling instead of some other?"

[b] Respondents in this column mentioned auto but used a common carrier.

TABLE 40

USE OF AIR, RAIL, BUS, AUTO, AND MIXED MODES ON MOST
RECENT BUSINESS AND NON-BUSINESS TRIPS BY DISTANCE, 1962
(Percentage distribution of trips by purpose and distance)

Mode used	Business			Non-Business		
	100-499 Miles	500-999 Miles	1000 Miles and Over	100-499 Miles	500-999 Miles	1000 Miles and Over
Air	21	42	67	3	15	30
Rail	5	8	2	4	5	11
Bus	9	4	1	9	9	6
Auto	62	42	26	81	65	45
Two or more modes	3	4	4	3	6	8
Total	100	100	100	100	100	100
Number of trips	302	91	93	1459	239	291

TABLE 41

DETERMINANTS OF CHOICE OF MODE ON MOST RECENT TRIP, 1955

(Percentage distribution of most recent trips)

Family Income
Distance of Trip
Number of Companions

Mode used	All Incomes				Under $3000				$3000-5999			
	Under 500 Miles		Over 500 Miles		Under 500 Miles		Over 500 Miles		Under 500 Miles		Over 500 Miles	
	Alone	Not Alone	Alone	Not Alone	Alone	Not Alone	Alone	Not Alone	Alone	Not Alone	Alone	Not Alone
Air	6	1	30	13	*	1	a	5	5	1	30	8
Rail	20	4	28	15	20	5	a	18	20	4	22	15
Bus	19	4	17	5	40	8	a	8	11	4	15	7
Auto	55	91	25	67	40	86	a	69	64	91	33	70
Total	100	100	100	100	100	100	a	100	100	100	100	100
Number of trips	301	1726	103	404	101	37	34	61	125	863	40	165

Mode used	$6000-9999				$10,000 and Over			
	Under 500 Miles		Over 500 Miles		Under 500 Miles		Over 500 Miles	
	Alone	Not Alone	Alone	Not Alone	Alone	Not Alone	Alone	Not Alone
Air	11	1	a	14	a	2	a	31
Rail	17	4	a	13	a	5	a	17
Bus	9	2	a	2	a	1	a	*
Auto	63	93	a	71	a	92	a	52
Total	100	100	a	100	a	100	a	100
Number of trips	46	378	19	108	29	114	10	70

* Less than one-half of one per cent.

a Columns totaling less than 40 trips were not percentagized.

TABLE 42

DETERMINANTS OF CHOICE OF MODE FOR VACATION AND PLEASURE TRIPS ONLY, 1956

(Percentage distribution of most recent trips by common carrier)

Mode used	All Distances	100-499 Mile Trip					500-999 Mile Trip					1000 Mile Trip or More				
		Under $3000	$3000 -5999	$6000 -9999	$10,000 & Over	All Incomes	Under $3000	$3000 -5999	$6000 -9999	$10,000 & Over	All Incomes	Under $3000	$3000 -5999	$6000 -9999	$10,000 & Over	All Incomes
Air	31	1	.14	25	61	17	11	31	53	a	35	42	48	75	86	62
Rail	46	41	50	46	39	46	50	50	37	a	43	67	48	34	24	45
Bus	32	63	43	31	4	42	43	19	10	a	24	33	8	3	9	14
Auto[b]	9	7	11	12	13	10	4	3	10	a	5	12	4	6	24	10
N.A.	2	*	1	*	4	1	*	*	*	a	*	12	*	*	9	1
Total[c]	120	112	119	114	121	116	108	103	110	a	107	166	108	118	152	132
Number of trips 459		70	97	52	23	252	28	32	19	11	96	24	25	32	21	106

Family Income — Distance of Trip

* Less than one-half of one per cent.

a Too few cases to be percentagized.

b Auto may be used in addition to common carrier.

c The total does not add to 100 because when several modes were used on the same trip each mode was counted.

TABLE 43

TOTAL NUMBER OF PEOPLE WHO WENT ON MOST RECENT LONG DISTANCE TRIP
BY AIR OR AUTO, 1962

(Percentage distribution of most recent non-business
trips of 500 miles or more by air or auto)

Mode used	All Trips	Total Number of People				
		One	Two	Three	Four	Five or More
Air	28	71	22	8	*	11
Auto	72	29	78	92	100	89
Total	100	100	100	100	100	100
Number of trips	427	105	130	71	53	46

* Less than one-half of one per cent.

TABLE 44

USE OF AIR, RAIL, BUS, AUTO, AND MIXED MODES ON MOST RECENT
NON-BUSINESS TRIPS BY DISTANCE AND WHETHER TRAVELED ALONE, 1962
(Percentage distribution of most recent non-business trips)

Mode used	Distance					
	100-499 Miles		500-999 Miles		1000 Miles or More	
	Went Alone	Not Alone	Went Alone	Not Alone	Went Alone	Not Alone
Air	12	1	36	6	51	18
Rail	11	3	14	2	15	8
Bus	30	5	20	5	10	4
Auto	41	89	24	81	10	66
Two or more modes	6	2	6	6	14	4
Total	100	100	100	100	100	100
Number of trips	239	1198	70	162	99	182

TABLE 45

SELECTION OF MODE ON LONG DISTANCE AIR AND AUTO TRIPS BY EXPERIENCE AS
AN AIR TRAVELER, 1962

(Percentage distribution of most recent non-business trips of 500 miles
or more by air or auto)

Mode used	All Trips	Prior Experience as an Air Traveler	
		Have Taken an Air Trip	Have Not Taken an Air Trip[a]
Air	28	39	19
Auto	72	61	81
Total	100	100	100
Number of trips	427	199	224

[a] This column includes both people who were not experienced and people whose
experience was not ascertained. If only those who in fact never had taken
an air trip were included, the proportion who went by air would be lower than
is shown.

TABLE 46

PREFERRED MODE IF COST HAD BEEN THE SAME, 1962[a]

(Percentage distribution of most recent non-business
trips of 500 miles or more by air or auto)

| Mode used | All Trips | Preferred Mode | | | |
		Air	Rail	Bus	Auto
Air	28	59	b	b	4
Auto	72	41	b	b	96
Total	100	100	b	b	100
Number of trips	427	163	9	6	229

[a] The question was: "If the cost had been the same no matter how you went, what kind of transportation would you have taken on this trip?"

[b] Too few cases to percentagize.

TABLE 47

EXPERIENCE AS AN AUTO TRAVELER BY FAMILY INCOME, 1955 AND 1962
(Percentage distribution of adults)

Experience as an auto traveler	All Adults		Family Income							
			Under $4000		$4000-5999		$6000-9999		$10,000 and Over	
	1955	1962	1955	1962	1955	1962	1955	1962	1955	1962
Have taken an auto trip	87	90	81	81	92	91	93	95	94	95
Have never taken an auto trip	11	9	17	17	7	8	5	4	3	4
Not ascertained	2	1	2	2	1	1	2	1	3	1
Total	100	100	100	100	100	100	100	100	100	100
Number of adults	8485	5329	3616	1417	2388	1228	1605	1564	646	884

TABLE 48

EXPERIENCE AS AN AUTO TRAVELER BY AGE, 1962
(Percentage distribution of adults)

| Experience as an auto traveler | All Adults | Age of Adult | | | | | |
		18-24	25-34	35-44	45-54	55-64	65 and Over
Have taken an auto trip	90	85	93	93	92	90	84
Have never taken an auto trip	9	10	6	7	8	9	14
Not ascertained	1	5	1	*	*	1	2
Total	100	100	100	100	100	100	100
Number of adults	5329	720	1048	1149	990	708	690

* Less than one-half of one per cent.

TABLE 49

NUMBER OF BUSINESS AND NON-BUSINESS AUTO TRIPS, 1962

(Percentage distribution of trips and travelers)

Number of auto trips taken	Business		Non-Business	
	Per Cent of Travelers 1962	Per Cent of Trips 1962	Per Cent of Travelers 1962	Per Cent of Trips 1962
1	32	4	32	7
2	15	3	16	6
3	9	3	13	8
4	5	2	8	6
5 - 9	15	10	16	20
10 - 19	11	15	10	23
20 - 29	5	12	3	12
30 - 39	2	7	1	6
40 and over	6	44	1	12
Total	100	100	100	100
Number of travelers	541		3146	
Number of trips		4922		15,736

TABLE 50

USE OF AUTO BY FAMILY INCOME, 1955 AND 1962
(Percentage distribution of adults)

| | All Adults | | Family Income | | | | | | | |
| | | | Under $2000 | | $2000-2999 | | $3000-3999 | | $4000-4999 | |
Use of Auto	1955	1962	1955	1962	1955	1962	1955	1962	1955	1962
Took one or more auto trips last year	55	64	31	40	42	46	51	55	56	57
For business reasons	2	3	2	2	2	2	1	5	2	3
For non-business reasons	48	54	27	35	38	41	46	46	51	49
For both business and non-business reasons	5	7	2	3	2	3	4	4	3	5
Did not take an auto trip last year	45	36	69	60	58	54	49	45	44	43
Total	100	100	100	100	100	100	100	100	100	100
Number of adults	8485	5329	1271	573	981	407	1364	438	1294	566

| | Family Income | | | | | | | | | |
| | $5000-5999 | | $6000-7499 | | $7500-9999 | | $10,000-14,999 | | $15,000 or Over | |
Use of Auto	1955	1962	1955	1962	1955	1962	1955	1962	1955	1962
Took one or more auto trips last year	68	66	66	72	73	74	70	79	75	87
For business reasons	2	3	3	3	1	3	2	4	5	5
For non-business reasons	59	55	59	61	63	62	57	65	58	67
For both business and non-business reasons	7	8	4	8	9	9	11	10	12	15
Did not take an auto trip last year	32	34	34	28	27	26	30	21	25	13
Total	100	100	100	100	100	100	100	100	100	100
Number of adults	1094	662	896	800	709	764	389	600	257	284

TABLE 51

PER CENT OF ALL AUTO TRIPS TAKEN BY ADULTS
IN SPECIFIED INCOME GROUPS, 1955 AND 1962
(Percentage distribution of trips and adults)

Family Income	1955		1962	
	Per Cent of Adults	Per Cent of Trips	Per Cent of Adults	Per Cent of Trips
Under $4000	44	24	28	13
$4000 - 5999	29	34	24	19
$6000 - 9999	19	28	31	39
$10,000 and over	8	14	17	29
Total	100	100	100	100
Number of trips		21,126		20,177
Number of adults	8231		5093	

TABLE 52

USE OF AUTO BY OCCUPATION OF ADULT, 1955 AND 1962
(Percentage distribution of adults)

Use of Auto	All Adults		Occupation of Adult					
			Professional, Technical		Managerial, Self-Employed		Clerical, Sales	
	1955	1962	1955	1962	1955	1962	1955	1962
Took one or more auto trips last year	55	64	76	79	64	76	63	74
For business reasons	2	3	5	7	6	10	3	6
For non-business reasons	48	54	55	50	42	43	54	59
For both business and non-business reasons	5	7	16	22	16	23	6	9
Did not take an auto trip last year	45	36	24	21	36	24	37	26
Total	100	100	100	100	100	100	100	100
Number of adults	8485	5329	476	405	637	402	787	507

Use of Auto	Craftsmen, Foremen, Operatives		Laborers, Service Workers		Occupation of Adult			
					Farmers, Farm Managers		Housewives, Retired, Students	
	1955	1962	1955	1962	1955	1962	1955	1962
Took one or more auto trips last year	60	69	45	43	50	55	50	61
For business reasons	3	3	2	3	5	5	*	1
For non-business reasons	52	61	40	38	35	40	49	57
For both business and non-business reasons	5	5	3	2	10	10	1	3
Did not take an auto trip last year	40	31	55	57	50	45	50	39
Total	100	100	100	100	100	100	100	100
Number of adults	1564	820	887	435	320	109	3606	2489

* Less than one-half of one per cent.

TABLE 53

USE OF AUTO BY AGE OF ADULT, 1955 AND 1962
(Percentage distribution of adults)

| Use of Auto | All Adults | | Age of Adult | | | | | |
| | | | 18 - 24 | | 25 - 34 | | 35 - 44 | |
	1955	1962	1955	1962	1955	1962	1955	1962
Took one or more auto trips last year	55	64	59	65	62	69	61	72
For business reasons	2	3	1	2	2	4	3	4
For non-business reasons	48	54	55	57	55	56	52	58
For both business and non-business reasons	5	7	3	6	5	9	6	10
Did not take an auto trip last year	45	36	41	35	38	31	39	28
Total	100	100	100	100	100	100	100	100
Number of adults	8485	5329	1009	720	1882	1049	1802	1149

| Use of Auto | Age of Adult | | | | | |
| | 45 - 54 | | 55 - 64 | | 65 and Over | |
	1955	1962	1955	1962	1955	1962
Took one or more auto trips last year	55	67	48	60	35	44
For business reasons	3	4	2	3	1	1
For non-business reasons	45	55	42	52	33	41
For both business and non-business reasons	7	8	4	5	1	2
Did not take an auto trip last year	45	33	52	40	65	56
Total	100	100	100	100	100	100
Number of adults	1509	990	1188	708	998	690

TABLE 54

USE OF AUTO BY STAGE IN THE FAMILY LIFE CYCLE, 1955 AND 1962
(Percentage distribution of adults)

| Use of Auto | All Adults | | Stage in the Family Life Cycle | | | | | | | | | |
| | | | Under 45, Single | | Under 45, Married No Children | | Married, Children | | Over 45, Married, No Children | | Over 45, Single | |
	1955	1962	1955	1962	1955	1962	1955	1962	1955	1962	1955	1962
Took one or more auto trips last year	55	64	54	58	69	74	61	72	51	61	33	41
For business reasons	2	3	1	2	2	6	3	3	1	4	1	1
For non-business reasons	48	53	49	49	61	58	52	59	46	52	30	37
For both business and non-business reasons	5	8	4	7	6	10	6	10	4	5	2	3
Did not take an auto trip last year	45	36	46	42	31	26	39	28	49	39	67	59
Total	100	100	100	100	100	100	100	100	100	100	100	100
Number of adults	8485	2729	868	275	685	155	3896	1248	1952	710	837	270

TABLE 55

USE OF AUTO BY SEX OF ADULT, 1955 AND 1962
(Percentage distribution of adults)

| Use of Auto | All Adults | | Sex of Adult | | | | | |
| | | | Male | | Female | | | |
	1955	1962	1955	1962	1955	1962
Took one or more auto trips last year	55	64	58	66	52	62
For business reasons	2	3	4	5	1	1
For non-business reasons	48	54	46	49	50	58
For both business and non-business reasons	5	7	8	12	1	3
Did not take an auto trip last year	45	36	42	34	48	38
Total	100	100	100	100	100	100
Number of adults	8485	5329	4034	2516	4438	2808

TABLE 56

USE OF AUTO BY RACE AND INCOME, 1955
(Percentage distribution of adults)

| | Under $4000 | | $4000 and Over | |
Use of Auto	White	Negro	White	Negrɔ
Took one or more auto trips last year	45	27	67	46
For business reasons	2	1	2	3
For non-business reasons	40	25	58	41
For both business and non-business reasons	3	1	7	2
Did not take an auto trip last year	55	73	33	54
Total	100	100	100	100
Number of adults	2941	556	4328	162

Income

Race

TABLE 57

USE OF AUTO BY RACE, 1955 AND 1962

(Percentage distribution of adults)

Use of Auto	All White Adults		All Negro Adults	
	1955	1962	1955	1962
Took one or more auto trips last year	58	68	30	35
For business reasons	2	4	1	2
For non-business reasons	51	57	28	31
For both business and non-business reasons	5	7	1	2
Did not take an auto trip last year	42	32	70	65
Total	100	100	100	100
Number of adults	7269	2275	718	264

TABLE 58

USE OF AUTO BY REGION, 1955 AND 1962
(Percentage distribution of adults)

Use of Auto	All Adults 1955	All Adults 1962	Northeast 1955	Northeast 1962	North Central 1955	North Central 1962	South 1955	South 1962	West 1955	West 1962
Took one or more auto trips last year	55	64	45	58	59	65	55	65	65	68
For business reasons	2	3	2	2	2	3	2	5	2	2
For non-business reasons	48	54	41	52	52	56	47	51	56	57
For both business and non-business reasons	5	7	2	4	5	6	6	9	7	9
Did not take an auto trip last year	45	36	55	42	41	35	45	35	35	32
Total	100	100	100	100	100	100	100	100	100	100
Number of adults	8485	5329	2339	1182	2689	1549	2300	1796	1156	801

TABLE 59

AUTO OWNERSHIP BY REGION, 1955 AND 1962[a]

(Percentage distribution of spending units)

Auto Ownership	All Spending Units 1955	1962	Northeast 1955	1962	North Central 1955	1962	South 1955	1962	West 1955	1962
Own	67	72	59	66	71	77	64	69	77	76
One car	59	58	54	55	63	60	57	55	66	61
Two or more cars	8	14	5	11	8	17	7	14	11	15
Do not own	33	28	41	34	29	23	36	31	23	24
Total	100	100	100	100	100	100	100	100	100	100
Number of spending units	3119	2117	897	497	1037	580	781	656	404	384

[a] This table is based on data from the 1955 and 1962 Surveys of Consumer Finances.

TABLE 60

USE OF AIR, RAIL, BUS, AND AUTO BY WHETHER LIVING IN THE NEW YORK AREA

1955, 1957, AND 1962

(Percentage distribution of adults)

	All Adults			New York Metropolitan Area		
	1955	1957	1962	1955	1957	1962
Use of air						
Took one or more air trips last year	7	9	11	12	15	15
Did not take any air trips last year[a]	93	91	89	88	85	85
Total	100	100	100	100	100	100
Use of rail						
Took one or more rail trips last year	10	11	7	13	15	11
Did not take any rail trips last year[a]	90	89	93	87	85	89
Total	100	100	100	100	100	100
Use of bus						
Took one or more bus trips last year	7	9	8	5	8	7
Did not take any bus trips last year[a]	93	91	92	95	92	93
Total	100	100	100	100	100	100
Use of auto						
Took one or more auto trips last year	55	61	64	42	40	47
Did not take any auto trips last year[a]	45	39	36	58	60	53
Total	100	100	100	100	100	100
Number of adults	8485	3150	5329	694	282	380

[a] Includes N.A. whether took any trips last year.

TABLE 60 continued

USE OF AIR, RAIL, BUS, AND AUTO BY WHETHER LIVING IN THE NEW YORK AREA
1955, 1957, AND 1962

	Megalopolis (Excluding N.Y. Metro Area)			Remainder of Country		
	1955	1957	1962	1955	1957	1962
Use of air						
Took one or more air trips last year	8	10	14	6	8	10
Did not take any air trips last year[a]	92	90	86	94	92	90
Total	100	100	100	100	100	100
Use of rail						
Took one or more rail trips last year	14	13	10	10	10	7
Did not take any rail trips last year[a]	86	87	90	90	90	93
Total	100	100	100	100	100	100
Use of bus						
Took one or more bus trips last year	6	6	7	7	10	9
Did not take any bus trips last year[a]	94	94	93	93	90	91
Total	100	100	100	100	100	100
Use of auto						
Took one or more auto trips last year	46	61	66	58	63	65
Did not take any auto trips last year[a]	54	39	34	42	37	35
Total	100	100	100	100	100	100
Number of adults	1176	384	552	6615	2484	4397

[a] Includes N.A. whether took any trips last year.

TABLE 61

AUTO OWNERSHIP IN THE NEW YORK METROPOLITAN AREA, SPRING OF 1962

(Percentage distribution of families)

Auto Ownership	All Families in the U.S.	All Families in the New York Metro Area	New York Metropolitan Area	
			Central City and Suburbs of 50,000 +	Suburban and Outlying Areas
Own	77	63	46	89
One	56	47	46	49
Two	19	15	*	37
Three or more	2	1	*	3
Do not own	23	37	54	11
Total	100	100	100	100
Number of families	1299	89	54	35

* Less than one-half of one per cent.

TABLE 62

AUTO OWNERSHIP WITHIN THE NEW YORK METROPOLITAN AREA BY BOROUGHS, 1962

(Percentage distribution of adults in the New York area)

Auto Ownership	All Adults in New York Area	Bronx	Queens	Brooklyn	Manhattan	Jersey City Newark	New York Suburbs	New Jersey Suburbs
Own	67[a]	38	65	33	41	70	89	83
One	53	38	55	33	37	70	63	59
Two	12	*	5	*	4	*	18	24
Three or more	2	*	5	*	*	*	8	*
Do not own	33	62	35	67	59	30	11	17
Total	100	100	100	100	100	100	100	100
Number of adults	380	29	56	42	49	20	74	110

[a] The proportion of all adults who live in families which own a car is slightly higher than the proportion of all families which have a car, which is shown in in Table 61.

TABLE 63

AUTO OWNERSHIP IN THE NEW YORK METROPOLITAN AREA AND THE NEXT ELEVEN LARGEST METROPOLITAN AREAS, 1958-1959[a]

(Percentage distribution of families living in the twelve largest metro areas)

Auto Ownership	Entire New York Metro Area	Eleven Next Largest Metro Areas
Own	<u>52</u>	<u>74</u>
One	44	59
Two	8	13
Three or more	*	2
Do not own	<u>48</u>	<u>26</u>
Total	100	100
Number of families	466	1270

* Less than one-half of one per cent.

[a] Based on data collected in the 1958-1959 Surveys of Consumer Finances.

TABLE 64

TYPE OF NEIGHBORHOOD IN THE NEW YORK METROPOLITAN AREA BY USE OF AUTO, 1962

(Percentage distribution of adults who live in the New York area)

Type of Neighborhood	All Adults	Use of Auto Last Year	
		Took One or More Auto Trips	Did Not Take Any Auto Trips
Low density	45	59	32
Under 2 miles out	*	*	*
2 - 5.9 miles	*	*	*
6 - 14.9 miles	20	31	11
15 miles and over	25	28	21
Medium density	19	17	21
Under 2 miles out	*	*	*
2 - 5.9 miles	3	2	4
6 - 14.9 miles	14	13	15
15 miles and over	2	2	2
High density	36	24	47
Under 2 miles out	4	4	4
2 - 5.9 miles	19	14	22
6 - 14.9 miles	13	6	20
15 miles and over	*	*	1
Total	100	100	100
Number of adults	369	171	195

*Less than one-half of one per cent.

TABLE 65

USE OF AUTO WITHIN THE NEW YORK METROPOLITAN AREA, 1962

(Percentage distribution of adults in the New York area)

Use of Auto	All Adults in New York Area	New York Metropolitan Area						
		Bronx	Queens	Brooklyn	Manhattan	Jersey City, Newark	New York Suburbs[a]	New Jersey Suburbs[b]
Took one or more auto trips last year	46	41	45	26	41	*	50	64
For business reasons	2	*	*	2	2	*	3	2
For non-business reasons	2	38	41	24	39	*	44	58
For both business and non-business reasons	42	3	4	*	*	*	3	4
Did not take an auto trip last year	54	59	55	74	59	100	50	36
Total	100	100	100	100	100	100	100	100
Number of adults	380	29	56	42	49	20	74	110

* Less than one-half of one per cent.

a Sample points involve Nassau, Westchester and Suffolk counties and Farmingdale and Islip township.

b Sample points include Union, Hudson, Essex and Bergen counties.

TABLE 66

USE OF SUPERHIGHWAYS BY SEX AND AGE, 1962
(Percentage distribution of respondents)

Sex	Per Cent Who Have Driven a Car On a Superhighway					
	18-24	25-34	35-44	45-54	55-64	65 and Over
Men	86	86	82	81	67	44
Women	47	61	52	43	31	18

TABLE 67

POSITIVE FEELINGS ABOUT DRIVING FAST BY SEX AND AGE, 1962
(Percentage distribution of respondents)

Sex	Per Cent Who Like Fast Driving					
	18-24	25-34	35-44	45-54	55-64	65 and Over
Men	41	28	32	25	22	9
Women	27	22	22	22	27	12

TABLE 68

SENTENCE COMPLETIONS ON PLANE TRIPS, 1958 AND 1962
(Percentage distribution of respondents)

Plane Trips Are:	1958	1962
Positive	50	47
Fascinating, educational, interesting	1	1
Exciting, adventurous, stimulating	5	3
Fun, entertaining	2	4
Convenient, easy	2	1
Comfortable, relaxing	2	1
Nice, pleasant	13	17
All right, O.K.	*	4
Fast, quick	20	10
Other positive comments	5	6
Negative comments	37	37
Dull, boring, tiresome	1	1
Dangerous, frightening	14	11
Expensive	7	9
Other negative comments	15	16
Other (don't know, no answer)	13	16
Total	100	100
Number of respondents	1456	2651

* Less than one-half of one per cent.

TABLE 69

GENERAL ADVANTAGES AND DISADVANTAGES OF AIR TRAVEL, 1955[a]

(Percentage distribution of respondents who have ever taken a trip)

General advantages of air	Per Cent of Respondents[b]
Speed; saves time	86
Inexpensive; reasonable	6
Safety	2
Comfort	5
Good passenger facilities (meals)	1
Cleanliness	2
Air minded; love planes; thrill of flight	8
Other advantages	3

General disadvantages of air	Per Cent of Respondents[b]
Fear of flying	76
Fear of air sickness	8
Expense	30
Health prevents flying	3
Don't see the scenery	2
Bad connections; inaccessibility	5
Other disadvantages	1
Number of respondents	900

[a] The questions were asked only in the fall of 1955. The questions were: "Why do you think some people travel by plane?" "What might keep some people from traveling by plane?"

[b] The table does not add to 100 because respondents were allowed to give more than one advantage and more than one disadvantage.

APPENDIX IV   275

TABLE 70

ADVANTAGES AND DISADVANTAGES OF AIR FOR THE RESPONDENT'S MOST RECENT TRIP, 1955[a]

(Percentage distribution of advantages and disadvantages)

Advantages and Disadvantages of Air Advantages	Per Cent of All Advantages and Disadvantages of Air
Cheaper	8
Safer	*
Faster	40
Comfortable, restful, good passenger facilities (e.g. meals)	6
Special event (e.g. honeymoon); adventure; wanted to see what it was like	3
Good (better) connections	8
Disadvantages of air	
(Too) expensive	9
Respondent or members of his family object to or fear flying	7
Bad connections	7
Hard to get to a plane; terminals are inconveniently located	8
Other advantages and disadvantages	4
Total	100
Number of adults who discussed air	104

* Less than one-half of one per cent.

[a] The question was: "How did you happen to choose this way of traveling instead of some other?" The question was asked in the context of a series of questions about a recent trip by common carrier.

TABLE 71

PLEASANT RECOLLECTIONS OF THE MOST RECENT AIR TRIP, 1955
(Percentage distribution of recollections)

Pleasant recollections	Per Cent of Recollections
Liked speed; saved time	40
Was comfortable, restful, less fatiguing	13
Liked the meals	6
Liked physical arrangements, clean, roomy, cool	12
Liked stewardess or other personnel	8
Enjoyed the scenery	6
Found it an exciting new experience	4
Is air-minded; loves to fly; thrilling	10
Other	1
Total	100
Number of adults who discussed air trip recollections	180

TABLE 72

UNPLEASANT RECOLLECTIONS OF THE MOST RECENT AIR TRIP, 1955
(Percentage distribution of recollections)

Unpleasant recollections	Per Cent of Recollections
Didn't like it because it was too expensive	6
Was afraid during flight; fears flying; felt unsafe	15
Too noisy; plane vibrated too much	4
Was too jarring; hit too many air-pockets	22
Take off or landing was too rough; too rough	8
Became air-sick	14
Was too cramped	6
Couldn't see scenery well	2
Other	4

Bad connections

Scheduling was bad for reasons of time (coach flights badly scheduled)	6
Scheduling was bad for reasons of place	2
Terminal inconveniently located	11
Total	100
Number of adults who discussed air trip recollections	107

TABLE 73

FEELINGS ABOUT WHETHER AIR TRAVEL IS SAFER NOW THAN TEN YEARS AGO
BY EXPERIENCE AS AN AIR TRAVELER, 1962

(Percentage distribution of respondents)

Feelings about air safety	All Respondents	Experience as an Air Traveler	
		Have Taken an Air Trip	Have Never Taken an Air Trip
Much safer now	6	8	4
Safer now	58	66	54
About the same	7	8	6
Not as safe now	10	6	13
Much less safe now	1	1	1
Don't know, not ascertained	18	11	22
Total	100	100	100
Number of respondents	2651	884	1738

TABLE 74

USE OF RAIL, BUS AND AUTO BY EXPERIENCE AS AN AIR TRAVELER, 1955 AND 1962
(Percentage distribution of adults)

| | All Adults | | Experience as an Air Traveler | | | |
| | | | Have Taken an Air Trip | | Have Never Taken an Air Trip | |
	1955	1962	1955	1962	1955	1962
Use of Rail						
Took one or more rail trips last year	11	7	19	12	8	6
For business reasons	2	1	5	3	1	1
For non-business reasons	9	6	13	8	7	5
For both business and non-business reasons	*	*	1	1	*	*
Did not take any rail trips last year	89	93	81	88	92	94
Total	100	100	100	100	100	100
Use of Bus						
Took one or more bus trips last year	8	9	9	10	6	8
For business reasons	3	1	2	1	*	1
For non-business reasons	5	8	7	8	6	7
For both business and non-business reasons	*	*	*	1	*	*
Did not take any bus trips last year	92	91	91	90	94	92
Total	100	100	100	100	100	100

TABLE 74 continued - USE OF RAIL, BUS AND AUTO BY EXPERIENCE AS AN AIR TRAVELER

| | All Adults | | Experience as an Air Traveler | | | |
| | | | Have Taken an Air Trip | | Have Never Taken an Air Trip | |
Use of Auto	1955	1962	1955	1962	1955	1962
Took one or more auto trips last year	55	64	72	75	51	58
For business reasons	2	3	4	5	2	3
For non-business reasons	48	54	57	57	46	51
For both business and non-business reasons	5	7	11	13	3	4
Did not take any auto trips last year	45	36	28	25	49	42
Total	100	100	100	100	100	100
Number of adults	8485	5329	1957	1676	6341	3586

* Less than one-half of one per cent.

TABLE 75

PER CENT OF EXPERIENCED AIR TRAVELERS
BY WHETHER LIVING IN THE NEW YORK AREA, 1955-1962

(The numbers in parentheses are the total number
of observations in the specified areas)

Survey year	All Adults	New York Metropolitan Area	Megalopolis (Excluding N. Y. Metro Area)	Remainder of Country
1955	23 (8485)	32 (694)	24 (1176)	22 (6615)
1957	27 (3150)	36 (282)	30 (384)	26 (2484)
1958	29 (1456)	36 (110)	(205)	28 (1141)
1960	28 (8329)	35 (725)	33 (878)	26 (6725)
1962	36 (5329)	45 (380)	42 (552)	34 (4397)

TABLE 76

YEAR OF FIRST AIR TRIP BY AGE OF ADULT, 1957 AND 1960

(Percentage distribution of adults)

	All Adults		18-24		25-44		45-64		65 and Over	
	1957	1960	1957	1960	1957	1960	1957	1960	1957	1960
Have ever taken an air trip	28	28	29	22	34	33	26	28	15	16
Year of first air trip										
Before 1940	2	2	*	*	?	1	3	4	2	2
1940 - 1945	7	4	2	1	14	7	11	5	8	1
1946 - 1949	4	4	2	*	5	6	3	4	1	2
1950 - 1955	12	9	16	7	10	12	5	7	2	6
1956 - 1957[a]	2		5		2		3		2	
1956 - 1958[b]		6		9		5		5		4
1959 - 1960		2		4		1		2		1
Year of first air trip not ascertained	1	1	4	1	1	1	1	1	*	*
Have never taken an air trip	72	72	71	78	66	67	74	72	85	84
Total	100	100	100	100	100	100	100	100	100	100
Number of adults	3149	8329	308	969	1317	3604	1022	2666	481	1039

Age of Adult at Time of Survey

* Less than one-half of one per cent.

a For 1957 data.

b For 1960 data.

TABLE 77

EXPERIENCE AS AN AIR TRAVELER BY FAMILY INCOME, 1955 AND 1962

(Percentage distribution of adults)

Family Income

Experience as an air traveler	All Adults		Under $2000		$2000-2999		$3000-3999		$4000-4999	
	1955	1962	1955	1962	1955	1962	1955	1962	1955	1962
Have taken an air trip	23	36	7	16	12	19	16	26	20	26
Have never taken an air trip	75	63	91	83	86	78	82	73	77	71
Not ascertained	2	1	2	1	2	3	2	1	3	3
Total	100	100	100	100	100	100	100	100	100	100
Number of adults	8485	5329	1271	573	981	407	1364	437	1294	566

Experience as an air traveler	$5000-5999		$6000-7499		$7500-9999		$10,000-14,999		$15,000 and Over	
	1955	1962	1955	1962	1955	1962	1955	1962	1955	1962
Have taken an air trip	28	29	33	37	36	47	47	59	71	59
Have never taken an air trip	70	70	65	62	62	52	49	40	27	40
Not ascertained	2	1	2	1	2	1	4	1	2	1
Total	100	100	100	100	100	100	100	100	100	100
Number of adults	1094	662	896	800	709	764	389	600	257	284

TABLE 78

EXPERIENCE AS AN AIR TRAVELER BY AGE OF ADULT, 1955 AND 1962
(Percentage distribution of adults)

Experience as an air traveler	All Adults		18 - 24		25 - 34		Age of Adult 35 - 44		45 - 54		55 - 64		65 +	
	1955	1962	1955	1962	1955	1962	1955	1962	1955	1962	1955	1962	1955	1962
Have taken an air trip	23	36	24	27	32	48	25	43	24	34	18	30	9	23
Have never taken an air trip	75	63	72	68	66	51	74	57	75	66	81	68	89	75
Not ascertained	2	1	4	5	2	1	1	*	1	*	1	2	2	2
Total	100	100	100	100	100	100	100	100	100	100	100	100	100	100
Number of adults	8485	5329	1009	720	1882	1048	1802	1149	1509	990	1188	708	998	690

* Less than one-half of one per cent.

TABLE 79

PER CENT OF ADULTS IN SPECIFIED INCOME GROUPS BY STAGE IN THE
FAMILY LIFE CYCLE AND BY WHETHER EXPERIENCED OR INEXPERIENCED AIR TRAVELER, 1955
(Percentage distribution of adults)

Stage in the Family Life Cycle

Family income	All Adults		Under 45, Single		Under 45, Married No Children	
	Experienced	Not Experienced	Experienced	Not Experienced	Experienced	Not Experienced
Under $3000	10	32	14	35	8	23
$3000 - 5999	41	45	37	34	41	47
$6000 - 9999	29	16	24	19	37	24
$10,000 - 14,999	9	3	11	5	11	4
$15,000 and over	9	1	11	3	3	*
Not ascertained	2	3	3	4	*	2
Total	100	100	100	100	100	100
Number of adults	1957	6341	258	579	210	464

Family income	Married, Children		Over 45, Married, No Children		Over 45, Single	
	Experienced	Not Experienced	Experienced	Not Experienced	Experienced	Not Experienced
Under $3000	8	21	9	40	29	52
$3000 - 5999	45	56	32	40	37	30
$6000 - 9999	30	18	25	13	23	10
$10,000 - 14,999	8	2	14	3	3	3
$15,000 and over	8	1	17	1	4	1
Not ascertained	1	2	3	3	4	4
Total	100	100	100	100	100	100
Number of adults	974	2838	361	1567	120	698

* Less than one-half of one per cent.

TABLE 80

NUMBER OF BUSINESS AND NON-BUSINESS AIR TRIPS, 1955, 1960, AND 1962

(Percentage distribution of trips and travelers)

Number of air trips taken	Business						Non-Business					
	Per Cent of Travelers			Per Cent of Trips			Per Cent of Travelers			Per Cent of Trips		
	1955	1960	1962	1955	1960	1962	1955	1960	1962	1955	1960	1962
1	43	40	40	7	6	8	72	70	69	45	41	38
2	13	18	17	5	6	7	14	16	15	18	19	16
3	9	8	10	5	4	6	5	7	6	10	13	10
4	8	7	8	6	4	6	3	3	4	7	6	10
5 - 9	14	13	11	14	13	15	5	3	4	12	9	13
10 - 19	4	7	10	9	13	24	1	1	1	8	7	6
20 - 29	3	4	2	13	14	10	*	*	1	*	5	7
30 - 39	4	1	*	24	9	3	*	*	*	*	*	*
40 and over	2	2	2	17	31	21	*	*	*	*	*	*
Total	100	100	100	100	100	100	100	100	100	100	100	100
Number of travelers	194	300	209				406	494	370			
Number of trips				1093	1863	1056				643	836	672

* Less than one-half of one per cent.

TABLE 81

USE OF AIR BY FAMILY INCOME, 1955 AND 1962
(Percentage distribution of adults)

	All Adults		Under $2000		$2000-2999		$3000-3999		$4000-4999	
Use of Air	1955	1962	1955	1962	1955	1962	1955	1962	1955	1962
Took one or more air trips last year	7	11	1	3	2	5	3	5	4	6
For business reasons	2	3	*	*	*	1	1	*	1	2
For non-business reasons	5	7	1	3	2	4	2	5	3	3
For both business and non-business reasons	*	1	*	*	*	*	*	*	*	1
Did not take an air trip last year	93	89	99	97	98	95	97	95	96	94
Total	100	100	100	100	100	100	100	100	100	100
Number of adults	8485	5329	1271	573	981	407	1364	438	1294	566

	$5000-5999		$6000-7499		$7500-9999		$10,000-14,999		$15,000 or Over	
Use of Air	1955	1962	1955	1962	1955	1962	1955	1962	1955	1962
Took one or more air trips last year	5	6	9	8	12	13	22	25	40	34
For business reasons	2	1	2	2	4	6	7	9	11	8
For non-business reasons	3	5	7	6	7	6	14	14	24	20
For both business and non-business reasons	*	*	*	*	1	1	1	2	5	6
Did not take an air trip last year	95	94	91	92	88	87	78	75	60	66
Total	100	100	100	100	100	100	100	100	100	100
Number of adults	1094	662	896	800	709	764	389	600	257	284

* Less than one-half of one per cent.

TABLE 82

PER CENT OF ALL AIR TRIPS TAKEN BY ADULTS
IN SPECIFIED INCOME GROUPS, 1955 AND 1962
(Percentage distribution of trips and adults)

Family income	1955		1962	
	Per Cent of Adults	Per Cent of Trips	Per Cent of Adults	Per Cent of Trips
Under $4000	44	7	28	6
$4000-5999	29	19	24	9
$6000-9999	19	24	31	25
$10,000 and over	8	50	17	60
Total	100	100	100	100
Number of trips		1573		1743
Number of adults	8231		5093	

TABLE 83

USE OF AIR BY OCCUPATION OF ADULT, 1955 AND 1962

(Percentage distribution of adults)

Use of Air	Occupation of Adult							
	All Adults		Professional, Technical		Managerial, Self-Employed		Clerical, Sales	
	1955	1962	1955	1962	1955	1962	1955	1962
Took one or more air trips last year	7	11	22	29	15	27	10	15
For business reasons	2	3	12	15	8	15	3	4
For non-business reasons	5	7	8	10	5	9	7	10
For both business and non-business reasons	*	1	2	4	2	3	*	1
Did not take an air trip last year	93	89	78	71	85	73	90	85
Total	100	100	100	100	100	100	100	100
Number of adults	8485	5329	476	405	637	402	787	507

Use of Air	Craftsmen, Foremen, Operatives		Laborers, Service Workers		Farmers, Farm Managers		Housewives, Retired, Students	
	1955	1962	1955	1962	1955	1962	1955	1962
Took one or more air trips last year	6	5	3	3	2	7	5	7
For business reasons	1	2	1	*	1	2	*	1
For non-business reasons	4	3	2	3	1	5	5	6
For both business and non-business reasons	1	*	*	*	*	*	*	*
Did not take an air trip last year	94	95	97	97	98	93	95	93
Total	100	100	100	100	100	100	100	100
Number of adults	1564	820	887	435	320	109	3606	2489

* Less than one-half of one per cent.

TABLE 84

USE OF AIR BY AGE OF ADULT, 1955 AND 1962

(Percentage distribution of adults)

Use of Air	All Adults		18-24		25-34		35-44	
	1955	1962	1955	1962	1955	1962	1955	1962
Took one or more air trips last year	7	11	8	11	6	12	7	13
For business reasons	2	3	1	2	2	4	3	6
For non-business reasons	5	7	7	9	4	7	3	6
For both business and non-business reasons	*	1	*	*	*	1	1	1
Did not take an air trip last year	93	89	92	89	94	88	93	87
Total	100	100	100	100	100	100	100	100
Number of adults	8485	5329	1009	720	1882	1048	1802	1149

Use of Air	45-54		55-64		65 and Over	
	1955	1962	1955	1962	1955	1962
Took one or more air trips last year	9	10	6	9	3	5
For business reasons	3	4	1	2	*	*
For non-business reasons	5	5	5	6	3	5
For both business and non-business reasons	1	1	*	1	*	*
Did not take an air trip last year	91	90	94	91	97	95
Total	100	100	100	100	100	100
Number of adults	1509	990	1188	708	998	691

* Less than one-half of one per cent.

TABLE 85

USE OF AIR BY STAGE IN THE FAMILY LIFE CYCLE, 1955 AND 1962
(Percentage distribution of adults)

| Use of Air | All Adults | | Stage in the Family Life Cycle | | | | | | | | | |
| | | | Under 45, Single | | Under 45, Married, No Children | | Married, Children | | Over 45, Married, No Children | | Over 45, Single | |
	1955	1962	1955	1962	1955	1962	1955	1962	1955	1962	1955	1962
Took one or more air trips last year	7	10	10	14	8	8	5	12	8	8	5	15
For business reasons	2	3	1	1	2	2	2	5	2	2	1	*
For non-business reasons	5	7	9	11	6	5	3	7	5	5	4	14
For both business and non-business reasons	*	*	*	2	*	1	*	*	1	1	*	1
Did not take an air trip last year	93	90	90	86	92	92	95	88	92	92	95	85
Total	100	100	100	100	100	100	100	100	100	100	100	100
Number of adults	8485	2729	868	275	685	155	3896	1248	1952	710	837	270

* Less than one-half of one per cent.

TABLE 86

USE OF AIR BY SEX OF ADULT, 1955 AND 1962
(Percentage distribution of adults)

| Use of Air | All Adults | | Sex of Adult | | | |
| | | | Male | | Female | |
	1955	1962	1955	1962	1955	1962
Took one or more air trips last year	7	11	9	13	5	8
For business reasons	2	3	4	6	*	1
For non-business reasons	5	7	4	6	5	7
For both business and non-business reasons	*	1	1	1	*	*
Did not take an air trip last year	93	89	91	87	95	92
Total	100	100	100	100	100	100
Number of adults	8485	5329	4034	2516	4438	2808

* Less than one-half of one per cent.

TABLE 87

USE OF AIR BY RACE AND INCOME, 1955

(Percentage distribution of adults)

Income				
Race				
	Under $4000		$4000 and Over	
Use of Air	White	Negro	White	Negro
Took one or more air trips last year	3	1	11	2
For business reasons	1	*	3	1
For non-business reasons	2	1	7	1
For both business and non-business reasons	*	*	1	*
Did not take an air trip	97	99	89	98
Total	100	100	100	100
Number of adults	2941	556	4328	162

* Less than one-half of one per cent.

TABLE 88

USE OF AIR BY RACE, 1955 AND 1962

(Percentage distribution of adults)

Use of Air	All White Adults		All Negro Adults	
	1955	1962	1955	1962
Took one or more air trips last year	8	12	1	3
For business reasons	2	4	*	1
For non-business reasons	5	7	1	2
For both business and non-business reasons	1	1	*	*
Did not take an air trip last year	92	88	99	97
Total	100	100	100	100
Number of Adults	7269	2275	718	264

* Less than one-half of one per cent.

TABLE 89

USE OF AIR BY REGION, 1955 AND 1962
(Percentage distribution of adults)

Use of Air	All Adults		Region							
			Northeast		North Central		South		West	
	1955	1962	1955	1962	1955	1962	1955	1962	1955	1962
Took one or more air trips last year	7	11	7	11	6	10	6	10	11	15
For business reasons	2	3	2	3	2	3	2	4	3	2
For non-business reasons	5	7	5	7	4	6	3	5	7	12
For both business and non-business reasons	*	1	*	1	*	1	1	1	1	1
Did not take an air trip last year	93	89	93	89	94	90	94	90	89	85
Total	100	100	100	100	100	100	100	100	100	100
Number of adults	8485	5329	2339	1182	2689	1549	2300	1796	1156	801

* Less than one-half of one per cent.

TABLE 90

PER CENT TAKING AN AIR TRIP IN YEAR

BY WHETHER LIVING IN THE NEW YORK AREA, 1955-1962

(The numbers in parentheses are the total number
of observations in the specified areas)

Survey year	All Adults	New York Metropolitan Area	Megalopolis (Excluding N. Y. Metro Area)	Remainder of Country
1955	7 (8485)	12 (694)	8 (1176)	6 (6615)
1957	9 (3150)	15 (282)	10 (384)	8 (2484)
1958	9 (1456)	14 (110)	8 (205)	9 (1141)
1960	9 (8329)	13 (725)	10 (878)	8 (6725)
1962	11 (5329)	15 (380)	14 (552)	10 (4397)

TABLE 91

USE OF AIR WITHIN THE NEW YORK METRO AREA, 1962

(Percentage distribution of adults in the New York area)

Use of Air	All Adults in New York Area	New York Metro Area					New York Suburbs[a]	New Jersey Suburbs[b]
		Bronx	Queens	Brooklyn	Manhattan	Jersey City, Newark		
Took one or more air trips last year	15	3	11	9	28	15	16	15
For business reasons	3	3	2	2	4	*	1	4
For non-business reasons	11	*	9	7	20	15	15	10
For both business and non-business reasons	1	*	*	*	4	*	*	1
Did not take an air trip last year	85	97	89	91	72	85	84	85
Total	100	100	100	100	100	100	100	100
Number of adults	380	29	56	42	49	20	74	110

* Less than one-half of one per cent.

a Sample points include Nassau, Westchester and Suffolk counties and Farmingdale and Islip township.

b Sample points include Union, Hudson, Essex, and Bergen counties.

TABLE 92

ATTITUDES TOWARD JET TRAVEL BY MODES OF TRAVEL USED LAST YEAR, 1957[a]

(Percentage distribution of respondents)

Attitudes toward jet travel	All Respondents	Modes Used Last Year[b]			Took No Trip Last Year
		Air	Rail	Bus, Auto	
Would like jet travel	33	67	45	38	23
Middle position: likes certain things about it but dislikes others	4	6	5	4	3
Would not like jet travel	51	20	45	48	59
Doesn't know whether would like jet travel	3	3	3	3	3
No difference between jets and other planes	3	2	1	3	3
Not ascertained	6	2	1	4	9
Total	100	100	100	100	100
Number of respondents	1493	125	161	1063	465

[a] The question was: "As you probably know, there are plans for developing jet planes for passenger service. How would you feel about traveling in a jet plane? What do you have in mind?"

[b] If a traveler used more than one mode, he appears in more than one column under "modes used last year".

TABLE 93

ATTITUDES TOWARD JET TRAVEL BY AGE OF PEOPLE WHO TOOK A TRIP LAST YEAR, 1957
(Percentage distribution of respondents)

Took a Trip Last Year

Attitudes toward jet travel	18-24	25-44	45-64	65 and Over
Would like jet travel	55	46	31	14
Middle position	1	4	5	5
Would not like jet travel	35	41	53	70
No difference between jets and other planes	6	3	3	3
Don't know	3	3	4	2
Not ascertained	*	3	4	6
Total	100	100	100	100
Number of respondents	68	477	353	119

* Less than one-half of one per cent.

TABLE 94

ATTITUDES TOWARD JET TRAVEL BY SEX OF PEOPLE WHO TOOK A TRIP LAST YEAR, 1957
(Percentage distribution of respondents)

Attitudes toward jet travel	Took a Trip Last Year	
	Men	Women
Would like jet travel	50	28
Middle position	4	4
Would not like jet travel	35	59
No difference between jet and other planes	4	2
Don't know	4	3
Not ascertained	3	4
Total	100	100
Number of respondents	485	542

TABLE 95

REASONS FOR ATTITUDES TOWARD JET TRAVEL BY SEX FOR PEOPLE WHO TOOK
A TRIP LAST YEAR, 1957

(Percentage distribution of respondents)

	Took a Trip Last Year	
Advantages of jet travel	Men	Women
Faster, save time	28	16
Safer	7	4
Quieter	2	1
More comfortable	4	4
Exciting, adventuresome	4	6
Likes new things, believes in being modern	3	1
Likes flying	8	4
Other reasons why would like jets	5	3
Disadvantages of jet travel		
Too fast	8	12
Too new to be safe	2	2
Unsafe for other reasons	4	6
"I'm afraid of jets" (personal reference)	5	13
Doesn't like flying	13	26
Other reasons why wouldn't like jets	4	5
Total	a	a
Number of respondents	485	542

a
 Columns will not add to 100 per cent because respondents were allowed to give
 more than one reason for liking or not liking jet planes.

TABLE 96

TIME REQUIRED FOR AIRPORT TRIPS BY DISTANCE OF TRIP, 1960

(Percentage distribution of respondents who took an air trip during the last 12 months)

Outgoing trip times	All	Distance of Trip	
		Under 1000 Miles	1000 Miles and Over
Both airport trips took less than 1/2 hour	12	18	6
At least one airport trip took 1/2 - 1 hour	32	35	30
At least one airport trip took 1 - 2 hours	34	40	30
At least one airport trip took 2 hours or more	19	6	32
Not ascertained	3	1	2
Total	100	100	100
Number of respondents	137	68	66

TABLE 97

KINDS OF APPOINTMENTS ON MOST RECENT BUSINESS TRIP, 1960

(Percentage distribution of respondents whose most recent air and rail trip
in the last 12 months was a business trip)

Appointments	All Business Travelers	Air	Rail
Talked to one person	2	4	*
Attended a convention	12	10	15
Met with a group of people	30	33	27
Several appointments	26	21	35
Combination	8	11	*
Not ascertained	22	21	23
Total	100	100	100
Number of respondents	77	52	26

TIME SPENT AT APPOINTMENTS ON MOST RECENT BUSINESS TRIP, 1960

Time spent at appointments	All Business Travelers	Air	Rail
Under 3 1/2 hours	8	6	11
3 1/2 hours to 6 hours	7	8	4
6 hours to 12 hours	18	13	27
12 hours and over	58	60	54
Not ascertained	9	13	4
Total	100	100	100
Number of respondents	77	52	26

* Less than one-half of one per cent.

TABLE 98

WHETHER RENTED AN AUTOMOBILE ON MOST RECENT AIR TRIP BY LENGTH OF TIME AWAY, 1962

(Percentage distribution of respondents who took an air trip during the last 12 months)

Whether rented automobile on recent air trip	All	Length of Time Away				
		Back Same Day	1-2 Days	3-6 Days	7-10 Days	11 or More Days
Did rent a car	11	*	10	15	17	9
Did not rent a car	87	100	88	83	83	89
Not ascertained	2	*	2	2	*	2
Total	100	100	100	100	100	100
Number of respondents	337	16	68	116	42	84

* Less than one-half of one per cent.

TABLE 99

REACTIONS TO REDUCED FARES AND FREE PLANE TRIPS
BY EXPERIENCE AS AN AIR TRAVELER, 1962

(Percentage distribution of respondents)

Reactions	All Respondents	Air Experience Have Taken an Air Trip	Have Never Taken an Air Trip
If plane fares were half			
Would take more trips	28	44	20
Probably would take more trips	3	3	3
Might take more trips	3	4	3
If plane travel were·free			
Would take more trips	28	31	26
Probably would take more trips	3	2	4
Might take more trips	3	2	3
Probably would not take more trips	3	2	4
Would not take more trips	26	10	34
Don't know, not ascertained	3	2	3
Total	100	100	100
Number of respondents	2651	884	1738

TABLE 100

PERCEIVED CHARACTERISTICS OF AIR TRAVELERS, 1955[a]

(Percentage distribution of adults)

Type of air traveler	Per Cent of Adults Mentioning this Characteristic
High status (important, rich, big shot)	25
Active (busy, in a hurry, efficient)	68
Modern (progressive, modern, sophisticated)	6
Courageous (not afraid)	6
Thrifty (economical)	2
Other characteristics	
Airminded, loves to fly	4
Doesn't like to spend (a long) time traveling; wants to spend less time away from family	2
Likes comfort	1
Other	4
Total	b
Number of adults	1035

[a] This table is based on the spring survey only. The question was: "Two businessmen often travel to a city 500 miles away. One always goes by air. The other always goes by rail. What would be your idea, what kind of person is the one who goes by air?"

[b] The table does not add to 100 as adults were allowed to mention more than one characteristic.

TABLE 101

PERCEIVED CHARACTERISTICS OF RAIL TRAVELERS, 1955[a]

(Percentage distribution of adults)

Type of Rail Traveler	Per Cent of Adults Mentioning This Characteristic
Status (average sort of person)	5
Less active (has time, is relaxed, takes life easier)	46
Conservative (old fashioned, established, older person, sensible)	18
Courage	
Afraid to fly, cautious	31
Afraid of air sickness (specific)	2
Thrifty (economical, needs to save money)	13
Other characteristics	
Railminded, loves trains	2
Enjoys travel, likes to spend longer at it	1
Likes comfort	2
Likes people	1
Likes to see the scenery	3
Needs (gets) a little extra rest	2
Has (heart condition) ailment that prevents him from flying (exclusive of air-sickness)	1
Doesn't own car, can't or doesn't like to drive	1
Convenient (no further information)	*
Total	b
Number of adults	1035

* Less than one-half of one per cent.

[a] This table is based on the spring survey only. The question was: "Two businessmen often travel to a city 500 miles away. One always goes by air. The other always goes by rail. What would be your idea, what kind of person is the one who goes by rail?"

[b] The table does not add to 100 as adults were allowed to mention more than one characteristic.

TABLE 102

GENERAL ADVANTAGES AND DISADVANTAGES OF RAIL TRAVEL, 1955[a]

(Percentage distribution of adults)

General advantages of rail	Per Cent of Adults
Cheap, cheaper, reasonable	9
Safer (better in bad weather)	19
Faster	11
Comfortable, restful, good passenger facilities, enjoys meeting people (likes club car)	38
Enjoys seeing the scenery	4
Avoids strain of driving car, can't drive, doesn't own car	21
Good connections	4
Convenient: no further information	12
Other	2
General disadvantages of rail	
Expensive	27
Dangerous (fear of train wrecks)	5
Slow (compared to air)	19
Uncomfortable (noise, sudden stops), fatiguing, monotonous	5
Train sickness	5
Trains are dirty	3
See less scenery	6
Inconvenient not to have car on arrival	2
Bad connections	15
Hard to get to a train; stations are inconveniently located	6
Total	b
Number of adults	900

[a] The question was asked only in the fall of 1955. The question was: "Why do you think some people travel by train?" "What might keep some people from traveling by train?"

[b] Table does not add to 100 per cent because respondents were permitted to cite more than one advantage and more than one disadvantage.

TABLE 103

ADVANTAGES AND DISADVANTAGES OF RAIL FOR THE MOST RECENT TRIP, 1957[a]

(Percentage distribution of advantages and disadvantages)

Advantages of rail	Per Cent of All Advantages and Disadvantages of Rail
Cheaper	6
Safer	4
Faster	8
Comfortable, restful; good passenger facilities (e.g. rest rooms, diner, club car)	19
Enjoy the scenery; sightseeing	3
Good (better) connections:	
Trains go to more places	3
Trains go at the right times	2
Trains are easy to reach; stations are conveniently located	5
Good connections; convenient; no further information	8
Disadvantages of rail	
(Too) expensive	3
Trains are slow	5
Bad connections; trains don't go to right places, enough places; are badly scheduled for reasons of destination	6
Trains don't go at right times; are badly scheduled for reasons of timing	2
Trains connect badly with one another or with other modes	1
Bad connections: no further information	1
Hard to get to a train; stations are inconveniently located	1
Other advantages and disadvantages	23
Total	100
Number of adults who discussed rail	220

[a] The question was: "How did you happen to choose this way of traveling instead of some other?"

TABLE 104

PLEASANT RECOLLECTIONS OF THE LAST RAIL TRIP, 1955
(Percentage distribution of recollections)

Pleasant recollections	Per Cent of Recollections
Liked it because it was cheap (cheaper)	1
Liked feeling of security or safety	3
Liked it because it was fast (faster)	4
Was comfortable, restful	26
Liked dining car, meals	14
Liked physical arrangements, clean, roomy, cool	20
Liked the service	4
Liked meeting people (club car)	5
Found it exciting; change from routine	3
Enjoyed the scenery	11
Enjoyed avoiding strain of driving car	4
Convenient: no other information	5
Total	100
Number of adults who discussed rail trip recollections	576

TABLE 105

UNPLEASANT RECOLLECTIONS OF THE LAST RAIL TRIP, 1955
(Percentage distribution of recollections)

Unpleasant recollections	Per Cent of Recollections
Didn't like it because it was too expensive	2
Too slow	17
Uncomfortable (noise, sudden stops), fatiguing	28
Train was dirty, unsanitary (e.g. rest rooms)	18
Dining car was too expensive	3
(Air conditioning) too cold	2
Service was poor	4
"It was crowded"	4
Didn't see enough scenery	4
Bad connections	14
Other	4
Total	100
Number of adults who discussed rail trip recollections	438

TABLE 106

EXPERIENCE AS A RAIL TRAVELER BY FAMILY INCOME, 1955 AND 1962

(Percentage distribution of adults)

| Experience as a rail traveler | All Adults | | Family Income | | | | | | | |
| | | | Under $4000 | | $4000-5999 | | $6000-9999 | | $10,000 and Over | |
	1955	1962	1955	1962	1955	1962	1955	1962	1955	1962
Have taken a rail trip	68	67	60	59	70	63	77	72	86	79
Have never taken a rail trip	30	31	38	39	28	35	21	26	12	19
Not ascertained	2	2	2	2	2	2	2	2	2	2
Total	100	100	100	100	100	100	100	100	100	100
Number of adults	8485	5329	3616	1417	2388	1228	1605	1564	646	884

TABLE 107

EXPERIENCE AS A RAIL TRAVELER BY AGE OF ADULT, 1962
(Percentage distribution of adults)

Experience as a rail traveler	All Adults	Age of Adult					
		18-24	25-34	35-44	45-54	55-64	65 and Over
Have taken a rail trip	67	43	65	74	70	70	74
Have never taken a rail trip	31	52	33	25	29	28	24
Not ascertained	2	5	2	1	1	2	2
Total	100	100	100	100	100	100	100
Number of adults	5329	720	1048	1149	990	708	690

TABLE 108

RAIL TRAVEL HISTORY BY AGE OF ADULT, 1957
(Percentage distribution of adults)

Rail travel history	All Adults	Age of Adult			
		18-24	25-44	45-64	65 and Over
Took a rail trip "last year"	11	13	9	13	11
Last rail trip was: 1954-1956	12	17	9	12	10
Last rail trip: 1950-1953	12	7	15	10	9
Last rail trip: 1946-1949	9	4	13	7	8
Last rail trip: 1940-1945	9	3	11	9	6
Last rail trip: 1939 or earlier	6	1	3	10	13
Year of last trip not known; can't remember; not ascertained	12	10	11	13	16
Never took a rail trip	29	45	29	26	27
Total	100	100	100	100	100
Number of adults	3149	308	1317	1022	481

TABLE 109

NUMBER OF BUSINESS AND NON-BUSINESS RAIL TRIPS, 1955 AND 1962

(Percentage distribution of trips and travelers)

Number of rail trips taken	Business				Non-Business			
	Per Cent of Travelers		Per Cent of Trips		Per Cent of Travelers		Per Cent of Trips	
	1955	1962	1955	1962	1955	1962	1955	1962
1	51	63	16	26	72	72	37	44
2	20	12	13	10	15	16	15	19
3	7	8	6	10	7	5	10	8
4	6	4	7	7	2	2	5	5
5 - 9	7	6	14	15	2	4	6	18
10 - 19	5	7	19	32	*	1	2	6
20 - 29	4	*	25	*	1	*	6	*
30 - 39	*	*	*	*	*	*	2	*
40 and over	*	*	*	*	1	*	17	*
Total	100	100	100	100	100	100	100	100
Number of travelers	162	73			748	323		
Number of trips			526	177			1480	534

* Less than one-half of one per cent.

TABLE 110

USE OF RAIL BY FAMILY INCOME, 1955 AND 1962
(Percentage distribution of adults)

	All Adults		Family Income — Under $2000		$2000-2999		$3000-3999		$4000-4999	
Use of Rail	1955	1962	1955	1962	1955	1962	1955	1962	1955	1962
Took one or more rail trips last year	10	7	6	5	7	8	8	8	10	4
For business reasons	2	1	*	*	*	1	1	*	1	1
For non-business reasons	8	6	6	5	7	7	7	8	9	3
For both business and non-business reasons	*	*	*	*	*	*	*	*	*	*
Did not take a rail trip last year	90	93	94	95	93	92	92	92	90	96
Total	100	100	100	100	100	100	100	100	100	100
Number of adults	8485	5329	1271	573	981	407	1364	438	1294	566

	$5000-5999		$6000-7499		$7500-9999		$10,000-14,999		$15,000 or Over	
Use of Rail	1955	1962	1955	1962	1955	1962	1955	1962	1955	1962
Took one or more rail trips last year	9	6	12	6	16	8	21	11	34	20
For business reasons	2	1	2	1	4	1	6	2	10	7
For non-business reasons	6	5	10	5	11	7	14	8	22	13
For both business and non-business reasons	1	*	*	*	1	*	1	1	2	*
Did not take a rail trip last year	91	94	88	94	84	92	79	89	66	80
Total	100	100	100	100	100	100	100	100	100	100
Number of adults	1094	662	896	800	709	764	389	600	257	284

* Less than one-half of one per cent.

TABLE 111

PER CENT OF ALL RAIL TRIPS TAKEN BY ADULTS
IN SPECIFIED INCOME GROUPS, 1955 AND 1962

(Percentage distribution of trips and adults)

Family income	1955		1962	
	Per Cent of Adults	Per Cent of Trips	Per Cent of Adults	Per Cent of Trips
Under $4000	44	29	28	24
$4000-5999	29	26	24	14
$6000-9999	19	22	31	31
$10,000 and over	8	23	17	31
Total	100	100	100	100
Number of trips		1930		747
Number of adults	8231		5093	

TABLE 112

USE OF RAIL BY OCCUPATION OF ADULT, 1955 AND 1962

(Percentage distribution of adults)

Use of Rail	All Adults		Professional, Technical		Laborers, Service Workers		Occupation of Adult Professional, Managerial, Self-Employed		Clerical, Sales	
	1955	1962	1955	1962	1955	1962	1955	1962	1955	1962
Took one or more rail trips last year	10	7	22	12	10	5	17	11	13	8
For business reasons	2	1	8	5	1	*	9	5	2	1
For non-business reasons	8	6	12	6	9	5	7	6	10	7
For both business and non-business reasons	*	*	2	1	*	*	1	*	1	*
Did not take a rail trip last year	90	93	78	88	90	95	83	89	87	92
Total	100	100	100	100	100	100	100	100	100	100
Number of adults	8485	5329	476	405	887	435	637	402	787	507

Use of Rail	Craftsmen, Foremen, Operatives		Farmers, Farm Managers		Housewives, Retired Students	
	1955	1962	1955	1962	1955	1962
Took one or more rail trips last year	13	5	4	3	9	7
For business reasons	6	1	1	*	*	*
For non-business reasons	7	4	3	3	9	7
For both business and non-business reasons	*	*	*	*	*	*
Did not take a rail trip last year	87	95	96	97	91	93
Total	100	100	100	100	100	100
Number of adults	1564	820	320	109	3606	2489

* Less than one-half of one per cent.

TABLE 113

USE OF RAIL BY AGE OF ADULT, 1955 AND 1962
(Percentage distribution of adults)

Use of Rail	All Adults		Age of Adult					
			18 - 24		25 - 34		35 - 44	
	1955	1962	1955	1962	1955	1962	1955	1962
Took one or more rail trips last year	10	7	12	8	8	5	10	7
For business reasons	2	1	1	1	1	1	2	2
For non-business reasons	8	6	11	7	7	4	8	5
For both business and non-business reasons	*	*	*	*	*	*	*	*
Did not take a rail trip last year	90	93	88	92	92	95	90	93
Total	100	100	100	100	100	100	100	100
Number of adults	8485	5329	1126	720	1882	1049	1802	1149

Use of Rail	45 - 54		55 - 64		65 and Over	
	1955	1962	1955	1962	1955	1962
Took one or more rail trips last year	13	7	11	11	7	8
For business reasons	3	1	1	2	*	*
For non-business reasons	9	6	10	9	7	8
For both business and non-business reasons	1	*	*	*	*	*
Did not take a rail trip last year	87	93	89	89	93	92
Total	100	100	100	100	100	100
Number of adults	1509	990	1188	708	998	690

* Less than one-half of one per cent.

TABLE 114

USE OF RAIL BY STAGE IN THE FAMILY LIFE CYCLE, 1955 AND 1962
(Percentage distribution of adults)

| Use of Rail | All Adults | | Stage in the Family Life Cycle | | | | | | | | | |
| | | | Under 45, Single | | Under 45, Married, No Children | | Married, Children | | Over 45, Married, No Children | | Over 45, Single | |
	1955	1962	1955	1962	1955	1962	1955	1962	1955	1962	1955	1962
Took one or more rail trips last year	10	7	13	12	8	3	9	6	12	9	11	10
For business reasons	2	1	1	1	1	*	2	1	2	1	*	1
For non-business reasons	8	6	12	11	7	3	7	5	10	8	11	9
For both business and non-business reasons	*	*	*	*	*	*	*	*	*	*	*	*
Did not take a rail trip last year	90	93	87	88	92	97	91	94	88	91	89	90
Total	100	100	100	100	100	100	100	100	100	100	100	100
Number of adults	8485	5329	868	275	685	155	3896	1248	1952	710	837	270

* Less than one-half of one per cent.

TABLE 115

USE OF RAIL BY SEX OF ADULT, 1955 AND 1962
(Percentage distribution of adults)

| Use of Rail | All Adults | | Sex of Adult | | | |
| | | | Male | | Female | |
	1955	1962	1955	1962	1955	1962
Took one or more rail trips last year	10	7	10	7	10	8
For business reasons	2	1	3	2	*	1
For non-business reasons	8	6	6	5	10	7
For both business and non-business reasons	*	*	1	*	*	*
Did not take a rail trip last year	90	93	90	93	90	92
Total	100	100	100	100	100	100
Number of adults	8485	5329	4034	2516	4438	2808

* Less than one-half of one per cent.

TABLE 116

USE OF RAIL BY RACE AND INCOME, 1955

(Percentage distribution of adults)

| Use of Rail | Under $4000 | | $4000 and Over | |
	White	Negro	White	Negro
Took one or more rail trips last year	<u>6</u>	<u>12</u>	<u>14</u>	<u>17</u>
For business reasons	*	1	3	1
For non-business reasons	6	11	10	15
For both business and non-business reasons	*	*	1	1
Did not take a rail trip last year	<u>94</u>	<u>88</u>	<u>86</u>	<u>83</u>
Total	100	100	100	100
Number of adults	2941	556	4328	162

* Less than one-half of one per cent.

TABLE 117

USE OF RAIL BY RACE, 1955 AND 1962

(Percentage distribution of adults)

Use of Rail	All White Adults		All Negro Adults	
	1955	1962	1955	1962
Took one or more rail trips last year	10	7	13	6
For business reasons	2	1	1	1
For non-business reasons	8	6	12	5
For both business and non-business reasons	*	*	*	*
Did not take a rail trip last year	90	93	87	94
Total	100	100	100	100
Number of adults	7269	2275	718	264

* Less than one-half of one per cent.

TABLE 118

USE OF RAIL BY REGION, 1955 AND 1962
(Percentage distribution of adults)

Use of Rail	All Adults		Region							
			Northeast		North Central		South		West	
	1955	1962	1955	1962	1955	1962	1955	1962	1955	1962
Took one or more rail trips last year	10	7	12	8	11	7	8	7	9	8
For business reasons	2	1	2	1	2	1	1	1	1	1
For non-business reasons	8	6	10	7	9	6	7	6	8	7
For both business and non-business reasons	*	*	*	*	*	*	*	*	*	*
Did not take a rail trip last year	90	93	88	92	89	93	92	93	91	92
Total	100	100	100	100	100	100	100	100	100	100
Number of adults	8485	5329	2339	1182	2689	1549	2300	1796	1156	801

* Less than one-half of one per cent.

TABLE 119

USE OF RAIL WITHIN THE NEW YORK METRO AREA, 1962

(Percentage distribution of adults in the New York area)

Use of Rail	All Adults in New York Area	New York Metro Area						
		Bronx	Queens	Brooklyn	Manhattan	Jersey City, Newark	New York Suburbs[a]	New Jersey Suburbs[b]
Took one or more trips last year	11	9	5	2	18	5	15	16
For business reasons	2	*	*	*	10	*	*	1
For non-business reasons	1	9	5	2	6	5	15	13
For both business and non-business reasons	8	*	*	*	2	*	*	2
Did not take a trip last year	89	91	95	98	82	95	85	84
Total	100	100	100	100	100	100	100	100
Number of adults	380	29	56	42	49	20	74	110

* Less than one-half of one per cent.

a Sample points include Nassau, Westchester and Suffolk counties and Farmingdale and Islip township.

b Sample points include Union, Hudson, Essex and Bergen counties.

TABLE 120

REACTIONS TO TRIPS BY BUS, 1962[a]

(Percentage distribution of respondents)

Trips Are:	Per Cent of Respondents
Positive, enthusiastic	37
Fascinating, educational	1
Exciting, adventurous	*
Fun, entertaining	2
Convenient, easy	1
Comfortable, relaxing	1
Nice, pleasant	11
All right, o.k.	10
Safe (r)	2
Cheap, practical	4
Fast, quick	*
Other positive comments	5
Negative comments	53
Dull, tiresome	16
Dangerous	1
Expensive	3
Tiring, fatiguing	5
Strong general negative comment (horrible, terrible)	13
Other negative comments	15
Other (don't know, no answer)	10
Total	100
Number of respondents	2651

* Less than one-half of one per cent.

[a] The question was: "Bus trips are ... ".

TABLE 121

REACTIONS TO BUS TRAVEL BY FAMILY INCOME

(Percentage distribution of respondents)

Reactions	All Respondents	Family Income								
		Under $2000	$2000 -2999	$3000 -3999	$4000 -4999	$5000 -5999	$6000 -7499	$7500 -9999	$10,000 -14,999	$15,000 or Over
Positive	18	27	26	27	20	18	15	13	9	7
Mildly positive	19	27	24	21	24	18	17	13	12	14
Negative	53	31	41	40	50	52	60	66	68	70
Other (don't know, no answer)	10	15	9	12	6	12	8	8	11	9
Total	100	100	100	100	100	100	100	100	100	100
Number of respondents	2651	364	222	225	288	321	386	348	262	120

TABLE 122

ADVANTAGES AND DISADVANTAGES OF BUS FOR THE MOST RECENT TRIP, 1957[a]

(Percentage distribution of advantages and disadvantages)

Advantages of bus	Per Cent of All Advantages and Disadvantages of Bus
Cheaper	22
Safer	1
Faster	6
See the scenery	7
More flexible schedule: stop when and where you want, stay longer	3
Better (good) connections:	
Buses go to more places; "only way you could get there"	8
Buses go at right times	5
Buses connect well with one another or with other modes	1
Buses are easy to reach; terminals are conveniently located	1
Good connections; convenient (no further information)	10
Disadvantages of bus	
Slow	8
Fatigue; lack of comfort	7
Bad connections:	
Buses don't go to right places, enough places; are badly scheduled for reasons of destination	1
Buses don't go at right times; are badly scheduled for reasons of timing	1
Buses connect badly with one another or with other modes	1
Hard to get a bus; terminals are inconveniently located	1
Other advantages and disadvantages of bus	17
Total	100
Number of adults who discussed bus	179

[a] The question was: "How did you happen to choose this way of traveling instead of some other?"

TABLE 123

EXPERIENCE AS A BUS TRAVELER BY FAMILY INCOME, 1955 AND 1962

(Percentage distribution of adults)

Experience as a bus traveler	All Adults		Family Income							
			Under $4000		$4000-5999		$6000-9999		$10,000 and Over	
	1955	1962	1955	1962	1955	1962	1955	1962	1955	1962
Have taken a bus trip	46	52	44	53	50	51	46	56	41	50
Have never taken a bus trip	51	46	53	45	47	47	52	43	53	48
Not ascertained	3	2	3	2	3	2	2	1	6	2
Total	100	100	100	100	100	100	100	100	100	100
Number of adults	8485	5329	3616	1417	2388	1228	1605	1564	646	884

TABLE 124

EXPERIENCE AS A BUS TRAVELER BY AGE OF ADULT, 1962
(Percentage distribution of adults)

Experience as a bus traveler	All Adults	Age of Adult					
		18-24	25-34	35-44	45-54	55-64	65 and Over
Have taken a bus trip	52	46	60	56	51	48	49
Have never taken a bus trip	46	49	39	43	48	50	49
Not ascertained	2	5	1	1	1	2	2
Total	100	100	100	100	100	100	100
Number of adults	5329	720	1048	1149	990	708	690

TABLE 125

NUMBER OF BUSINESS AND NON-BUSINESS BUS TRIPS, 1955 AND 1962
(Percentage distribution of trips and travelers)

Number of bus trips taken	Business				Non-Business			
	Per Cent of Travelers		Per Cent of Trips		Per Cent of Travelers		Per Cent of Trips	
	1955	1962	1955	1962	1955	1962	1955	1962
1	56	68	20	25	71	68	52	35
2	13	16	10	11	16	14	12	14
3	9	7	10	7	3	6	3	9
4	6	*	9	*	2	5	4	11
5 - 9	10	7	23	15	5	4	11	12
10 - 19	6	*	28	*	2	3	7	19
20 - 29	*	*	*	*	1	*	7	*
30 - 39	*	*	*	*	*	*	*	*
40 and over	*	2	*	42	*	*	4	*
Total	100	100	100	100	100	100	100	100
Number of travelers	68	44			512	413		
Number of trips			184	123			1367	812

* Less than one-half of one per cent.

TABLE 126

USE OF BUS BY FAMILY INCOME, 1955 AND 1962
(Percentage distribution of adults)

Use of Bus	All Adults		Under $2000		$2000-2999		$3000-3999		$4000-4999	
	1955	1962	1955	1962	1955	1962	1955	1962	1955	1962
Took one or more bus trips last year	7	9	8	14	7	12	7	12	6	8
For business reasons	1	1	*	1	*	1	*	1	*	*
For non-business reasons	6	8	8	13	7	11	7	11	6	7
For both business and non-business reasons	*	*	*	*	*	*	*	*	*	1
Did not take a bus trip last year	93	91	92	86	93	88	93	88	94	92
Total	100	100	100	100	100	100	100	100	100	100
Number of adults	8485	5329	1271	573	981	407	1364	438	1294	566

Use of bus	$5000-5999		$6000-7499		$7500-9999		$10,000-14,999		$15,000 or Over	
	1955	1962	1955	1962	1955	1962	1955	1962	1955	1962
Took one or more bus trips last year	6	8	5	5	6	7	5	6	5	5
For business reasons	1	1	*	*	1	*	1	1	1	1
For non-business reasons	5	7	5	5	5	7	4	5	4	4
For both business and non-business reasons	*	*	*	*	*	*	*	*	*	*
Did not take a bus trip last year	94	92	95	95	94	93	95	94	95	95
Total	100	100	100	100	100	100	100	100	100	100
Number of adults	1094	662	896	800	709	764	389	600	257	284

* Less than one-half of one per cent.

TABLE 127

PER CENT OF ALL BUS TRIPS TAKEN BY ADULTS
IN SPECIFIED INCOME GROUPS, 1955 AND 1962
(Percentage distribution of trips and adults)

Family income	1955		1962	
	Per Cent of Adults	Per Cent of Trips	Per Cent of Adults	Per Cent of Trips
Under $4000	44	48	28	47
$4000-5999	29	28	24	24
$6000-6999	19	18	31	21
$10,000 and over	8	6	17	8
Total	100	100	100	100
Number of trips		1551		899
Number of adults	8231		5093	

TABLE 128

USE OF BUS BY OCCUPATION, 1955 AND 1962
(Percentage distribution of adults)

Use of Bus	All Adults		Professional, Technical		Occupation of Adult					
					Managerial, Self-Employed		Clerical, Sales		Housewives, Retired, Students	
	1955	1962	1955	1962	1955	1962	1955	1962	1955	1962
Took one or more bus trips last year	7	9	10	9	6	6	7	9	6	9
For business reasons	1	1	3	*	2	2	1	*	*	*
For non-business reasons	6	8	6	7	4	4	6	9	6	9
For both business and non-business reasons	*	*	1	2	*	*	*	*	*	*
Did not take a bus trip last year	93	91	90	91	94	94	93	91	94	91
Total	100	100	100	100	100	100	100	100	100	100
Number of adults	8485	5329	476	405	637	402	787	507	3606	2489

Use of Bus	Craftsmen, Foremen, Operatives		Laborers, Service Workers		Farmers, Farm Managers	
	1955	1962	1955	1962	1955	1962
Took one or more bus trips last year	5	6	9	10	3	7
For business reasons	*	1	1	1	1	2
For non-business reasons	5	5	8	9	2	5
For both business and non-business reasons	*	*	*	*	*	*
Did not take a bus trip last year	95	94	91	90	97	93
Total	100	100	100	100	100	100
Number of adults	1564	820	887	435	320	109

* Less than one-half of one per cent.

TABLE 129

USE OF BUS BY AGE OF ADULT, 1955 AND 1962
(Percentage distribution of adults)

Use of Bus	All Adults		18 - 24		25 - 34		35 - 44	
	1955	1962	1955	1962	1955	1962	1955	1962
Took one or more bus trips last year	7	9	11	13	6	7	5	5
For business reasons	1	1	*	1	1	1	1	1
For non-business reasons	6	8	10	12	5	6	4	4
For both business and non-business reasons	*	*	1	*	*	*	*	*
Did not take a bus trip last year	93	91	89	87	94	93	95	95
Total	100	100	100	100	100	100	100	100
Number of adults	8485	5329	1009	720	1882	1049	1802	1149

Use of bus	45 - 54		55 - 64		65 and Over	
	1955	1962	1955	1962	1955	1962
Took one or more bus trips last year	6	7	8	11	8	10
For business reasons	1	*	1	1	1	*
For non-business reasons	5	7	7	10	7	10
For both business and non-business reasons	*	*	*	*	*	*
Did not take a bus trip last year	94	93	92	89	92	90
Total	100	100	100	100	100	100
Number of adults	1509	990	1188	708	998	690

* Less than one-half of one per cent.

TABLE 130

USE OF BUS BY STAGE IN THE FAMILY LIFE CYCLE, 1955 AND 1962

(Percentage distribution of adults)

| Use of Bus | All Adults | | Stage in the Family Life Cycle | | | | | | | | | |
| | | | Under 45, Single | | Under 45, Married No Children | | Married, Children | | Over 45, Married No Children | | Over 45, Single | |
	1955	1962	1955	1962	1955	1962	1955	1962	1955	1962	1955	1962
Took one or more bus trips last year	7	9	12	12	9	7	5	7	6	7	10	15
For business reasons	1	1	1	*	1	2	1	*	1	*	1	*
For non-business reasons	6	8	10	11	8	5	4	7	5	7	9	14
For both business and non-business reasons	*	*	1	1	*	*	*	*	*	*	*	1
Did not take a bus trip last year	93	91	88	88	91	93	95	93	94	93	90	85
Total	100	100	100	100	100	100	100	100	100	100	100	100
Number of adults	8485	5329	868	275	685	155	3896	1248	1952	710	837	270

* Less than one-half of one per cent.

TABLE 131

USE OF BUS BY SEX OF ADULT, 1955 AND 1962
(Percentage distribution of adults)

| Use of Bus | All Adults | | Sex of Adult | | | | | |
| | | | Male | | Female | | | |
	1955	1962	1955	1962	1955	1962		
Took one or more bus trips last year	7	9	6	6	7	10
For business reasons	1	1	1	1	*	*
For non-business reasons	6	8	5	5	7	10
For both business and non-business reasons	*	*	*	*	*	*
Did not take a bus trip last year	93	91	94	94	93	90
Total	100	100	100	100	100	100
Number of adults	8485	5329	4034	2516	4438	2808

* Less than one-half of one per cent.

TABLE 132

USE OF BUS BY RACE, 1955 AND 1962

(Percentage distribution of adults)

Use of Bus	All White Adults		All Negro Adults	
	1955	1962	1955	1962
Took one or more bus trips last year	7	8	7	15
For business reasons	1	1	*	2
For non-business reasons	6	7	7	12
For both business and non-business reasons	*	*	*	1
Did not take a business trip last year	93	92	93	85
Total	100	100	100	100
Number of adults	7269	2275	718	264

* Less than one-half of one per cent.

TABLE 133

USE OF BUS BY REGION, 1955 AND 1962
(Percentage distribution of adults)

	All Adults		Northeast		North Central		South		West	
Use of Bus	1955	1962	1955	1962	1955	1962	1955	1962	1955	1962
Took one or more bus trips last year	7	9	5	7	6	7	9	10	7	10
For business reasons	1	1	1	*	1	*	1	1	*	1
For non-business reasons	6	8	4	7	5	7	8	9	7	9
For both business and non-business reasons	*	*	*	*	*	*	*	*	*	*
Did not take a bus trip last year	93	91	95	93	94	93	91	90	93	90
Total	100	100	100	100	100	100	100	100	100	100
Number of adults	8485	5329	2339	1182	2689	1549	2300	1796	1156	801

* Less than one-half of one per cent.

TABLE 134

USE OF BUS WITHIN THE NEW YORK METRO AREA, 1962

(Percentage distribution of adults in the New York area)

Use of Bus	All Adults in New York Area	New York Metro Area						
		Bronx	Queens	Brooklyn	Manhattan	Jersey City, Newark	New York Suburbs[a]	New Jersey Suburbs[b]
Took one or more bus trips last year	7	6	5	5	12	5	5	11
For business reasons	*	*	*	*	*	*	*	*
For non-business reasons	7	*	5	5	12	5	5	11
For both business and non-business reasons	*	6	*	*	*	*	*	*
Did not take a bus trip last year	93	94	95	95	88	95	95	89
Total	100	100	100	100	100	100	100	100
Number of adults	380	29	56	42	49	20	74	110

* Less than one-half of one per cent.

a Sample points include Nassau, Westchester and Suffolk counties and Farmingdale and Islip township.

b Sample points include Union, Hudson, Essex and Bergen counties.

TABLE A-I

DEFINITION OF INDEPENDENT VARIABLES USED FOR ESTIMATION OF
MULTIPLE DISCRIMINANT FUNCTION SCALES AND FOR MULTIPLE
REGRESSION ANALYSES

Variable	Symbol or Abbreviation	Range of Values
1. Experience as an air traveler prior to beginning of survey year	EXP	1 if experienced 0 if otherwise
2. Sex	SEX	1 if female 0 if male
3. Place of residence	METRO	1 if lives in one of the twelve largest metropolitan areas 0 if otherwise
4. Family income $3000-5999	Y_1	1 adult falls in this group 0 if otherwise
5. Family income $6000-9999	Y_2	1 adult falls in this group 0 if otherwise
6. Family income $10,000 or over	Y_3	1 adult falls in this group 0 if otherwise
7. Occupation	OCC	1 if occupation of adult is professional, technical, self-employed, managerial or sales 0 if otherwise
8. Education of head	EDUC	1 head is at least a high school graduate 0 if otherwise
9. Automobile ownership	AUTO	1 family owns one or more automobiles 0 if otherwise

TABLE A-2

ESTIMATES OF REGRESSION EQUATIONS FOR TOTAL NON-BUSINESS AND BUSINESS TRAVEL
STRATIFIED BY LIFE CYCLE, FOR YEARS 1955 AND 1962

Stage in the Family Life Cycle

Variable	Under 45 Single		Under 45 Married, No Children		Married, Children		Over 45 Married, No Children		Over 45 Single	
	1955	1962	1955	1962	1955	1962	1955	1962	1955	1962
C	.6912	.7307	.9131	.8642	.5162	.5552	.3070	.5130	.4105	.5585
EXP	.3557** (.1028)	.5507** (.0964)	.1276 (.1159)	.4173** (.1112)	.3311** (.0540)	.2381** (.0417)	.3291** (.0811)	.1806* (.0621)	.6034** (.1281)	.3216** (.0901)
SEX	-.1024 (.0883)	-.1382 (.0833)	-.0147 (.1004)	-.0287 (.1026)	-.0387 (.0450)	-.0404 (.0404)	.0451 (.0540)	-.0271 (.0527)	.0861 (.0886)	-.0167 (.0860)
METRO	-.0960 (.0929)	-.4178** (.0905)	-.3075* (.1045)	-.5404** (.1182)	-.2667** (.0497)	-.2614** (.0415)	-.1291* (.0604)	-.3252** (.0579)	-.2681** (.0883)	-.2509* (.0874)
Y_1	.0172 (.1080)	.0011 (.1132)	.3661* (.1522)	-.2988* (.1427)	.1408* (.0590)	.1033 (.0650)	.3513** (.0658)	.2105** (.0663)	.0573 (.0957)	.0320 (.0980)
Y_2	.1521 (.1304)	.0768 (.1244)	.5867** (.1699)	.0802 (.1519)	.4591** (.0746)	.3254** (.0671)	.3625** (.0895)	.5080** (.0755)	.0080 (.1497)	.0404 (.1241)
Y_3	.2696 (.1542)	.4201** (.1370)	.7736** (.2300)	-.1402 (.1698)	.7069** (.1069)	.6479** (.0759)	.8124** (.1198)	.7814** (.0897)	.2758 (.2104)	.0908 (.1672)
OCC	.1875 (.1238)	.2633* (.1118)	.3391* (.1424)	.1043 (.1428)	.1622* (.0619)	.2552** (.0510)	.2465** (.0818)	-.0224 (.0754)	.4186** (.1256)	.4622** (.1253)
EDUC	.5714** (.0929)	.4716** (.0938)	-.0766 (.1051)	.3780** (.1070)	.1530** (.0454)	.1958** (.0418)	.3333** (.0670)	.3470** (.0602)	.2999** (.0921)	.4574** (.0920)
AUTO	.3071** (.1050)	.0722 (.1074)	.3289* (.1489)	.4037* (.1490)	.3817** (.0614)	.3887** (.0688)	.2682** (.0648)	.3772** (.0708)	.1388 (.0906)	.1149 (.0864)
R^2	.2094	.2109	.1279	.1985	.1498	.1727	.2613	.2262	.1677	.1807
N	435	533	358	342	1908	2451	980	1303	449	521

* Coefficient is 2 times its standard deviation.
** Coefficient is 3 times its standard deviation.

TABLE A-3

ESTIMATES OF REGRESSION EQUATIONS FOR NON-BUSINESS AIR TRAVEL
STRATIFIED BY LIFE CYCLE, FOR YEARS 1955 AND 1962

Stage in the Family Life Cycle

Variable	Under 45 Single		Under 45 Married, No Children		Married, Children		Over 45 Married, No Children		Over 45 Single	
	1955	1962	1955	1962	1955	1962	1955	1962	1955	1962
C	-.0101	-.0003	-.0391	-.0291	.0014	-.0159	-.0235	-.0077	-.0198	.0147
EXP	.2673**	.2674**	.2301**	.1290**	.0651**	.1015**	.2128**	.1169**	.1949**	.2516**
	(.0368)	(.0382)	(.0380)	(.0377)	(.0112)	(.0125)	(.0240)	(.0173)	(.0310)	(.0294)
SEX	-.0009	.0153	.0408	.0383	.0109	.0194	.0261	.0135	.0224	-.0305
	(.0316)	(.0330)	(.0330)	(.0348)	(.0093)	(.0121)	(.0160)	(.0147)	(.0214)	(.0281)
METRO	.0807*	.0719*	.0405	.0304	.0038	.0443**	.0325	.0647**	.0109	.0212
	(.0332)	(.0359)	(.0343)	(.0401)	(.0103)	(.0125)	(.0179)	(.0161)	(.0214)	(.0285)
Y_1	-.0015	.0775	.0551	-.0597	-.0057	-.0218	-.0040	.0085	.0049	-.0029
	(.0386)	(.0449)	(.0500)	(.0484)	(.0122)	(.0195)	(.0195)	(.0185)	(.0232)	(.0320)
Y_2	-.0144	.0272	.1283*	.0173	.0327*	-.0253	.0492	-.0167	.0435	-.0210
	(.0466)	(.0493)	(.0558)	(.0515)	(.0154)	(.0201)	(.0265)	(.0210)	(.0362)	(.0405)
Y_3	.1973**	.1165*	.1567*	.0098	.2014**	.0844**	.1264**	.1263**	.2130**	.0851
	(.0552)	(.0543)	(.0755)	(.0575)	(.0221)	(.0228)	(.0355)	(.0250)	(.0509)	(.0546)
OCC	.0158	.0343	.0449	.0684	-.0147	.0124	-.0573*	.0205	.0041	.0615
	(.0443)	(.0443)	(.0468)	(.0484)	(.0128)	(.0153)	(.0242)	(.0210)	(.0304)	(.0409)
EDUC	.0747*	.0660	.0094	.0161	.0244*	.0447**	.0063	.0433*	.0423	.0841*
	(.0332)	(.0372)	(.0345)	(.0363)	(.0094)	(.0125)	(.0199)	(.0167)	(.0223)	(.0300)
AUTO	-.0280	-.0665	-.0644	.0396	-.0126	.0013	.0260	-.0241	-.0228	-.0211
	(.0376)	(.0426)	(.0489)	(.0505)	(.0127)	(.0206)	(.0192)	(.0197)	(.0219)	(.0282)
R^2	.2113	.1591	.1466	.0798	.1050	.0968	.1521	.1343	.1622	.1990
N	435	533	358	342	1908	2451	980	1303	449	521

* Coefficient is 2 times its standard deviation.
** Coefficient is 3 times its standard deviation.

TABLE A-4

ESTIMATES OF REGRESSION EQUATIONS FOR NON-BUSINESS RAIL TRAVEL
STRATIFIED BY LIFE CYCLE, FOR YEARS 1955 AND 1962

| | \multicolumn{10}{c}{Stage in the Family Life Cycle} |
Variable	Under 45 Single		Under 45 Married, No Children		Married, Children		Over 45 Married, No Children		Over 45 Single	
	1955	1962	1955	1962	1955	1962	1955	1962	1955	1962
C	.1437	.0812	.1099	.0800	.0785	.0112	.0463	.0735	.0734	.1035
EXT	.1153* (.0438)	.0326 (.0339)	-.0012 (.0451)	.0394 (.0301)	.0317 (.0166)	.0148 (.0108)	.0295 (.0330)	.0522* (.0202)	.0816 (.0545)	.0982* (.0343)
SEX	-.0156 (.0377)	-.0246 (.0292)	.0640 (.0391)	-.0047 (.0278)	.0307* (.0139)	.0265* (.0105)	.0549* (.0220)	.0283 (.0171)	.0196 (.0377)	-.0130 (.0327)
METRO	.0078 (.0396)	-.0347 (.0318)	.0136 (.0407)	.0079 (.0320)	-.0143 (.0153)	.0062 (.0108)	-.0157 (.0246)	.0449* (.0188)	-.0290 (.0376)	-.0005 (.0333)
Y_1	-.0141 (.0461)	.0608 (.0398)	-.0539 (.0593)	-.0022 (.0387)	.0334 (.0182)	-.0028 (.0169)	.0548* (.0268)	.0212 (.0216)	.0036 (.0407)	.0256 (.0373)
Y_2	.0268 (.0556)	.0615 (.0437)	-.0514 (.0662)	-.0083 (.0412)	.0497* (.0230)	.0151 (.0174)	.1603** (.0364)	.0429 (.0245)	-.0371 (.0636)	.0106 (.0472)
Y_3	.1397* (.0658)	.0662 (.0481)	.1488 (.0896)	-.0215 (.0460)	.1351** (.0330)	.0527* (.0197)	.1990** (.0487)	.0874*** (.0292)	.0405 (.0894)	.0653 (.0636)
OCC	-.0370 (.0528)	.0433 (.0392)	.0589 (.0555)	-.0094 (.0387)	-.0093 (.0191)	.0035 (.0132)	.0203 (.0333)	-.0407 (.0245)	.0281 (.0534)	.0188 (.0477)
EDUC	.1262** (.0396)	.0718* (.0329)	.0465 (.0409)	.0246 (.0290)	.0509** (.0140)	.0121 (.0108)	.0030 (.0273)	.0404* (.0196)	-.0806* (.0392)	-.0122 (.0350)
AUTO	-.1124* (.0448)	-.0850* (.0377)	-.0448 (.0580)	-.0513 (.0404)	-.0912** (.0189)	-.0054 (.0179)	-.0422 (.0263)	-.0820** (.0230)	.0097 (.0385)	-.0535 (.0329)
R^2	.0725	.0318	.0429	.0164	.0346	.0153	.0492	.0433	.0251	.0231
N	435	533	358	342	1908	2451	980	1303	449	521

* Coefficient is 2 times its standard deviation.
** Coefficient is 3 times its standard deviation.

TABLE A-5

ESTIMATES OF REGRESSION EQUATIONS FOR NON-BUSINESS BUS TRAVEL
STRATIFIED BY LIFE CYCLE, FOR YEARS 1955 AND 1962

Stage in the Family Life Cycle

Variable	Under 45 Single 1955	Under 45 Single 1962	Under 45 Married, No Children 1955	Under 45 Married, No Children 1962	Married, Children 1955	Married, Children 1962	Over 45 Married, No Children 1955	Over 45 Married, No Children 1962	Over 45 Single 1955	Over 45 Single 1962
C	.1196	.2428	.1166	.1359	.1216	.0931	.1084	.0842	.1352	.1635
EXP	-.0146 (.0418)	.0305 (.0380)	.0830 (.0427)	.0324 (.0351)	.0140 (.0136)	.0146 (.0111)	-.0209 (.0252)	.0351* (.0179)	.0731 (.0466)	.0726 (.0404)
SEX	.0410 (.0359)	.0104 (.0328)	.0392 (.0370)	.0350 (.0324)	.0036 (.0113)	.0278* (.0108)	.0331* (.0168)	.0425* (.0152)	.0065 (.0322)	.0416 (.0386)
METRO	-.0800* (.0378)	-.0781* (.0356)	-.0143 (.0385)	.0031 (.0373)	-.0281* (.0125)	-.0193 (.0111)	-.0358 (.0188)	.0145 (.0167)	-.0688* (.0321)	-.0623 (.0392)
Y_1	.0901* (.0439)	.0244 (.0446)	.0811 (.0561)	-.0389 (.0451)	-.0207 (.0149)	.0054 (.0173)	.0392* (.0205)	-.0095 (.0191)	-.0215 (.0348)	.0769 (.0440)
Y_2	.0208 (.0530)	-.0033 (.0490)	.0713 (.0626)	-.0796 (.0480)	-.0109 (.0188)	-.0127 (.0179)	.0632* (.0278)	.0125 (.0217)	-.0612 (.0544)	-.0281 (.0557)
Y_3	.0047 (.0627)	-.0353 (.0539)	.0319 (.0847)	-.0994 (.0536)	-.0069 (.0269)	-.0059 (.0202)	.0486 (.0373)	-.0507 (.0259)	.0048 (.0765)	-.0468 (.0751)
OCC	-.0638 (.0503)	-.0249 (.0440)	.0090 (.0524)	-.0096 (.0451)	-.0184 (.0156)	-.0080 (.0136)	.0205 (.0254)	-.0301 (.0217)	.0157 (.0456)	.0869 (.0562)
EDUC	.0745* (.0377)	.1252** (.0369)	-.0064 (.0387)	.0384 (.0338)	-.0129 (.0114)	-.0097 (.0111)	-.0155 (.0209)	.0389* (.0173)	.0448 (.0335)	.0504 (.0413)
AUTO	-.0251 (.0427)	-.1958** (.0423)	-.1184* (.0548)	-.0606 (.0470)	-.0493** (.0155)	-.0419* (.0183)	-.0997** (.0202)	-.0635** (.0204)	-.0649 (.0329)	-.1202** (.0388)
R^2	.0364	.0717	.0273	.0314	.0131	.0100	.0310	.0296	.0332	.0557
N	435	533	358	342	1908	2451	980	1303	449	521

* Coefficient is 2 times its standard deviation.
** Coefficient is 3 times its standard deviation.

TABLE A-6

ESTIMATES OF REGRESSION EQUATIONS FOR NON-BUSINESS AUTO TRAVEL STRATIFIED BY LIFE CYCLE, FOR YEARS 1955 AND 1962

Stage in the Family Life Cycle

Variable	Under 45 Single		Under 45 Married, No Children		Married, Children		Over 45 Married, No Children		Over 45 Single	
	1955	1962	1955	1962	1955	1962	1955	1962	1955	1962
C	.4078	.3537	.4434	.4516	.2707	.3430	-.0235	.2773	.1875	.2483
EXP	.1800* (.0737)	.3147** (.0689)	.0083 (.0801)	.1778* (.0796)	.1522** (.0388)	.0614* (.0302)	.2128** (.0240)	.0911* (.0446)	.3068** (.0936)	.0977 (.0642)
SEX	-.0462 (.0634)	-.0412 (.0596)	-.0143 (.0694)	.0567 (.0735)	.0289 (.0323)	.0298 (.0292)	.0261 (.0160)	.0080 (.0378)	.0930 (.0647)	.0860 (.0613)
METRO	-.0361 (.0667)	-.3027** (.0647)	-.1852* (.0723)	-.3404** (.0847)	-.1943** (.0357)	-.1362** (.0300)	.0325 (.0179)	-.2308** (.0416)	-.1821* (.0645)	-.2535** (.0622)
Y_1	.0115 (.0775)	.0734 (.0810)	.3711** (.1052)	-.1196 (.1022)	.1449** (.0424)	.0598 (.0470)	-.0040 (.0195)	.1590** (.0476)	.0238 (.0698)	.0206 (.0698)
Y_2	.0944 (.0936)	.0708 (.0889)	.4841** (.1174)	.1169 (.1088)	.3835** (.0536)	.2629** (.0485)	.0492 (.0265)	.3448** (.0542)	.0477 (.1093)	.0761 (.0884)
Y_3	.1342 (.1107)	.3172** (.0980)	.5836** (.1590)	.1180 (.1216)	.2990** (.0768)	.3961** (.0548)	.1264** (.0355)	.4335** (.0644)	-.0214 (.1536)	.0625 (.1191)
CCC	.1431 (.0888)	.0316 (.0799)	.1756 (.0984)	.0226 (.1022)	-.0273 (.0445)	-.0355 (.0369)	-.0573* (.0242)	-.1134* (.0541)	.2001* (.0917)	.1676 (.0892)
EDUC	.3654** (.0666)	.3204** (.0670)	.0260 (.0726)	.2387** (.0766)	.0913* (.0326)	.1421** (.0302)	.0063 (.0199)	.1876** (.0432)	.2301** (.0673)	.3149** (.0655)
AUTO	.3137** (.0753)	.1767* (.0768)	.3197** (.1029)	.3646** (.1067)	.3709** (.0441)	.3376** (.0497)	.0260 (.0192)	.3847** (.0509)	.2327** (.0661)	.1675** (.0616)
R^2	.1925	.1798	.1584	.1641	.1233	.1107	.1521	.1906	.1496	.1546
N	435	533	358	342	1908	2451	980	1303	449	521

* Coefficient is 2 times its standard deviation.
** Coefficient is 3 times its standard deviation.

TABLE A-7

A MULTIPLE CLASSIFICATION ANALYSIS OF MAJOR FACTORS AFFECTING TOTAL NON-BUSINESS AND
BUSINESS TRAVEL BY ALL MODES COMBINED FOR YEARS 1955 AND 1962

	Stage in the Family Life Cycle									
	Under 45, Single				Under 45, Married No Children				Married, Children	
	1955		1962		1955		1962		1955	
Variable	Number of Cases	Adjusted Deviations From Mean of 1.20	Number of Cases	Adjusted Deviations From Mean of 1.23	Number of Cases	Adjusted Deviations From Mean of 1.53	Number of Cases	Adjusted Deviations From Mean of 1.37	Number of Cases	Adjusted Deviations From Mean of 1.14
Family Income										
Less than $3000	139	-.07	149	-.10	53	-.40	62	.10	354	-.21
$3000-5999	159	-.05	151	-.10	179	-.04	112	-.19	1054	-.07
$6000-9999	85	.08	132	-.02	98	-.18	97	.18	384	.25
$10,000 or more	52	.20	101	.32	28	.37	71	-.04	116	.49
Air Experience										
Experienced	108	.27	157	.39	96	.09	117	.27	443	.25
Not experienced	327	-.09	376	-.16	262	-.03	225	-.14	1465	-.08
Education of head										
High School	147	.38	369	.15	192	-.04	227	.13	896	.08
Less	288	-.19	164	-.33	166	.04	115	-.25	1012	-.07
Auto Ownership										
Owns	305	.09	415	.02	304	.05	295	.06	1620	.06
Does not own	130	-.22	118	-.06	54	-.28	47	-.35	288	-.32
Place of residence										
Large metro area	148	-.06	197	-.26	123	-.20	83	-.41	501	-.20
Other	287	.03	336	.15	235	.11	260	.13	1107	.07
Occupation										
Professional, etc.	60	.16	97	.22	53	.29	54	.09	319	.14
Other	375	-.03	436	-.05	305	-.05	288	-.02	1589	-.03

TABLE A-7 continued

A MULTIPLE CLASSIFICATION ANALYSIS OF MAJOR FACTORS AFFECTING TOTAL NON-BUSINESS AND BUSINESS TRAVEL BY ALL MODES COMBINED FOR YEARS 1955 AND 1962

	Married, Children		Stage in the Family Life Cycle							
			Over 45, Married No Children				Over 45, Single			
	1962		1955		1962		1955		1962	
Variable	Number of Cases	Adjusted Deviations From Mean of 1.36	Number of Cases	Adjusted Deviations From Mean of .94	Number of Cases	Adjusted Deviations From Mean of 1.21	Number of Cases	Adjusted Deviations From Mean of .90	Number of Cases	Adjusted Deviations From Mean of .84
Family Income										
Less than $3000	253	-.28	343	-.27	393	-.31	226	-.03	270	-.02
$3000-5999	825	-.17	390	.08	399	-.10	157	.02	128	.01
$6000-9999	911	.05	162	.09	298	.20	47	-.02	86	.02
$10,000 or more	462	.37	85	.54	213	.47	19	.24	37	.07
Air Experience										
Experienced	934	.15	153	.28	347	.13	53	.53	143	.23
Not experienced	1517	-.09	827	-.05	956	-.05	396	-.07	378	-.09
Education of head										
High School	1517	.07	286	.24	501	.21	155	.20	159	.32
Less	934	-.12	694	-.10	802	-.13	294	-.10	362	-.14
Auto Ownership										
Owns	2247	.03	711	.07	1078	.07	236	.07	273	.05
Does not own	204	-.36	269	-.19	225	-.31	213	-.07	248	-.06
Place of residence										
Large metro area	675	-.19	282	-.09	345	-.24	140	-.18	156	-.18
Other	1776	.07	698	.04	958	.09	309	.08	365	.08
Occupation										
Professional, etc.	530	.20	145	.21	211	-.02	56	.37	63	.41
Other	1921	-.06	835	-.04	1092	.00	393	-.05	458	-.06

TABLE A-8

DEFINITION OF DEPENDENT AND INDEPENDENT VARIABLES USED FOR
ESTIMATION OF REGRESSION EQUATIONS FOR CHOICE OF
MODE IN INTERCITY TRAVEL

I. Dependent Variables for
    Indicated Mode Choices

    Dependent Variable   Range of Values

    Choice between:

    1. Non-business air and non-   1 if non-business air trip
       business automobile   0 if non-business automobile trip

    2. Non-business common carrier   1 if non-business common carrier
       and non-business automobile   trip
                                          0 if non-business automobile trip

    3. Business air and   1 if business air trip
       business automobile   0 if business automobile trip

II. Independent Variables

     Independent Variables
     Reflecting Travel Tastes
     and Experience   Range of Values

     1. Experience as an air traveler   1 if experienced
        prior to beginning of survey   0 otherwise
        year

     2. Travel frequency   1 if took 5 or more trips in
                                             year preceding interview
                                          0 otherwise

     3. Positive comments on   1 if made such comments
        auto travel   0 otherwise

     4. Danger of air travel   1 if mentions
                                          0 otherwise

     5. Positive comments on   1 if made such comments
        air travel   0 otherwise

     6. Positive comments on   1 if made such comments
        bus travel   0 otherwise

TABLE 4 -8 continued

Independent Variables Reflecting Travel Tastes and Experience	Range of Values
7. Preference for air travel	1 if stated air best way to travel 0 otherwise
8. Preference for auto travel	1 if stated auto best way to travel 0 otherwise
9. Ever driven on super-highway	1 if driven on superhighway 0 otherwise

Independent Variables Reflecting Distance of Trip	
10. Length of trip	1 if 300-599 miles 0 otherwise
11. Length of trip	1 if 1000 miles or more 0 otherwise
12. Length of time away	1 if 11 days or more 0 otherwise

Independent Variables Reflecting Supply of Travel	
13. Region: Northeast	1 if lives in Northeast 0 otherwise
14. Region: North Central	1 if lives in North Central 0 otherwise
15. Region: West	1 if lives in West 0 otherwise
16. Automobile ownership	1 if family owns one or more automobiles 0 otherwise

TABLE A-8 continued

Independent Variables
Reflecting Supply of Travel   Range of Values

17. Distance to center of central   1 if lives in or within 50
    city of nearest Standard   miles of SMSA of 350,000
    Metropolitan Statistical   or more
    Area of 350,000 to 1,500,000   0 otherwise

Independent Variables
Reflecting Income

18. Family income $5000-9999   1 belongs to this income class
                                     0 otherwise

19. Family income $10,000   1 belongs to this income class
    or more   0 otherwise

Independent Variables
Reflecting Price

20. Air cheapest   1 if indicated air cheapest mode
                                     0 otherwise

21. Rail cheapest   1 if indicated rail cheapest mode
                                     0 otherwise

22. Bus cheapest   1 if indicated bus cheapest mode
                                     0 otherwise

23. Number who went   1 if two or more
                                     0 otherwise

Independent Variables
Reflecting Demographic
Characteristics

24. Stage in the family life   1 if belongs to this life cycle
    cycle: young single, young   class
    married without children   0 otherwise

25. Stage in the family life   1 if belongs to this life cycle
    cycle: married, children   class
                                     0 otherwise

TABLE A-9

ESTIMATE OF REGRESSION EQUATION FOR FACTORS AFFECTING
THE CHOICE OF BUSINESS AIR TRAVEL OVER
BUSINESS AUTOMOBILE TRAVEL

| Variable[1] | Mode Choice | |
| | Business Air and Business Automobile | |
	Coefficient	Standard Error
C	.07	
Experience	.01	(.05)
Travel frequency	-.02	(.05)
Positive auto	.04	(.04)
Air danger	.07	(.09)
Positive air	.04	(.05)
Prefer air	.09	(.05)
Superhighway	.05	(.06)
Length 300-999	.28	(.05)**
Length 1000 +	.49	(.06)**
No. went (2 +)	-.26	(.04)**
Time away	-.19	(.07)*
Air cheapest	.30	(.06)**
Northeast	.09	(.06)
North Central	-.02	(.05)
West	.02	(.07)
L.C. - young	.15	(.09)
L.C. - married, children	.07	(.05)
Auto ownership	-.04	(.09)
Metro area	-.01	(.07)
Income $5000-9999	.13	(.06)*
Income $10,000 +	.19	(.06)**
R^2	.44	
N	348	

[1] Defined in Table A-8.

* Coefficient is 2 times its standard deviation.

** Coefficient is 3 times its standard deviation.

TABLE A-10

MULTIPLE CLASSIFICATION ANALYSIS OF MAJOR FACTORS AFFECTING CHOICE
OF BUSINESS AIR TRAVEL OVER BUSINESS AUTOMOBILE TRAVEL

Variable	Number of Cases	Adjusted Deviations from Mean of .47
I. Distance		
Length of trip		
100-299 miles	167	-.19
300-999 miles	111	.09
1000 miles or over	70	.30
Length of time away from home		
Eleven days or more	38	-.17
Less than eleven days	310	.02
II. Income		
Family income		
Less than $5000	76	-.12
$5000-9999	138	.00
$10,000 or over	134	.07
III. Price		
Cheapness		
Air the cheapest mode	47	.26
Air not the cheapest mode	301	-.04
Number who went		
Two or more	138	-.16
One	210	.10
IV. Tastes and Experience		
Preference for air travel		
Indicated air as best way to travel	154	.05
Did not prefer air travel	194	-.04
Danger of air travel		
Mentions danger of air travel	23	.07
Does not mention danger of air travel	325	.00
Experience as an air traveler		
Experienced prior to survey year	205	.01
Not experienced prior to survey year	143	-.01
Travel frequency		
Took 5 trips or more during year	205	-.01
Took less than 5 trips during year	143	.01
Positive comments concerning air travel		
Made such comments	231	.01
Did not make such comments	117	-.03
Positive comments concerning auto travel		
Made such comments	202	.02
Did not make such comments	146	-.03

TABLE A-10 continued - MULTIPLE CLASSIFICATION ANALYSIS OF MAJOR FACTORS AFFECTING
CHOICE OF BUSINESS AIR TRAVEL OVER BUSINESS AUTOMOBILE TRAVEL

Variable	Number of Cases	Adjusted Deviations from Mean of .47
V. Tastes and Experience		
Ever driven on a superhighway		
Driven on a superhighway	291	.01
Never driven on a superhighway	57	-.04
VI. Supply		
Automobile ownership		
Does not own an automobile	21	.03
Owns one or more automobiles	327	.00
Region		
Northeast	64	.08
Northcentral	100	-.03
West	40	.00
Southeast	144	-.01
Residence		
Lives in or within 50 miles of a		
metropolitan area of 350,000 to 1,500,000	42	-.01
Lives elsewhere	306	.00
VII. Demographic		
Stage in the family life cycle		
Under 45: single, married without children	31	.09
Married, children	237	.01
Over 45: single, married without children	80	-.06

TABLE A-11

ESTIMATE OF REGRESSION EQUATION FOR FACTORS AFFECTING
THE CHOICE OF NON-BUSINESS AIR TRAVEL
OVER NON-BUSINESS AUTOMOBILE TRAVEL

Variable[1]	Mode Choice	
	Non-Business Air and Non-Business Auto	
	Coefficient	Standard Error
C	.20	
Experience	.03	(.01)**
Travel frequency	.01	(.01)
Positive auto	-.02	(.01)*
Air danger	.00	(.02)
Positive air	.02	(.01)*
Prefer air	.04	(.01)**
Superhighway	.00	(.01)
Length 300-999	.06	(.01)**
Length 1000 +	.25	(.02)**
No. went (2 +)	-.22	(.01)**
Time away	-.02	(.02)
Air cheapest	.48	(.03)**
Northeast	-.01	(.02)
North Central	-.01	(.01)
West	.00	(.02)
L.C. - young	.02	(.02)
L.C. - married, children	.00	(.01)
Auto ownership	-.02	(.02)
Metro area	.00	(.02)
Income $5000-9999	.00	(.01)
Income $10,000 +	.02	(.02)
R^2	.40	
N	1602	

[1] Defined in Table A-8.

* Coefficient is 2 times its standard deviation.

** Coefficient is 3 times its standard deviation.

TABLE A-12

MULTIPLE CLASSIFICATION ANALYSIS OF MAJOR FACTORS AFFECTING
CHOICE OF NON-BUSINESS AIR TRAVEL OVER NON-BUSINESS AUTOMOBILE TRAVEL

Variable	Number of Cases	Adjusted Deviations from Mean of .10
I. Price		
Cheapness		
Air the cheapest mode	63	.46
Air not the cheapest mode	1539	-.02
Number who went		
Two or more	1304	-.04
One	298	.18
II. Distance		
Length of trip		
100-299 miles	913	-.05
300-999 miles	478	.01
1000 miles or over	211	.20
III. Demographic		
Stage in the family life cycle		
Under 45: single, married without children	222	.02
Married, children	786	.00
Over 45: single, married without children	594	-.01
IV. Income		
Family income		
Less than $5000	592	.00
$5000-9999	717	.00
$10,000 or over	293	.02
V. Tastes and Experience		
Preference for air travel		
Indicated air as best way to travel	519	.03
Did not prefer air travel	1083	-.01
Experience as an air traveler		
Experienced prior to survey year	639	.02
Not experienced prior to survey year	963	-.01
Travel frequency		
Took 5 trips or more during year	585	.01
Took less than 5 trips during year	1017	.00

Maximum potential positive deviations from variables not included in this table: -.0

Maximum potential negative deviations from variables not included in this table: .0

TABLE A-13

ESTIMATE OF REGRESSION EQUATION FOR FACTORS AFFECTING
THE CHOICE OF NON-BUSINESS COMMON-CARRIER TRAVEL
OVER NON-BUSINESS AUTOMOBILE TRAVEL

| | Mode Choice | |
| | Non-Business Common Carrier and Non-Business Auto | |
Variable[1]	Coefficient	Standard Error
C	.46	
Experience	.01	(.02)
Travel frequency	.02	(.02)
Positive auto	-.02	(.02)
Air danger	-.01	(.03)
Positive air	.01	(.02)
Positive bus	.01	(.02)
Prefer auto	-.03	(.02)
Superhighway	-.04	(.02)*
Length 300-999	.05	(.02)*
Length 1000+	.19	(.03)**
No. went (2 +)	-.32	(.02)**
Time away	.01	(.02)
Air cheapest	.45	(.04)**
Rail cheapest	.44	(.04)**
Bus cheapest	.38	(.02)**
Northeast	-.01	(.02)
North Central	.00	(.02)
West	-.04	(.02)*
L.C. - young	.00	(.02)
L.C. - married, children	.00	(.02)
Auto ownership	-.09	(.02)**
Metro area	.01	(.02)
Income $5000-9999	.00	(.02)
Income $10,000 +	.01	(.02)
R^2	.45	
N	1880	

[1] Defined in Table A-8.

* Coefficient is 2 times its standard deviation.

** Coefficient is 3 times its standard deviation.

TABLE A-14

MULTIPLE CLASSIFICATION ANALYSIS OF MAJOR FACTORS AFFECTING CHOICE
OF NON-BUSINESS COMMON CARRIER TRAVEL OVER NON-BUSINESS AUTOMOBILE TRAVEL

Variable	Number of Cases	Adjusted Deviations from Mean of .23
I. Price		
<u>Cheapness</u>		
Rail the cheapest mode	55	.35
Air the cheapest mode	66	.36
Bus the cheapest mode	299	.29
Auto the cheapest mode	1460	-.09
<u>Number who went</u>		
Two or more	1411	-.08
One	469	.24
II. Supply		
<u>Automobile ownership</u>		
Does not own an automobile	293	.08
Owns one or more automobiles	1587	-.01
<u>Region</u>		
Northeast	394	.00
Northcentral	450	.01
West	309	-.03
Southeast	727	.01
III. Distance		
<u>Length of trip</u>		
100-299 miles	1049	-.04
300-999 miles	572	.01
1000 miles or more	259	.15
IV. Demographic		
<u>Stage in the family life cycle</u>		
Under 45: single, married without children	262	.00
Married, children	882	.00
Over 45: single, married without children	736	.00
V. Tastes and Experience		
<u>Travel frequency</u>		
Took 5 or more trips during year	672	.01
Took less than 5 trips during year	1208	-.01
<u>Preference for automobile travel</u>		
Indicated automobile as best way to travel	765	-.02
Did not prefer automobile travel	1115	.01

APPENDIX IV 359

TABLE A-14 continued - MULTIPLE CLASSIFICATION ANALYSIS OF MAJOR FACTORS AFFECTING
CHOICE OF NON-BUSINESS COMMON CARRIER TRAVEL OVER NON-BUSINESS AUTOMOBILE TRAVEL

Variable	Number of Cases	Adjusted Deviations from Mean of .23
V. Tastes and Experience		
Experience as an air traveler		
Experienced prior to survey year	729	.01
Not experienced prior to survey year	1151	.00
Ever driven on a superhighway		
Driven on a superhighway	1221	-.02
Never driven on a superhighway	659	.03
VI. Income		
Family income		
Less than $5000	740	.00
$5000-9999	816	.00
$10,000 or more	324	.01

Maximum potential positive deviations from variables not included in this table:
.06.

Maximum potential negative deviations from variables not included in this table:
-.05.

Appendix Table S-I: Approximate Sampling Errors of Percentages for "Per Adult" Responses
(expressed in percentages)

Reported Percentage		100	200	300	400	500	700	1000	1500	2000	2500	3000	4200	5500	8500
								Number of Adults							
50		10.0	7.1	5.8	5.0	4.5	3.8	3.2	2.6	2.2	2.0	1.8	1.5	1.3	1.1
		18.8	13.4	11.0	9.6	8.6	7.3	6.2	5.3	4.7	4.2	4.0	3.5	3.2	2.9
30 or 70		9.2	6.5	5.3	4.6	4.1	3.5	2.9	2.4	2.0	1.8	1.7	1.4	1.2	1.0
		17.2	12.3	10.1	8.8	7.9	6.7	5.7	4.8	4.3	3.9	3.6	3.2	3.0	2.6
20 or 80		8.0	5.7	4.6	4.0	3.6	3.0	2.5	2.1	1.8	1.6	1.5	1.2	1.1	0.9
		15.0	10.7	8.8	7.6	6.9	5.9	5.0	4.2	3.7	3.4	3.2	2.8	2.6	2.3
10 or 90		6.0	4.2	3.5	3.0	2.7	2.3	1.9	1.5	1.3	1.2	1.1	0.9	0.8	0.7
		11.3	8.1	6.6	5.7	5.2	4.4	3.7	3.2	2.8	2.5	2.4	2.1	1.9	1.7
5 or 95		4.4	3.1	2.5	2.2	1.9	1.6	1.4	1.1	1.0	0.9	0.8	0.7	0.6	0.5
		8.2	5.9	4.8	4.2	3.7	3.2	2.7	2.3	2.0	1.8	1.7	1.5	1.4	1.3
1 or 99		2.0	1.4	1.2	1.0	0.9	0.8	0.6	0.5	0.4	0.4	0.4	0.3	0.3	0.2
		3.7	2.7	2.1	1.9	1.7	1.4	1.2	1.0	0.9	0.8	0.8	0.7	0.6	0.6

Appendix Tables-II: Sampling Errors of Differences for "Per Adult" Responses
(expressed in percentages)

Size of Subgroup

For percentages around 35% and 65%

Size of Subgroup	8000	5000	4000	2000	1500	1250	1000	700	500	300	200	100
8000	1.6-4.1	1.8-4.4	1.9-4.6	2.5-5.5	2.8-6.0	3.0-6.4	3.4-6.9	3.9-7.9	4.6-9.1	5.9-11.4	7.2-13.7	10.1-19.0
5000		2.0-4.7	2.1-4.9	2.6-5.7	2.9-6.2	3.2-6.6	3.5-7.1	4.0-8.1	4.7-9.2	5.9-11.5	7.2-13.8	10.1-19.1
4000			2.2-5.1	2.7-5.9	3.0-6.4	3.2-6.7	3.5-7.2	4.1-8.2	4.7-9.3	6.0-11.6	7.2-13.9	10.1-19.2
2000				3.2-6.6	3.4-7.0	3.6-7.4	3.9-7.8	4.4-8.7	5.0-9.8	6.2-11.9	7.4-14.2	10.2-19.4
1500					3.6-7.4	3.8-7.7	4.1-8.2	4.6-9.1	5.2-10.1	6.3-12.2	7.5-14.4	10.3-19.6
1250						4.0-8.0	4.2-8.5	4.7-9.3	5.3-10.3	6.4-12.4	7.6-14.6	10.4-19.7
1000							4.5-8.9	4.9-9.7	5.5-10.6	6.6-12.7	7.8-14.8	10.5-19.9
700								5.4-10.4	5.9-11.3	6.9-13.2	8.0-15.3	10.7-20.2
500									6.3-12.2	7.2-14.0	8.4-15.9	11.0-20.7
300										8.2-15.6	9.1-17.3	11.5-21.8
200											10.0-18.9	12.2-23.1
100												14.1-26.6

For percentages around 20% and 80%

Size of Subgroup	8000	5000	4000	2000	1500	1250	1000	700	500	300	200	100
8000	1.3-3.3	1.4-3.5	1.5-3.7	2.0-4.4	2.3-4.8	2.4-5.1	2.7-5.5	3.2-6.3	3.7-7.3	4.7-9.1	5.7-11.0	8.0-15.2
5000		1.6-3.8	1.7-3.9	2.1-4.6	2.4-5.0	2.5-5.3	2.8-5.7	3.2-6.4	3.8-7.4	4.8-9.2	5.8-11.1	8.1-15.3
4000			1.8-4.1	2.2-4.7	2.4-5.1	2.6-5.4	2.8-5.8	3.3-6.6	3.8-7.5	4.8-9.3	5.8-11.1	8.1-15.4
2000				2.5-5.3	2.7-5.6	2.9-5.9	3.1-6.2	3.5-7.0	4.0-7.8	5.0-9.5	5.9-11.4	8.2-15.5
1500					2.9-5.9	3.1-6.2	3.3-6.5	3.7-7.2	4.1-8.1	5.1-9.8	6.0-11.5	8.2-15.7
1250						3.2-6.4	3.4-6.8	3.8-7.4	4.2-8.2	5.1-9.9	6.1-11.7	8.3-15.8
1000							3.6-7.1	3.9-7.7	4.4-8.5	5.3-10.2	6.2-11.8	8.4-15.9
700								4.3-8.3	4.7-9.0	5.5-10.6	6.4-12.2	8.6-16.2
500									5.1-9.8	5.8-11.2	6.7-12.7	8.8-16.6
300										6.5-12.5	7.3-13.8	9.2-17.4
200											8.0-15.1	9.8-18.5
100												11.3-21.3

For percentages around 10% and 90%

8000	0.9-2.5	1.1-2.7	1.2-2.8	1.5-3.3	1.7-3.6	1.8-3.8	2.0-4.1	2.4-4.7	2.8-5.4	3.5-6.8	4.3-8.2	-------
5000		1.2-2.8	1.3-2.9	1.6-3.4	1.8-3.7	1.9-3.9	2.1-4.2	2.4-4.8	2.8-5.5	3.6-6.9	4.3-8.3	-------
4000			1.3-3.0	1.6-3.5	1.8-3.8	1.9-4.0	2.1-4.3	2.5-4.9	2.8-5.6	3.6-7.0	4.4-8.3	-------
2000				1.9-4.0	2.1-4.2	2.2-4.4	2.3-4.7	2.6-5.2	3.0-5.9	3.7-7.1	4.5-8.5	-------
1500					2.2-4.5	2.3-4.6	2.4-4.9	2.7-5.4	3.1-6.1	3.8-7.3	4.5-8.6	-------
1250						2.4-4.8	2.5-5.1	2.8-5.6	3.2-6.2	3.9-7.4	4.6-8.8	-------
1000							2.7-5.3	3.0-5.8	3.3-6.4	3.9-7.6	4.7-8.9	-------
700								3.2-6.2	3.5-6.8	4.1-7.9	4.8-9.2	-------
500									3.8-7.3	4.3-8.4	5.0-9.5	-------
300										4.9-9.4	5.5-10.4	-------
200											6.0-11.3	-------

For percentages around 5% and 95%

8000	0.7-1.8	0.8-1.9	0.8-2.0	1.1-2.4	1.2-2.6	1.3-2.8	1.5-3.0	1.7-3.4	2.0-4.0	2.6-4.9	3.1-6.0	-------
5000		0.9-2.1	0.9-2.1	1.2-2.5	1.3-2.7	1.4-2.9	1.5-3.1	1.8-3.5	2.0-4.0	2.6-5.0	3.1-6.0	-------
4000			1.0-2.2	1.2-2.6	1.3-2.8	1.4-2.9	1.5-3.1	1.8-3.6	2.1-4.1	2.6-5.1	3.2-6.1	-------
2000				1.4-2.9	1.5-3.1	1.6-3.2	1.7-3.4	1.9-3.8	2.2-4.3	2.7-5.2	3.2-6.2	-------
1500					1.6-3.2	1.7-3.4	1.8-3.6	2.0-3.9	2.3-4.5	2.8-5.3	3.3-6.3	-------
1250						1.7-3.5	1.8-3.7	2.1-4.1	2.3-4.6	2.8-5.4	3.3-6.4	-------
1000							1.9-3.9	2.1-4.2	2.4-4.6	2.9-5.5	3.4-6.5	-------
700								2.3-4.5	2.6-4.9	3.0-5.8	3.5-6.7	-------
500									2.8-5.3	3.1-6.1	3.6-6.9	-------
300										3.6-6.8	4.0-7.5	-------
200											4.4-8.2	-------

Appendix Table S-III: Approximate Sampling Errors of Percentages for "Per Interview" Responses
(expressed in percentages)

Reported Percentage	Number of Interviews										
	100	200	300	400	500	700	1000	1500	2000	3000	4200
50	10.0	7.1	5.8	5.0	4.5	3.8	3.2	2.6	2.2	1.8	1.5
	12.7	9.1	7.6	6.7	6.1	5.3	4.6	3.9	3.4	2.9	2.6
30 or 70	9.2	6.5	5.3	4.6	4.1	3.5	2.9	2.4	2.0	1.7	1.4
	11.6	8.4	6.9	6.1	5.6	4.8	4.2	3.5	3.2	2.7	2.3
20 or 80	8.0	5.7	4.6	4.0	3.6	3.0	2.5	2.1	1.8	1.5	1.2
	10.2	7.3	6.0	5.3	4.9	4.2	3.7	3.1	2.8	2.3	2.0
10 or 90	6.0	4.2	3.5	3.0	2.7	2.3	1.9	1.5	1.3	1.1	0.9
	7.6	5.5	4.5	4.0	3.6	3.2	2.8	2.3	2.1	1.8	1.5
5 or 95	4.4	3.1	2.5	2.2	1.9	1.6	1.4	1.1	1.0	0.8	0.7
	5.5	4.0	3.3	2.9	2.7	2.3	2.0	1.7	1.5	1.3	1.1

Appendix Table S-IV: **Sampling Errors of Differences for "Per Interview" Responses**
(expressed in percentages)

Size of Subgroup	2000	1500	1000	700	500	300	200	100
	For percentages from about 35% to 65%							
2000	3.2-4.9	3.4-5.2	3.9-5.7	4.4-6.3	5.0-7.0	6.2-8.3	7.4-9.8	10.2-13.2
1500		3.7-5.5	4.1-6.0	4.6-6.5	5.2-7.2	6.3-8.4	7.5-9.9	10.3-13.3
1000			4.5-6.5	4.9-7.0	5.5-7.6	6.6-8.9	7.8-10.2	10.5-13.5
700				5.4-7.4	5.9-8.0	6.9-9.2	8.0-10.5	10.7-13.8
500					6.3-8.6	7.2-9.7	8.4-11.0	11.0-14.1
300						8.2-10.7	9.1-11.9	11.5-14.8
200							10.0-12.9	12.2-15.7
100								14.1-18.0
	For percentages around 20% and 80%							
2000	2.5-3.9	2.7-4.1	3.1-4.6	3.5-5.0	4.0-5.6	5.0-6.6	5.9-7.8	8.2-10.6
1500		2.9-4.4	3.3-4.8	3.7-5.2	4.1-5.8	5.1-6.7	6.0-7.9	8.2-10.6
1000			3.6-5.2	3.9-5.6	4.4-6.1	5.3-7.1	6.2-8.2	8.4-10.8
700				4.3-6.0	4.7-6.4	5.5-7.4	6.4-8.4	8.6-11.0
500					5.1-6.8	5.8-7.8	6.7-8.8	8.8-11.3
300						6.5-8.6	7.3-9.5	9.2-11.8
200							8.0-10.3	9.8-12.6
100								11.3-14.4

Size of Subgroup

For percentages around 10% and 90%

Sample size								
2000	1.9-2.9	2.1-3.1	2.3-3.4	2.6-3.8	3.0-4.2	3.7-5.0	4.5-5.9	6.1-7.9
1500		2.2-3.3	2.4-3.6	2.7-3.9	3.1-4.3	3.8-5.0	4.5-6.0	6.2-8.0
1000			2.7-3.9	3.0-4.2	3.3-4.6	3.9-5.3	4.7-6.1	6.3-8.1
700				3.2-4.5	3.5-4.8	4.1-5.5	4.8-6.3	6.4-8.3
500					3.8-5.1	4.3-5.8	5.0-6.6	6.6-8.5
300						4.9-6.4	5.5-7.1	6.9-8.9
200							6.0-7.7	7.3-9.4
100								8.5-10.8

For percentages around 5% and 95%

Sample size							
2000	1.4-2.1	1.5-2.3	1.7-2.5	1.9-2.7	2.2-3.0	2.7-3.6	3.2-4.3
1500		1.6-2.4	1.8-2.6	2.0-2.9	2.2-3.1	2.8-3.7	3.3-4.3
1000			1.9-2.8	2.1-3.0	2.4-3.3	2.9-3.9	3.4-4.4
700				2.3-3.2	2.6-3.5	3.0-4.0	3.5-4.6
500					2.8-3.7	3.1-4.2	3.6-4.8
300						3.6-4.7	4.0-5.2
200							4.4-5.6

Age
  distribution among regions,
    1956: 67-68
  (See also Air, Auto, Rail, and
    Bus travel)
Air fares, changes in
  response to, 115-116
Air safety
  attitudes toward, 86-87; 1962:
    153-158
  and air experience, 88
  federal government work,
    knowledge of, 1962: 156-161
  trends in, 1962: 153
Air travel, Ch. IV
  attitudes toward, 83-87, 118-
    119; 1955: 6,8-11, 32-34,
    130-133; 1956: 138-142;
    1957: 88-90; 1958: 8-11,
    27-28; 1962: 15-19, 25-28,
    142-152
  business, 99, 112-113; 1955: 37-
    38, 48, 136-137, 165; 1956:
    79, 84-87; 1960: 44-46;
    1962: 98-101
    frequency of travel, 1955: 37,
      48, 137; 1956: 79, 84-87
    by income, 1955: 48, 165
    by industry, 1955: 38, 136
    and modern communications,
      112-113; 1960: 45
    most recent trip, 1960: 44-46;
      1962: 98-101
    by occupation, 99; 1955: 37-
      136
  business and non-business, 37-
    38, 51, 95-96; 1955: 30-32,
    128-129, 158; 1956: 8, 11,
    77-78; 1958: 6-7; 1960: 29,
    31; 1962: 35, 37, 85-95,
    101-102
    first air trip, 1955: 30-32,
      128-129
    frequency of travel, 38, 95-
      96; 1960: 29, 31; 1962: 35-
      37
    by income, 1955: 158; 1956: 8,
      11
    most recent trip, 1962: 85-95,
      101-102
    number and class of flights,
      1958: 6-7
    by region, 1956: 77-78
  by coach,   1955: 76, 167; 1956:
    113-114, 1957: 17-24, 72-73,
    86-87

experience with, 88-94; 1955: 26-
  28, 65, 124, 155, 157; 1958:
  5-6; 1960: 28, 38-40; 1962:
  116-121
  by age, 92-94
  and attitude toward air safety,
    88
  by cohort age groups, 1960: 38-
    40
  by family life cycle, 1962:
    120-121
  first trips, year of, 90-91;
    1957: 25-30; 1960: 34-37
  by income, 91-92; 1955: 26-27;
    1958: 5-6
  by occupation, 1955: 26,28,
    155
  trends, 89-90
  and use of other modes, 89
by first class, 1955: 76, 167;
  1956: 113-114; 1957: 17-24,
  72-73, 86-87
frequent travelers, reinterviewed
  in summer of 1962, 1962: 87-
  106
future of, 81-82, 116
by jet, attitudes toward, 107-110;
  1957: 114-139; 1958: 12-17
long distance trips, 1960: 53-77;
  1962: 107-115
  business, 1960: 63-65
  non-business, 1962: 107-115
  purpose of, 1960: 63-64
most recent trip, 1955: 76-78,
  166-168; 1956: 111-121, 127-
  128,136-137; 1957: 83-86; 1960
  17-19, 41-51; 1962: 84-108
  alternate mode considered, 1956:
    136-137; 1960: 49, 51
  by distance, 1956: 119-121;
    1957: 83-84; 1960: 17-18
  number who went, 1955: 76, 166;
    1956: 111-112; 1957: 83-86
  preferred mode, 1962: 104-105
  purpose of, 1956: 122, 124;
    1960: 19-20
  business, 1960: 44-46; 1962:
    98-101
  business and non-business, 1962:
    85-95, 101-102
  non-business, 1956: 125-126
non-business, 99, 102; 1955: 35-
  36, 66-70, 74, 134-135, 160,
  163-164; 1956: 79-83, 125-126;
  1960: 32-33
  by age, 99

Air, continued
  by family life cycle, 102;
    1960: 32-33
  frequency of travel, 1955: 35,
    36, 66, 69, 74, 134, 135, 164;
    1956: 79-83
  by income, 1955: 68, 70, 160,
    163; 1960: 32-33
  most recent trip, 1956: 125-
    126
  by occupation, 1955: 160
  prediction of, 1955: 35-36
  price changes, response to, 115-
    116
  by purpose, 1955: 124-125, 127,
    157; 1956: 5-15, 19-21, 69-
    70; 1957: 7-16, 70-71;
    1960: 4, 28-30; 1962: 25, 27,
    35-59, 63, 67-74, 81-83
    and age, 1962: 50-53
    and auto ownership, 1962: 81-
      83
    and education, 1962: 44, 46-47
    and experience, 1955: 124;
      1960: 28-29; 1962: 35, 38-40
    and family life cycle, 1956:
      12-13; 1957: 12-13; 1962: 54-
      56
    and income, 1955: 127; 1956:
      8-10; 1957: 7-12; 1960: 4,
      29-30; 1962: 40, 42-44
    and occupation, 1955: 125;
      1956: 19-21; 1957: 15-16;
      1962: 44, 48-50
    and reactions to plane trips,
      1962: 25-26
    and region, 1956: 69-70;
      1957: 70-71; 1962: 68, 70-71
    and size of place, 1956: 14-
      15; 1957: 12, 14; 1962: 58-
      60
    and type of neighborhood, 1962:
      63, 67-68
  and rented cars, 114
  safety, 1962: 153-162
  by supersonic transport, 107, 110
  time to reach airport, 111
  total, 96-106
    by age, 99-102; 1960: 13-14,
      34-36; 1962: 3
    by family life cycle, 102
    by income, 96-98; 1955: 5, 7,
      26, 28, 31-32, 66, 71, 111;
      1960: 13-15; 1962: 2
    in megalopolis, 105-106

    in New York area, 105-106;
      1962: 72-74, 78-79
    by occupation, 98-99; 1960: 15-
      16, 34-35
    by race, 102-103
    by region, 104-105; 1960: 11-12
    by sex, 102
    by size of place, 1955: 6, 7,
      30, 42, 74-75, 126, 161;
      1960: 12-13
  trends in, 1956: 129-132; 1960:
    2-10
    frequency of travel, 1960: 5-7
    by income, 1960: 2-5, 8-9
    by distance and number who
      went, 1956: 129-132; 1962: 33
    number of revenue passengers,
      1960: 7
    proportion traveling by air,
      1962: 33
  expansion of number of, 183-188
Attitudes
  toward air safety, 86-87; 1962:
    153-158
  toward air travel, 83-87, 118-
    119; 1955: 6, 8-11, 32-34, 130-
    133; 1956: 138-142; 1957: 88-
    90; 1958: 8-11, 27-28; 1962:
    15-19, 25-28, 142-152
  toward auto travel, 6-13; 1955:
    63-64, 156; 1956: 151-152;
    1957: 93, 96-97; 1958: 27-28;
    1962: 15-24
  toward jets, 1957: 114-139; 1958:
    12-17
  toward rail travel, 118-123;
    1955: 43-46, 141-144; 1956:
    144-148; 1957: 88, 91-94; 1962:
    18-19
  toward travel, 6-13; 1955: 24;
    1956: 91-105; 1958: 21-27;
    1962: 7-19
  (See also Air, Rail, Bus and
    Auto travel)
Auto ownership, 61-62
  and air travel, 1962: 81-83
  and auto travel, 1962: 81-83
  and bus travel, 1962: 81-83
  and common carrier travel, 1962:
    79-80
  in New York area, 76-77
  and rail travel, 1962: 81-83
  by region, 74
Auto travel, Ch. III

Auto, continued
  attitudes toward, 6-13; 1955:
    63-64, 156; 1956: 151-152;
    1957: 93, 96-97; 1958: 27-
    28; 1962: 15-24
  business, 67-69; 1955: 62-63,
    165; 1956: 79, 84-87
  business and non-business, 37-38,
    51
    frequency of travel, 38, 64-65,
      1962: 35, 37
    by income, 1955: 158; 1956: 50-
      53
  experience with, 60-61, 63; 1955:
    57-59, 65, 153-154
    by age, 61, 63
    by income, 60, 61; 1955: 57, 59,
      153
    by occupation, 1955: 57-58, 154
  frequent travelers, reinterviewed
    in summer of 1962, 1962: 87-
    106
  long distance trips, 1960: 53-77;
    1962: 107-115
    experience with, 1960: 54-57,
      60
    non-business, 1962: 107-115
    purpose of most recent trip,
      1960: 63-64
  most recent trip, 1955: 76, 166;
    1956: 111-112, 120-122, 124,
    126, 128; 1957: 83-86; 1962:
    84-105
    by distance, 1956: 120-121;
      1957: 83-84
    by number who went, 1955: 76,
      166; 1956: 111-112; 1957:
      83, 85-86
    preferred mode, 1962: 104-105
    by purpose and distance, 1956:
      122, 124
    business and non-business,
      1962: 84-102
    non-business, 1956: 126,128
  non-business, 69-71; 1955: 66, 68,
    70, 163-164; 1956: 79-83
    by age, 69-70
    by family life cycle, 70-71
    frequency of travel, 1956: 79-
      83
    by income, 1955: 66, 68, 70,
      163-164
  by purpose, 1955: 75-76, 153-154,
    157; 1956: 46-47, 50-52, 54-
    59; 1957: 61-69, 78-79; 1962:

    35-56, 58-60, 66-68, 70-71,
    81-83
  and age, 1962: 50-52
  and air experience, 1962: 35,
    38-40
  and auto ownership, 1962: 81-
    83
  and education, 1962: 44, 46-47
  and family life cycle, 1956:
    54-55; 1957: 65-66; 1962: 54-
    56
  and income, 1955: 153; 1956:
    50-52; 1957: 61-64; 1962: 42-
    44
  and occupation, 1955: 154; 1956:
    58-59; 1957: 68-69; 1962: 44,
    48-50
  and region, 1956: 75-76; 1957:
    78-79; 1962: 68, 70-71
  and size of place, 1956: 56-57,
    1957: 65, 67; 1962: 54, 58-60
  and rented cars, 114; 1958: 44;
    1962: 122-133
  self-driving automobile, 1960:
    70-79
  on superhighways, 79-80; 1962:
    134-145
    attitudes toward speed, 79,80;
      1962: 141-145
    experience with, 79-80; 1962:
      134-145
  total, 65-78
    by age, 69-70
    by family life cycle, 70-71;
      1955: 72-74
    by income, 65-67
    in megalopolis, 74
    in New York area, 74, 76; 1956:
      75-78; 1962: 77-78
    by occupation, 67-69; 1955: 60,
      62
    by race, 71-72
    by region, 73-74
    by size of place, 1955: 62, 74-
      75, 77, 155, 161

Barriers to travel, 10-13, 157-158
  (See also Attitudes toward travel)
Bus travel, Ch. VI
  attitudes toward, 140-142; 1955:
    54-56, 152; 1956: 149-150;
    1957: 93,95; 1962: 15-19,29-32
  business, 1955: 54, 165; 1956:
    79, 84-87
  business and non-business, 37-38;
    51

Bus, continued
    frequency of travel, 38, 146;
        1962: 35, 37
    by income, 1955: 158; 1956: 36,
        39
    by region, 1956: 77-78
    and type of neighborhood, 1962:
        65, 67-68
experience with, 143-145; 1955:
    50-51, 65, 149-150, 157
    by age, 144-145
    by income, 143-144
non-business, 1955: 66, 68, 70,
    163-164; 1956: 79-83
most recent trip, 1955: 76, 78,
    166-168; 1956: 111-112, 118-
    127, 136-137; 1957: 83-86;
    1960: 17-20; 1962: 85-108
    alternate mode considered,
        1956: 136-137
    by distance, 1956: 120-121;
        1957: 83-84; 1960: 17-18
    by number who went, 1955: 76,
        166; 1956: 111-112; 1957:
        83, 85-86
    and package tours, 1955: 78,
        168; 1956: 117-118
    place of ticket purchase, 1955:
        76, 167; 1956: 115-116
    preferred mode, 1962: 104-105
    by purpose, 1956: 122-124;
        1960: 19-20
    business and non-business,
        1962: 85-86, 89, 91-92, 94-
        95, 98-99, 101-102
    non-business, 1956: 126-128
by purpose, 1955: 149-151, 157;
    1956: 34-45, 73-74; 1957: 53-
    60, 75, 77-78; 1960: 8, 10,
    19-20; 1962: 3, 29, 31, 35-
    65, 68-71, 81-83
    and age, 1962: 50, 52-53
    and air experience, 1962: 35,
        38-40
    and attitudes toward bus travel,
        1962: 29, 31
    and auto ownership, 1962: 81-83
    and education, 1962: 44, 46-47
    and family life cycle, 1956:
        40-41; 1957: 53-57; 1962: 54-
        56
    and income, 1955: 149; 1956:
        36-38; 1957: 53-56; 1962: 42-
        43
    and occupation, 1955: 150; 1956:
        44-45; 1957: 58, 60; 1962: 48-
        50

    and region, 1956: 73-74; 1957:
        75, 77-78; 1962: 68-71
    and size of place, 1956: 42-43;
        1957: 58-59; 1962: 58-61
total, 146-156
    by age, 150-151; 1960: 13-14;
        1962: 3
    by family life cycle, 151-152
    by income, 147-148; 1955: 52-
        54, 66, 71; 1960: 13, 15;
        1962: 2
    in megalopolis, 154
    in New York area, 154; 1956:
        73-74, 78-79; 1962: 72-73,
        76, 78
    by occupation, 149-150; 1960:
        15-16
    and package tours, 1955: 78,
        168
    by race, 152
    by region, 154-156; 1960: 11-12
    by sex, 152; 1960: 13-14
    by size of place, 1955: 54, 74-
        75, 151, 161; 1960: 12-13
trends in, 1956: 129, 131-132;
    1960: 8, 10; 1962: 34
(See Air, Auto, Bus, and Rail
    travel)

Car ownership
    (See Auto Ownership)
Choice of mode, Ch. II, 158-159;
    1956: 119-154; 1957: 99-113;
    1962: 13-32
    determinants of, 41-58
        by age, 43
        availability, 41, 44-46
        distance of trip, 43, 51, 54,
            57
        experience with air travel, 57-
            58
        financial considerations, 41-
            46, 48-49, 52-53
        income, 42, 52-54
        number who went, 56-57
        price, 41-46, 48-49, 53-55
        purpose of trip, 43, 51
        quality and preferences, 41-44,
            46-50, 57-58
    division of travel market, 36-40
        business and non-business trips,
            37-38
        by mileage, 39-40
    multivariate analysis of, 175-179

Common carrier travel
  most recent trip, 1956: 107-110,
    129-135; 1957: 81-83
  alternate modes considered,
    1960: 21-25
  date of, 1956: 107-108
  by distance, 1957: 81
  number of modes used, 1957: 83
  number who went, 1956: 129-135
  by purpose of trip, 1956: 109-
    110; 1957: 81-82
  total, 1955: 72-73; 1957: 4-6;
    1960: 11-26; 1962: 61-62, 79-
    81
  by age, 1960: 13-14
  by income, 1957: 4-5; 1960: 2-3,
    13, 15
  trends in, 1960: 1-10
  (See also Air, Bus, or Rail travel)
Communications, modern
  business air travel, 112-113
Concentration of travel, 23-24
  methodological implications of,
    24-27
Consumer attitudes, 3

Definition of trip, 1955: 3; 1956:
  vi; 1957: iii
Determinants, of choice of mode
  (See Choice of mode, Determinants
  of)

Education
  (See Air, Auto, Bus, and Rail
  travel)
Expanding the sample, 1955: 94-98
Experience
  (See Air, Auto, Bus, and Rail
  travel)

Family life cycle
  (See Air, Auto, Bus, and Rail
  travel)
Frequency of travel, 14-27
  by age, 1962: 50-51
  by income, 1955: 111,118
  by mode, 1956: 79-87; 1957: 3
    1962: 35, 37
  multivariate analysis of, 162-174
  by opinions about the best way to
    travel, 1962: 18-19
  by reactions to reduced plane
    fares, 1962: 147, 149-150
  by reactions to trips by plane,
    bus, and auto, 1962: 16-18
  by region, 1962: 68-69

by size of place, 1962: 54, 57
(See also Frequent Travelers,
  non-travelers, air, auto, bus,
  and rail travel)
Frequent travelers, 14-15, 17,19-21
  concentration of travel, 23-24
  methodological implications of,
    24-27
  by income, 14-15
  in megalopolis, 20
  in New York area, 20-21
  by region, 19-21
  reinterviewed in summer of 1962,
    1962: 84-106
  cheapest mode, 1962: 103-104
  convenience of other modes,
    1962: 97-101
  distance traveled, 1962: 87-83
  length of time away, 1962: 94-
    97
  number of children who went,
    1962: 91-94
  number who went, 1962: 90-91
  preferred mode, 1962: 104-106
  use of rented auto, 1962: 107

Graphs, list of, 201-203

High frequency travelers, 14-15,
  17, 19-21; 1955: 10, 12, 114-116;
  1956: 48-49

Implications for future research,
  1960: 89-92
Income
  distribution among regions, 1956:
    63-64
  (See also Air, Auto, Bus, and
  Rail travel)
Interstate and defense highway
  program, 2, 3, 139
Interviewing methods, 182

Jet travel
  attitudes toward, 107-110; 1957:
    114-139; 1958: 12-17

Lodgings
  experience with different types,
    1958: 39
  by income, 1958: 39
  on next trip, 1958: 42-43
  opinions of different types, 1953:
    40-42
Long distance trips
  choice between air or auto, 1960:

Long distance trips, continued
    53-77; 1962: 107-115
    (See also Air and Auto travel)

Megalopolis
    frequent travelers in, 20
    (See also Air, Auto, Bus, and
    Rail travel)
Methodology, survey, 181-190
Mode, choice of
    (See also Choice of mode)
Most recent trip
    (See Air, Auto, Bus, Common
    carrier, and rail travel)
Motives for travel, 6-10, 157
    (See also Attitudes toward travel)
Multivariate analysis, 161-179
    of choice of mode, 175-179
    of frequency of travel, 162-174

New York Central territory
    age distribution in, 1956: 67-68
    and air travel, 1956: 69-70
    and auto travel, 1956: 75-76
    and bus travel, 1956: 73-74
    definition of, 1956: 60
    income distribution in, 1956: 63-
    64
    occupation distribution in, 1956:
    65-66
    and rail travel, 1956: 71-72
    size of place distribution in,
    1956: 61-62
    use of all modes compared, 1956:
    77-78
New York metropolitan area
    age distribution in, 1956: 67-68
    and air travel, 105-106; 1956: 69-
    70, 77-78; 1962: 72-74, 78-79
    and auto travel, 74-76; 1956: 75-
    78; 1962: 77-79
    and bus travel, 154; 1956: 73-74,
    78-79; 1962: 72-73, 76, 78
    definition of, 1956: 60, 88-90
    frequent travelers, 20-21
    income distribution in, 1956: 63-
    64
    occupation distribution in, 1956:
    65-66
    population shifts, 77-78
    and rail travel, 136-137; 1956:
    71-72, 78-79; 1962: 75, 78
    size of place distribution, 1956:
    61-62
Non-business travel
    (See Air, Auto, Bus and Rail travel)

Non-travelers, 16-18, 22; 1955: 12,
    14, 116-117
    by age, 17-18, 22; 1955: 12, 14,
    117
    by income, 16-17, 22; 1955: 12,
    116
    by size of place, 1955: 14, 117
Number of air trips
    expansion of, 183-188
Number of modes used, 1955: 68, 75,
    159, 162
Number of trips
    (See Frequency of travel)

Occupation
    distribution among regions, 1956:
    65-66
    (See also Air, Auto, Bus and Rail
    travel)
Overseas travel, 31-33; 1958: 18-20;
    1960: 79-87
    experience with, 31-33; 1958: 18-
    20; 1960: 82-87
    by age, 33
    areas visited, 1958: 19
    by family life cycle, 31-32
    by income, 31; 1958: 20
    by prior experience, 32-33
    by sex, 1958: 18
    year of first overseas trip,
    1960: 82-87

Package tours
    comments on, 1962: 164, 167-169
    experience with, 1955: 78, 168;
    1956: 117-118; 1962: 164-165
    reactions to, 1962: 164, 166,
    169-171
Policy decisions, 2,3
Publications
    list of, 191
Questionnaires, 1955: 99-104; 1957:
    145-149; 1958: 51-54; 1960: 94-99;
    1962: 172-176

Rail travel, Ch. V
    attitudes toward, 118-123; 1955:
    43-46, 141-144; 1956: 144-
    148; 1957: 88, 91-94; 1962:
    18-19
    business, 1955: 48-49, 147-148,
    165; 1956: 79, 84-87
    business and non-business, 37-38,
    38, 51, 128; 1955: 47, 140,
    158; 1956: 24, 27, 77-78;
    1957: 31, 34; 1962: 84-101

Rail, continued
  by coach, 1955: 76, 167; 1956:
      113-114; 1957: 40-45, 75-76,
      86-87
  decline in, 117, 138
  experience with, 124-127; 1955:
      39-40, 65, 138-139, 157; 1957:
      46-52
    by age, 125-126
    first trip, year of, 127
    by income, 124-125
  by first class, 1955: 76, 167;
      1956: 113-114; 1957: 40-45,
      75-76, 86-87
  most recent trip, 1955: 76, 166-
      167; 1956: 111-116, 119-128,
      136-137; 1957: 83-87; 1960:
      17-25, 45-46; 1962: 84-108
    alternate mode considered, 1956:
      136-137
    by distance, 1956: 119-121; 1957:
      83-84; 1960: 17-18
    by number who went, 1955: 76,
      166; 1956: 111-112; 1957: 83,
      85-86
    and package tours, 1955: 78,
      168,; 1956: 117-118
    preferred mode, 1962: 104-105
    by purpose, 1956: 122, 124;
      1960: 19-20
    by business, 1960: 45-46
    business and non-business, 1962:
      89-102
    non-business, 1956: 125-127
  non-business, 1955: 46-47, 66, 68,
      70, 146, 160, 163-164; 1956:
      79-83
  by purpose, 1955: 138, 157; 1956:
      22-33, 71-72; 1957: 31-39, 72,
      74-75; 1960: 8, 10; 1962: 35-
      60, 64-71, 81-83
    by age, 1962: 50, 52-53
    and air experience, 1962: 35, 38-
      40
    and auto ownership, 1962: 81-83
    and family life cycle, 1956: 28-
      29; 1957: 35-36; 1962: 54-56
    and income, 1955: 138; 1956: 24-
      26; 1957: 31-34; 1962: 42-44
    and occupation, 1956: 32-33;
      1957: 35, 38-39; 1962: 48-50
    and region, 1956: 71-72; 1957:
      72, 74-75; 1962: 68, 70-71
    and size of place, 1956: 30-31;
      1962: 58-60
  total, 129-138

    by age, 132, 134; 1960: 13-14
    by family life cycle, 132-134
    by income, 130-131; 1955: 39-
      42, 66, 71; 1960: 13, 15
    in Megalopolis, 136
    in New York area, 136-137;
      1956: 71-72, 78-79; 1962: 72-
      73, 75, 78
    by occupation, 131-133; 1960:
      15-16
    by race, 135
    by region, 136-138; 1960: 11-12
    by size of place, 1955: 43, 74-
      75, 161; 1960: 12-13
  trends in, 1956: 129, 131-132;
      1960: 8, 10; 1962: 34
Region
  distribution of use of four
      modes, 1956: 77-78
  (See also Air, Auto, Bus and
      Rail travel)
Rented cars
  use of, 114; 1958: 44; 1962: 122-
      133
    and air travel, 114; 1962: 125-
      129
    by auto ownership, 1962: 125,
      127
    by auto ownership for those who
      live in suburban areas, 1962:
      131, 133
    by distance from center of
      metro area, 1962: 131-132
    by family life cycle, 1962:
      125-126
    by frequency of travel last
      year, 1962: 122-123
    by income, 1958: 44; 1962: 122,
      124
    by income for those who live in
      suburban areas, 1962: 128,
      130
    purpose of trip, 1958: 44

Safety in air travel
  (See Air safety)
Sampling errors, 189-190; 1955: 83-
      97; 1956: 155-157; 1957: 140-142;
      1958: 45-46; 1960: 101-111; 1962:
      177-184
Sampling methods, 181; 1955: 83-87;
      1956: iv-vi; 1957: iii; 1958: 1
Shares
  of air trips, 98
    by income groups, 98

Shares, continued
  of auto trips, 66-67
    by income groups, 66-67
  of bus trips, 148
    by income groups, 148
  of rail trips, 130
    by income groups, 130
Size of place
  distribution among regions, 1956:
    61-62
  (See also Air, Auto, Bus and
    Rail travel)
Summary of findings, Ch. VII, 1956:
  1956: 1-4; 1957: 1-2; 1958: 2-4;
  1962: 1-6
Superhighways
  experience with, 79-80; 1962: 134-
    145
Survey of Consumer Finances, 28, 61,
  74
Survey methodology, 181-190

Tables and charts
  lists of, 193-200; 1955: 105-110;
    1956: ix-xii; 1957: vi-ix;
    1962: 185-189
Total travel, Ch. I, VII; 1955: 9-
    25, 112, 114-123, 163-165;
    1956: 48-49; 1962: 40-41, 44-
    45, 50-51, 54, 57, 68-69
  business, 1955: 20, 122-123, 165
  business and non-business, 1955:
    10, 12, 14, 19-20, 112, 114-
    116; 1956: 48-49
    by high frequency travelers,
      1955: 10, 12, 114-116; 1956:
      48-49
  by income, 1955: 16-17, 163-164
  most recent trip, 4-5
    by purpose, 4-5
  non-business, 1955: 120-121, 163-
    164
  by occupation, 1955: 18, 119

  total frequency of travel, 1955:
      10, 13
    by age, 1962: 50-51
    by education, 1962: 44-45
    by income, 1955: 111, 118; 1962:
      40-41
    by region, 1962: 68-69
    by size of place, 1962: 54, 57
Travel
  theory of, 1955: 20-25
Trip
  definition of, 1955: 3; 1956: vi;
    1957: iii
  (See Air, Auto, Bus, Common
    Carrier or Rail travel)
Type of neighborhood
  definition, 1962: 61, 67
  distribution of adults in New
    York area, 1962: 72, 74, 78

Vacation travel, 28-30; 1955: 79-
    82, 169-171; 1958: 29-38
  destination, 1958: 29-32
  distance of, 1955: 80-81, 169-
    171
    by income, 1955: 170
    by length of vacation, 1955: 81
  expenditure on, 28-29
    by income, 29
  experience with, 28; 1955: 80
    by income, 28; 1955: 80
    by length of vacation, 1955:
      80
  frequency of, 29-30; 1955: 79,
    169
  mode used, 1958: 36-37
  and non-business air trips, 1955:
    81-82, 168
  paid vacations, 1955: 79
  payment for, 1958: 36-38
  plans for, 1958: 32-33
  vacation time, 1958: 34-36
    choice of, 1958: 34-36